PENGUIN BOOKS

ECHOES DOWN THE CORRIDOR

Arthur Miller was born in New York City in 1915 and studied at the University of Michigan. His plays include *All My Sons* (1947), *Death of a Salesman* (1949), *The Crucible* (1953), *A View from the Bridge* and *A Memory of Two Mondays* (1955), *After the Fall* (1964), *Incident at Vichy* (1965), *The Price* (1968), *The Creation of the World and Other Business* (1972), and *The American Clock* (1980). He has also written two novels, *Focus* (1945) and *The Misfits*, which was filmed in 1960, and the text for *In Russia* (1969), *In the Country* (1977), and *Chinese Encounters* (1979), three books of photographs by Inge Morath. His most recent works include a memoir, *Timebends* (1987), and the plays *The Ride Down Mt. Morgan* (1991), *The Last Yankee* (1993), *Broken Glass* (1994), which won the Olivier Award for Best Play of the London Season, and *Mr. Peters' Connections* (1999). He has twice won the New York Drama Critics Circle Award, and in 1949 he was awarded the Pulitzer Prize.

Steven R. Centola, who collaborated with the author to edit this collection, is Professor of English at Millersville University and is the coeditor of Arthur Miller's *Theater Essays*.

Collected Essays | 1944–2000

Arthur

Echoes Down the Corridor

Miller

Edited by Steven R. Centola

Penguin Books

PENGUIN BOOKS
Published by the Penguin Group
Penguin Putnam Inc., 375 Hudson Street,
New York, New York 10014, U.S.A.
Penguin Books Ltd, 27 Wrights Lane, London W8 5TZ, England
Penguin Books Australia Ltd, Ringwood, Victoria, Australia
Penguin Books Canada Ltd, 10 Alcorn Avenue, Toronto, Ontario, Canada M4V 3B2
Penguin Books (N.Z.) Ltd, 182–190 Wairau Road, Auckland 10, New Zealand

Penguin Books Ltd, Registered Offices: Harmondsworth, Middlesex, England

First published in the United States of America by Viking Penguin,
a member of Penguin Putnam Inc., 2000
Published in Penguin Books 2001

3 5 7 9 10 8 6 4 2

The following selections were previously published, some under different titles:
"Lost Horizon" appeared in *American Theater;* "Thoughts on a Burned House" in *Architectural Digest;* "Making Crowds," "Miracles," "What's Wrong with This Picture?" and "The Night Ed Murrow Struck Back" in *Esquire;* "The Bored and the Violent," "The Limited Hang-Out: The Dialogues of Richard Nixon as a Drama of the Antihero," and "Notes on Realism" in *Harper's;* A Boy Grew in Brooklyn" and "University of Michigan" in *Holiday;* "After the Spring" in *House & Garden;* "The Sin of Power" and "Ibsen's Warning" in *Index on Censorship;* "Concerning the Boom" in *International Theatre Annual;* "Suspended in Time" in *Life;* "A Modest Proposal for the Pacification of the Public Temper," "Dinner with the Ambassador," and "The Measure of the Man" in *The Nation;* "The Parable of the Stripper" in *The New Republic;* "The Nazi Trials and the German Heart" in *The New York Herald Tribune;* "Get It Right: Privatize Executions," "Let's Privatize Congress," "Clinton in Salem," and "The Price—The Power of the Past" in *The New York Times;* "The Face in the Mirror: Anti-Semitism Then and Now" in *The New York Times Book Review;* "Guilt and *Incident at Vichy,*" "The Battle of Chicago: From the Delegates' Side," "On True Identity," and Uneasy About Germans: After the Wall" in *The New York Times Magazine;* "Kidnapped?" in *The Saturday Evening Post;* "Tennessee Williams' Legacy: An Eloquence and Amplitude of Feeling" in *TV Guide;* and "Rain in a Strange City" in *Travel and Leisure.*
"The Good Old American Pie" appeared in *Censored Books: Critical Viewpoints,* edited by Nicholas J. Karolides, Lee Burress, and John M. Kean (Scarecrow Press, 1993); "The Pure in Heart Need No Lawyers" in *The Atlantic Monthly* and later in *Chinese Encounters* by Inge Morath and Arthur Miller (Farrar Strauss Giroux, 1979); "The Opera House in Tashkent" in *In Russia* by Inge Morath and Arthur Miller (Viking, 1969); "A Genuine Countryman" in *Blair & Ketchum's Country Journal* and later in *In the Country* by Inge Morath and Arthur Miller (Viking, 1977); and "Belief in America" in *Situation Normal* (Reynal & Hitchcock, 1944). "On Mark Twain's *Chapters from My Autobiography*" was published as the introduction to the 1966 Oxford University Press edition of *Chapters from My Autobiography.*
The following selections are reprinted by permission of Viking Penguin:
"*Salesman* at Fifty" from *Death of a Salesman,* fiftieth anniversary edition, copyright Arthur Miller, 1999 and an excerpt from *Salesman in Beijing,* copyright © Arthur Miller, 1983, 1984.
"*The Crucible* in History" was presented as a Massey Lecture at Harvard University, May 1999.

THE LIBRARY OF CONGRESS HAS CATALOGED THE HARDCOVER EDITION AS FOLLOWS:
Miller, Arthur, 1915–
Echoes down the corridor: collected essays,
1944–2000 / Arthur Miller; edited by Stephen Centola.
p.   cm.
ISBN 0-670-89314-5 (hc.)
ISBN 0 14 20.0005 1 (pbk.)
I. Centola, Stephen.   II. Title.
PS3525.15156 A6 2000
814'.52—dc21   00–040427

Printed in the United States of America
Set in Bodoni Book • Designed by Jaye Zimet

[*Acknowledgments*]

I would like to thank Arthur Miller for his friendship, support, and wise counsel in selecting the essays for this collection; Michael Millman and Zelimir Galjanic for their assistance in the preparation of the manuscript; Michelle Sampson for helping me with the research; and my wife, Susan, and our children, Tamara, Paul, and Devon, for their love, kindness, and understanding. I dedicate this book to my deceased father, Mario, whose lifelong example taught me that personal sacrifice and hard work define the essence of the phrase "labor of love."

—*Steven R. Centola*

For Inge

Contents

Looking through the score of essays I have published over the past half century, I find myself surprised at how many were involved with the political life of the times. I hadn't quite realized. By political I don't mean the question of who should be elected to office but rather the life of the community and its apparent direction. This preoccupation, brought back to mind by this collection, reminds me once again of how the "givens" of any generation change and how the dominant literary tradition of one time loses relevance in another.

To one growing up in the Thirties, the new force in one's awareness, as in so much of the cultural comment, was, of course, the failure of capitalism and the promise of socialism. The depth of that failure is all but incommunicable anymore, and the redolence of the cure even less so. The notion of the artist as activist was new and initially thrilling. One looked back with envy not only at the social realist Zola and his historic pamphlets that changed French political consciousness, but also at Tolstoy's and Dostoyevsky's pamphleteering, and even at Chekhov, seemingly a most private recorder of sensibility and quiet longing, who still found time to make a trip across the breadth of Russia, in an open carriage no less, to report on conditions of political prisoners on Sakhalin Island. And of course there was the long, illustrious line of British-Irish artist-politicos, most recently Shaw, who was still writing plays and trying to make sense of Britain's society. In contrast—at least it seemed so to me—American writers were far less involved in the nation's political life; and indeed for many critics the political itself was irreconcilable in principle with esthetic feeling or art in general. Or so it seemed.

So the young in the Thirties were self-consciously raising the banners of social protest and commitment, a prideful distinction challenging the ivory tower in which most writers seemed to have lived in the glamorous and rather silly Twenties. Very little of the writing of that exciting new dispensation has survived, having died with the issues with which it was so tightly bound up. The few surviving works of high art, like Henry Roth's *Call It Sleep*, while powerfully depicting the poverty and squalor of the city life of working-class people, were essentially aimed elsewhere, at the subjective experiences of the author, in fact, and his personal sensations of life in a certain time and place.

But one took it for granted, and without really giving it much thought, that the very idea of "writer" had less to do with the entertainer (which he has fundamentally become) and everything to do with remaking humanity in one way or another (and of course winning fame at the same time). And this meant politics and social commitment and indeed embodied a rather short view. But this was inevitable when one lived as though in a permanent emergency, as it were, a time-passage which would end with either the triumph or defeat of fascism, including the fascism of the heart which was all around us. Germany and Italy, two of the great cultures of Europe, had already been taken over by that plague. And at home it was a time, after all, when lynching was not uncommon in the South, when the Ford plant had tear gas in its sprinkler systems in case workers pulled a sit-down strike, and the private Ford police had the right to enter any employee's house to see if he was living as Ford thought he should; when there were discreet signs in front of New Jersey summer hotels reading, "No dogs or Jews"; when a boatload of Jews allowed by Hitler to leave Germany was not allowed to land in an American port and was forced to return to Germany to deliver its cargo to the ovens. It was a time when autoworkers, newly organized and freshly aware of the idea of social justice, would still insist on separate white and black picket lines. I cannot recall seeing a black New York policeman then, and of course the armed forces were tightly segregated.

The point of remarking on all this now is that Americans and Europeans, Jews and non-Jews alike, had silenced themselves, declining to protest what they knew was happening in Germany; non-Jews, because they no doubt feared that their concern—if they felt any—would open the country to a flood of refugees; Jews, lest drawing attention to themselves would make them even better targets at home than they already were. But then, not very many people thought it particularly odd that the new reformist labor movement, with all its newly born social idealism, was also thoroughly racist.

It seems to me that all this has wildly changed now, that people on every side are easily given to protest loudly at what they see as injustice to themselves or others. The "givens" of this new century are of an entirely different order from those that existed in most of the last. But the "givens" have shifted back and forth in several directions in the sixty years since the Thirties.

There was a kind of implicit cease-fire on social criticism during World War II after the explosively contentious years of the Depression. (I wrote *All My Sons* during the war, expecting much trouble, but the war ended just as I was completing the play, leaving some room for the unsayable, which everyone knew—that the war had made some people illicit, sometimes criminal fortunes.) The Fifties began the Cold War's religiously imposed silencing of any sharp criticism, lest the Communists benefit therefrom, and the cap was blown off again in the Sixties with the drug culture and the anti–Vietnam War movement. I can't recall anything at all happening in the Seventies, and by the Eighties the Reagan trance was in place and writers—so it seems to me now—felt surrounded by an ever expanding suburbia of the mind, which, as I write in the new century, has flowered into a culture of entertainment that absorbs whatever is dropped on it like a sponge, mixing everything into a general dampness beyond all definition. In a word, more dramatic work in movies especially (far less in theater) is built around themes of social importance than ever in memory, but none of it seems able to resist the public's transformation of all information—even the most alarming kind—into something like a good time. There was a time when a novel, John Steinbeck's *Grapes of Wrath*, would rouse Congress to pass legislation to ameliorate conditions in the transient labor camps in the West, an inconceivable event now when congressmen are unlikely even to be aware of a novel, let alone to take it seriously as a picture of real people's lives rather than the lives of entertainment people.

But to a greater or lesser extent through the decades the popular culture, where my plays existed, has always made it difficult to get at all serious about life. Nor was this a purely American phenomenon. It took many long years for Bernard Shaw, as great an agitator as he was, to get Ibsen produced in Britain, where he was assumed to be a madman; and I can say from personal experience that even into the Fifties there was an overwhelming resistance to serious considerations of contemporary life in the British theater. Indeed, it was the American play that the avant-garde looked to as an example of what they should be doing in England, few and far apart as those plays were on Broadway.

In any case, I have been spouting off over the years away from the stage as well as on it, and this collection is part of the record of the things that interested me enough to write about over the past half century.

A Note on the Selection

Although Arthur Miller's reputation will forever rest on his significant achievements in the theater, he has also produced an extraordinary body of nonfiction prose. In his introduction to *The Theater Essays of Arthur Miller*, Robert A. Martin praised Miller's enormous contribution to the field of theater criticism, writing that "Arthur Miller's essays on drama and theater may well represent the single most important statement of critical principles to appear in England or America since the Prefaces of George Bernard Shaw" (xx). Certainly no other American playwright has written as extensively and judiciously about the theater and his own body of work as Arthur Miller—and few, if any, have done so with such skill and elegance.

With the publication of *The Theater Essays of Arthur Miller*, attention was finally directed toward Miller's extraordinary work in the area of theater criticism. Since he is a prolific writer whose accomplishments in this genre have been considerable, it seemed imperative that someone locate and collect selected essays written by the playwright over the past six decades. With this goal in mind, I collaborated with the playwright to assemble the present collection.

Arthur Miller's achievement as an essayist is extraordinary. From the start of his career until the present, he has used the essay form as a way of providing insightful commentary on the urgencies of social change affecting, and sometimes transforming, not just American society, but also the international community. For this reason, Miller can be thought of as a chronicler of the historical procession of the twentieth century. Acknowledging the importance of this role in an interview in 1999, Miller remarked that "the function of a writer is to remember, to be a rememberer" (quoted in Bigsby, "The Shearing Point"). His essays demonstrate his fervent commitment to this purpose. Nothing escapes Miller's piercing scrutiny as he discusses such subjects as the Holocaust, the Nazi War Crimes Trials, the Great Depression, the Cold War, McCarthyism, the Vietnam War, anti-Semitism, censorship, juvenile delinquency, the Watergate scandal, capital punishment, and the oppression of dissident writers in foreign countries, in an effort to understand the sources of human misery and conflict in the twentieth century. In one memorable essay after another, he captures the frenzied spirit of a schizophrenic age and records poignant observations on the political unrest and moral decline rampant in this century.

His historical vision is enlarged by his remarkable ability to synthesize past and present circumstance and to find in the immediate event a corresponding analogue whose example is instructive and perhaps even curative to a national psyche fractured by its own internal contradictions. Everything is interrelated, and time is but a flimsy veil that sometimes masks the underlying connective tissue that binds all of human experience together. But it is not just the past and the present, or the world and America, that are united in Miller's work. Throughout these essays, Miller also interweaves his criticism of American cultural myths and political disasters with his personal reminiscences and individual reading of the workings and failures of history. As a result, not all of these essays are political in nature. Some are quite personal; yet even in these pieces it is obvious that the thematic center of his drama is also the unmistakable fulcrum of his essays. According to Robert A. Martin, the vital link between Miller's essays and his drama is his intense pursuit of "the twin concepts of truth and morality as the highest priority in his work" (*Theater Essays*, xxi). These principles undoubtedly motivate everything he writes. Christopher Bigsby agrees and identifies this "moral imperative" as the matrix behind Miller's aesthetics and artistic vision. Bigsby writes: "For Miller, beyond the fantasies, the self-deceptions, the distortions of private and public myths are certain obligations which cannot be denied. The present cannot be severed from the past nor the individual from his social context; that, after all, is the basis of his dramatic method and of his moral faith" (*Modern American Drama*, 124).

Certainly, at least part of the value of this collection derives from the fact that it gives us a glimpse at the private man behind the public screen of notoriety. Given his larger-than-life stature and disciplined effort to avoid associating his characters with himself, the private person named Arthur Miller, and not the writer, may seem to his audiences to hide in plain sight in his plays. After all, one measure of Miller's success as a playwright has been his ability to create characters who generally appear to have nothing in common with their creator. When asked whether he sees himself in any of his characters, Miller explained that "There's no *one* [character] who's actually me, that I'm sure of. But a writer projects himself into every one of his characters—you can't write convincingly about a character unless you identify with him" ("Responses," 822). Interestingly enough, this capacity for what Keats calls negative capability perhaps also has much to do with Miller's success as an essayist. Miller seems to know exactly how to engage his reader. Seduced by his conversational tone and disarming candor, the reader is swept away by the force of his prose and has difficulty not succumbing to the illusion that he is experiencing an identification with the playwright. Miller removes the persona conferred by his profession and international renown and writes passionately about his feelings, concerns, and interests. In his vignettes about particular episodes of his life, he gives charming accounts of fondly remembered personal experience. In "A Boy Grew in Brooklyn," for instance, he reflects on his childhood and writes movingly about his family and the Brooklyn neighborhood in which he lived during the Great Depression. He takes a similar approach in essays that discuss his involvement in theatrical productions, his student days at the University of Michigan, the fire that nearly burned down his entire house, his fondness for gardening, and his appreciation of the poetic value of the Brooklyn Bridge.

Miller skillfully modulates his tone and style from essay to essay and thereby avoids strident articulation of his social conviction while developing a unique rhetorical approach in each piece that simultaneously engages, entertains, and informs the reader. In his essays, as in his plays, Miller never hesitates to tackle issues and opponents head-on. He does not pull his punches and writes with a muscular prose style that is quite robust. On occasion, he uses his remarkably quick wit and biting satire to reduce an issue to utter absurdity. His searing social commentary, for instance, takes on a Swiftian flavor in such pieces as "A Modest Proposal for the Pacification of the Public Temper," "The Limited Hang-Out: The Dialogues of Richard Nixon as a Drama of the Antihero," "On True Identity," and "Get It Right: Privatize Executions." At other times, however, he completely abandons the ironic approach and addresses his subject with a serious tone in chiseled prose. This is the characteristic style of "The Bored and the Violent," "The Sin of Power," "The Good Old American Apple Pie," "Notes on Realism," and many other essays in this collection. Yet some of the selections appear almost meditative in tone and nostalgically reflect on intensely lived and felt personal experience. In fact, his work at times seems more like poetry than prose, as is the case in the impressionistically styled "Rain in a Strange City." Miller has a journalist's penchant for facts, a novelist's eye for detail, and a playwright's ear for linguistic patterns and speech rhythms, but he also has a poetic sensibility.

He can be quite humorous and playful and is oftentimes remarkably skillful in forming the perfect turn of phrase to drive home a point. Perhaps more than anything else, a look at Miller's work as an essayist reinforces the impression that this world-renowned playwright has tremendous talent as a writer. Reading the essays, both for their content and for their form, sheds light on his use of language as a playwright and leaves no doubt that Miller is a writer who is extremely conscious of stylistic matters and is very much in control of his craft.

While most of the selections for this collection do not deal directly with the theater, several in this area have been included since this has been Miller's abiding interest throughout his entire adult life. A few discuss issues that have concerned Miller since the start of his career, such as the value of a federally subsidized theater. However, others represent significant pieces that the playwright has written since the publication of the last edition of *The Theater Essays of Arthur Miller* in 1996. "*Salesman* at Fifty" commemorates the fiftieth anniversary of the original Broadway production of *Death of a Salesman* and discusses successful productions of the play abroad as evidence of its success in proving that there is only one humanity. "*The Crucible* in History" is a previously unpublished essay that originally was given as a speech at Harvard University in 1999. It is a wonderful discussion of the cultural forces and historical context that affected Miller's creation of this famous play and eventually led to his awareness of striking parallels between the seventeenth-century witch-hunts in Salem and McCarthyism in twentieth-century American society. "*The Price*—The Power of the Past" discusses the most recent Broadway production of this play, in 1999, and the lasting significance of its themes. "Notes on Realism," also written in 1999, is a brilliant discussion of various considerations central to an understanding of American theatrical accomplishments in the twentieth century. The volume ends with a splendid new essay written especially for this collection on a subject that has interested the playwright since the start of his career: "Subsidized Theatre." Pointing out the inherent risks historically associated with the commercial theater in New York, Miller cogently explains how a subsidized theater would benefit writers, directors, actors, and designers of serious intentions while simultaneously providing American audiences with the opportunity to experience the best in new American dramatic achievement.

In addition to presenting essay selections, this book also includes excerpts from Miller's books of reportage. In these longer works of prose nonfiction, Miller also displays his tremendous talent for working in this genre. The first of these is excerpted from *Situation Normal* (1944), which reports Miller's experiences visiting army camps during the Second World War. The selection from this book has been given the title "Belief in America." It is a fascinating report on Miller's conversation with a veteran named Watson during the playwright's effort to find out what motivates American soldiers in combat. The excerpt from *In Russia* (1969) is entitled "The Opera House in Tashkent." This blithe piece offers a humorous account of a night at the opera during the Millers' visit to Russia. Excerpted from *In the Country* (1977), "A Genuine Countryman" is an evocative portrait of an elderly man from western Connecticut who lived a simple country life and attempted to resist the changes affecting his world. "The Pure in Heart Need No Lawyers" is a selection from Miller's book *Chinese Encounters* (1979). In this excerpt, Miller expresses concerns about the absence of a legal code in Communist China and draws parallels between the Puritan persecutions in Salem in 1692 and the oppressive purges by the Gang of Four in China. Finally, the memoir dated March 31 from *Salesman in Beijing* (1984) is included as a representative selection from this important autobiographical work that chronicles Miller's work as director of an all-Chinese cast during rehearsals for the historic performance of *Death of a Salesman* in the People's Republic of China. Like the other essays chosen for this text, these selections demonstrate Miller's enormous skill and tremendous range as a writer of this genre.

A brief word on the structure of this book and its title seems necessary before bringing this note to a close. For the most part, the essays that follow are arranged chronologically, with a few notable exceptions. Since so much of Miller's work has been shaped by his formative experiences, it seemed logical to start the book with two autobiographical selections dealing with his childhood in Brooklyn and his student days at the University of Michigan. The penultimate piece also deviates from the chronological progression of the whole. "Notes on Realism" not only puts everything else written by the playwright in perspective, but also encapsulates an entire history of the American theater. The final spot is reserved for "Subsidized Theater," a remarkable rewrite of an essay originally composed over fifty years ago, which closes the circle of powerful resoundings in this volume by reaffirming Miller's belief in the importance of the theatrical experience for the survival of the human spirit.

The title *Echoes Down the Corridor* comes from *The Crucible*, a play that has gained the distinction of being Miller's most frequently produced work and possibly his most popular drama. Serving as the title to the play's epilogue, which briefly recounts the repercussions emanating from the Salem hangings, it also fits this collection perfectly for several reasons. On a literal level, these essays function as echoes of Miller's work in the theater. An echo is said to be a reflection or a repetition of a sound wave. The reverberations heard in these selections clearly reflect the primary thematic interests in Miller's plays. An echo also can be viewed as a vehicle for momentarily recovering the past in the present. The echoes registered in these selections have the effect of reviving for the reader the people and past historical events discussed by Miller. In essence, therefore, the title reflects a central thematic concern in Miller's entire body of work: the necessity of viewing the past as a living presence in today's reality. These echoes have not died. For decades they have continued to sound their reverberations down the corridor of time, and their tone is as clear and strong today as when they were first heard. For Miller, then, even though the corridor of time and history may be long, dark, and mysterious, the echoes resounding within it remain vibrant and resonate with powerful significance in our lives. One can only speculate whether these echoes will continue to speak to future generations, but, given both the magnitude and the quality of Miller's impressive achievements, it is safe to conclude that his work and reputation as one of the twentieth century's most important writers will certainly endure.

Steven R. Centola

Works Cited

Bigsby, Christopher. *Modern American Drama, 1945–1990*. Cambridge: Cambridge University Press, 1992.

———. "The Shearing Point: Arthur Miller and the Holocaust." Arthur Miller and the Holocaust. Kean University, Union, N.J., February 28, 1999.

Martin, Robert A. "Introduction to the Original Edition." *The Theater Essays of Arthur Miller*. Eds. Robert A. Martin and Steven R. Centola. New York: Da Capo Press, 1996.

Miller, Arthur. "Responses to an Audience: Question and Answer Session." *Michigan Quarterly Review* (Fall 1998): 817–27.

Echoes Down the Corridor

A Boy Grew in Brooklyn

Nobody can know Brooklyn, because Brooklyn is the world, and besides it is filled with cemeteries, and who can say he knows those people? But even aside from the cemeteries it is impossible to say that one knows Brooklyn. Three blocks from my present house live two hundred Mohawk Indians. A few blocks from them are a group of Arabs living in tenements in one of which is published an Arabic newspaper. When I lived on Schermerhorn Street I used to sit and watch the Muslims holding services in a tenement back yard outside my window, and they had a real Moorish garden, symmetrically planted with curving lines of white stones laid out in the earth, and they would sit in white robes—twenty or thirty of them, eating at a long table, and served by their women who wore the flowing purple and rose togas of the East. All these people, plus the Germans, Swedes, Jews, Italians, Lebanese, Irish, Hungarians and more, created the legend of Brooklyn's patriotism, and it has often seemed to me that their having been thrown together in such abrupt proximity is what gave the place such a Balkanized need to proclaim its never-achieved oneness.

But this is not the Brooklyn I know or was brought up in. Mine was what is called the Midwood section, which now has no distinguishing marks, but thirty years ago was a flat forest of great elms through which ran the elevated Culver Line to Coney Island, two and a half miles distant. My Brooklyn consisted of Jews, some Italians, a few Irish—and a Mr. Dunham, whom I remember only because he was reputed to carry a gun as part of his duties as a bank guard.

Children going to school in those days could be watched from the back porch and kept in view for nearly a mile. There were streets, of course, but the few houses had well-trodden trails running out of their back doors which connected with each other and must have looked from the air like a cross section of a mole run; these trails were much more used than the streets, which were as unpaved as any in the Wild West and just as muddy. Today everything is paved and your bedroom window is just far enough away from your neighbor's to leave room to swing the screens out when fall comes.

My aunts and uncles, who moved there right after World War I, could go to Manhattan on the Culver Line for a nickel (although my cousins always climbed around the turnstile, which was easy, so long as you didn't mind hanging from iron railings a hundred feet or so above the street), but they had to buy potatoes in hundred-pound sacks because there was no grocery store within four miles. And they planted tomatoes, and they canned fruits and vegetables, and kept rabbits and chickens and hunted squirrels and other small game. The Culver Line cars were made of wood, like trolleys hooked together, and clattered above the cemeteries and the elms, and I must say there was something sweet about it when you got aboard in the morning and there was always the same conductor who knew you and even said good morning.

I don't precisely know why, but Brooklyn in my memory has always been full of characters and practical jokers. I suppose it is really a collection of villages which all seem the same to the stranger's eye, but are not; and characters thrive and express their special ways in a village atmosphere. My father was one, and is the last of those Mohicans as he sits in front of his frame house of a Sunday afternoon, remembering, as he glances down the tree-lined block, the old friends and screwballs who lived in each of the houses and are now resting peacefully in the cemetery that spreads out two blocks away, their pinochle decks laid down forever, their battles done.

My father, a large, square-headed man who looks like a retired police captain, and has that kind of steady severity, is likely to feel the need, from time to time, to "start something." Years ago, he sat down on the Culver Line one morning, and seeing a neighbor whom he regarded as particularly gullible, moved over to him and in his weightiest manner, began:

"You hear my brother-in-law got back from Florida?"

"Yes, I heard," said the neighbor. "What does he do down there? Just fish and like that?"

"Oh, no," my father said, "haven't you heard about his new business?"

"No. What?"

"He raises cockroaches there."

"Cockroaches! What does he do with the cockroaches?"

"What does he do with the cockroaches? Sells them!"

"Who wants cockroaches?"

"Who wants cockroaches! There's a bigger demand for cockroaches than for mink. Of course they gotta be of a certain breed. He breeds them down there. But they're all purebred."

"But what good are they?"

"Listen," my father confided, lowering his voice. "Don't say I even mentioned it, but if you happen to see any cockroaches around, in your house, or anywhere like that, my brother-in-law would appreciate it if you brought them all to him. Because I tell you why, see—he's raising them up here now, right in his house, but in Brooklyn it's against the law, you understand?—but once in a while a couple of them escape, and he's bashful to ask people, but you'd be doing him a big favor if you happen to catch any, bring them to him. But be very careful. Don't hurt them. He'll pay five dollars for any purebred cockroach anybody brings him."

"Five dollars!"

"Well, listen, that's his business. But don't tell anybody I told you because it's against the law, you know?"

Having planted this seed, my father left the neighbor. A week or so later my uncle's doorbell rang, and there was the man, considerably insecure in his mind, but there nevertheless, with a matchbox full of cockroaches. For three whole days my uncle refused to play casino with my father.

There is Ike Samuels, who runs—or rather sits outside—the hardware store. Ike's way with women who come in not knowing precisely what they want is something not easily described. I have watched him double-talking a *Hausfrau* for better than ten minutes; but when they come in with complaints he rises to a height of idiotic evasion that is positively lyrical. I was myself a victim of his for years, as a boy. We lived three blocks from his store, and often as I passed he would open his eyes against the sunlight where he sat in his rocker beside the door, and say, "Raining on Ocean Parkway?"

For years I answered him seriously because he has a remorseless poker face and thick lenses on his eyeglasses that make a clear view of his eyes impossible. Out of respect, at first, I described the weather three blocks away; but later I began to doubt myself and came to wonder, now and then, whether it *had* been raining there while the sun shone here.

But that was the least of Ike Samuels. I happened to be in his store one morning when a woman entered. Like so many of them at eleven A.M., she had a coat on top of her nightgown—and in her hands was an electric broiler which Ike had repaired only a week before. She strode in, a large woman with lumpy hair that, in her anger at the broiler, she had neglected to comb, and she plunked the broiler down on the counter.

"You said you fixed it!" she began.

"What is the trouble?" Ike said.

"It don't heat! My husband came home last night, I put four lamb chops in, we could've dropped dead from hunger, it was like an ice box in there!"

Ike took the top off the broiler and made as though to examine its works. There was a silence. He peered this way and that inside it, and I could tell that he was winding up for a stroke that would resound through his whole day. Looking up at her like a detective on the scent, he asked, "What did you say you put in here?"

Suspecting, perhaps, that she had in fact done something wrong, she parried: "What do you mean what did I put in here?"

Like a prosecutor, Ike leaned in toward her: "Answer my question, madam; what did you put in this broiler?"

Her voice smaller now, off balance, she replied, "I said—lamb chops."

"Lamb chops!" Ike rolled his eyes at the ceiling, where the mops and pails hung. "Lamb chops she puts in!"

Close to tears now, the woman began to plead, "Well, what's the matter with lamb chops?"

"What's the matter with lamb chops!" Ike roared indignantly. "Can't you read, lady? What night school did you go to? Look!" With which he turned the broiler upside down and pointed to the brass plate riveted to the bottom, on which were embossed the long serial numbers of the manufacturer's patents, and the Underwriters' Laboratory seal.

She bent over to peer at the tiny numbers and the few words. And before she could fix her eyes Ike was on her. "It's plain as day. 'No Lamb Chops,' it says; this is written by naval architects, graduate engineers from the Massachusetts Institute of Technology—'No lamb chops'—and you throw lamb chops in there. What do you want from me, lady? I fixed it for steak!"

Her eyes were distraught now, utterly bewildered. "But he likes lamb chops," she pleaded.

And now, having won the initiative, he came around the counter and escorted her to the door. "Now look, don't be discouraged. I'll do my best, and I'll fix it for lamb chops. I got a license for that, but you gotta have a double affixative on the forspice."

"Could you put one on?" she asked, exhausted.

"For you anything, darling," he said, and sent her on her way.

It was a village, even down to the feeble-minded Danny, who hung around Ike's store, and when you came by he would point at you and say, "Navarre 8-7135," because his pride lay in remembering everybody's phone number. If he overheard Ike talking about somebody's aunt, he would interject, "Dewey 9-0518," which, in his mind, identified the aunt. "Ulster 5-8009 is getting married, Ike," he announced one morning. Asked who the bride was, he answered, "Navarre 8-6661." But he had his dignity, which he enforced. If they started kidding him, he would get off the barrel and leave, saying, "I gotta see a party."

It was a village, and while to the stranger's eye one street was no different from another, we all knew where our "neighborhood" somehow ended, and the line of demarcation was never more than three blocks away. Beyond that, a person was somehow a stranger.

It was a village with village crimes. I don't recall any time when the cops had to be called. Everyone was so well and thoroughly known that the frown of his neighbors was enough law to keep things in line. When we stole from the candy store, when we played handball against the druggist's window and broke it, it was enough for the offended proprietor to let it be known to the parents. Although I must add that Mr. Dozik, the pharmacist, had it a little harder. The wall of his building was perfect for handball, and poor Dozik had to be all the time giving us water from his soda fountain. He tried putting up billboards that projected from the wall, but we played around them, until finally he had his soda fountain removed. Mr. Dozik is the first man in history to discover that boys cannot play handball where there is no cold drinking water.

He's still there as he was then—a kind of doctor who knows what ails everybody; a man who sewed up the arms, hands and ears of all my cousins and remembers every stitch.

It was a village with no stream, however, so my cousins and I would get up at four in the morning and climb around the turnstile of the Culver Line, and go rickety-rackety down the two-mile track to Coney Island and fish off the rocks and bring home flounder or sea bass—even in winter, when the wind was raw off the ocean.

I got to know those village winters especially well because I delivered rolls and bread every morning for the bakery before I went to school. There were no gloves warm enough to keep the icy cold of the handlebars away from my fingers, so I wore long woolen plaid stockings that came up to my elbows, and with the basket over the front wheel piled high with bags of bread, rolls and bagels, I would ride forth through the streets at four-thirty in the morning.

In the spring and fall it was lovely and one could sing out loud for the beauty of it, but when the snow fell, or worse yet, when the streets were covered with ice, a special kind of hell broke loose. Bread means something very special to these people. A man rising to breakfast in those houses *expects* his bagel, or his rye bread, or his onion roll or whatever it is he craves most. Give a bagel man an onion roll and his whole day is ruined, while for a rye-bread man a bagel is beneath contempt, especially for breakfast when one's taste buds are fresh and quivering and so very delicately attuned to flavors.

So it used to be with a somewhat trembling care that I would guide the bike down the streets when there was ice, because each bag was filled with its special order, and each one marked in crayon with its proper address. I would slowly ride down the center of the street, carefully holding to the crown of the road, and the cold cats would follow me, meowing and pleading for warmth and food, and the dark sky of winter was merciless over my head. And there came a time, once, when the bike suddenly slid out from under me, and the bags tumbled out of the wire basket, and many broke, and others just opened because they were overstuffed, and as I sat there on the ice, I could see bagels, onion rolls, whole rye breads, sliding out over the sheet ice in all directions. Few people can imagine how far a bagel will slide on clean ice. I know.

And besides, the baker had gallstones. I hadn't the heart to return and tell him of this catastrophe. So I went about on the empty street, gathering up the cargo, some of which had come to a stop three quarters of a block away. I then sat on the ice, flashlight gleaming, trying to put things back into the proper bags. Some were easy, because the bags had been packed so tightly that the impressions made by the hump of a rye bread's back and the circle of a bagel were unmistakable. But most were simply bags, like any other bags, and I finally just stuffed them as best I could, spreading the bagels through the lot, and offering, in short, what I thought was a nice variety to each customer. I had, as amateur mechanics do when they try to assemble a machine that has been taken apart, several pieces left over, which I simply ate before delivering the bags.

I returned to the bakery to leave the bike, and already the phone was ringing, or more accurately, burning. The baker looked ghastly. In his whole life nothing like this had happened. Utterly baffled, he listened to Mrs. 1690 screaming in his ear for her onion rolls, her husband is going to be shaved in five minutes! And Mrs. 1277 asking when in her nine years of dealing with him she had ever ordered rye bread! And the poor man turned to me, his two overcoats making him look like a mountain of horrification, and I explained at last. But it remained a tragedy from which, as far as I could tell, he never fully recovered.

I do not think I am painting it more serene than it was. There was a rhythm and a flowing to the days that began with the men trekking to Avenue M from all the side streets in the early morning, and like a column of ants climbing up the long steep stairs to the Culver Line, and it ended toward nightfall when they trekked down again and dispersed into their houses. We walked three miles to James Madison High School, and the ambitious track men among us trotted all the way, stopping only to look at the girl setting out the blackberry tarts in the window of the Ebinger Bakery. I do not think there were any intellectuals among us and as far as I can remember the greatest thing anybody could do was to get on the football team, or run like hell, or swim a couple of miles in the ocean in the summer. I know that in later years, when I began to publish, my old high-school teachers looked through their records in an attempt to remember me, but not one of them could. I was, in fact, thoroughly invisible during the entire four years, and this is by all odds my most successful accomplishment so far. Because the idea all of us subscribed to, was to get out onto the football field with the least possible scholastic interference, and I can fairly say we were none of us encumbered by anything resembling a thought.

The first ripple of what may properly be called the Outside World was felt one day when a crowd of people formed at the doors of The Bank of the United States—which was not even in our neighborhood, being five blocks away. To be succinct about it, the thing had closed. This in itself did not bother me particularly because, while I had been a depositor to the tune of twelve dollars, I had withdrawn the entire amount the very day before to buy Joey Backus's Columbia racer. What did bother me was that the day after the bank closed I got hungry, left the bike in front of our house, went inside for some bread and jam, and came out to find no bike, and a block can never look as empty as it does to a boy whose bike should be on it and isn't. In that emptiness lay the new reality.

With this incident I was introduced to the Depression Age. Suddenly, overnight, in fact, the postman became an envied character because he could not lose his job and even had a paid vacation. Our postman, unlike some others, did not flaunt his new superiority but went right on opening our front door, coming into the living room and calling up to my mother to read her the mail: "Nothing important, Mrs. Miller. Gas bill, electric bill, and a card from your sister. She says she's enjoying the hotel and will be home next Friday," with which he simply went out, just as he always had.

But other things had begun to change, sometimes in a weird way. The government soon took over practically every mortgage on the block, and the result was that all the housewives started making more and better coffee. When the man came to our house to collect the payments, my mother, for one, got out the coffeepot and her wonderful coffeecake, and he would sit down and before he could say a number she was stuffing him, and for about a year or so this collector always left our block bloated, and not with money either. It got so he would never mention the mortgage, but just sit there and wait to be served.

There was a lot of tension, though, in that time, and in a little while you could see grown men sitting on the porches in the middle of a weekday afternoon, and the trotters to Madison High were thinned out as one after another had to go looking for work. And the line of breadwinners coming down the stairs of the Culver Line had the slump of humiliation and bewilderment in their shoulders, and there were stores empty now, and when you ripped your shirt it was a minor tragedy, and every now and then, toward midnight, there were voices raised in loud argument within the houses. It got so bad that one night, after dinner, my grandfather put down his paper—he who had been a Republican all his life and believed, if you pressed him hard enough, that what America needed was a king like they had in Austria—my grandfather turned to me with his great bald head and the bags under his eyes like von Hindenburg's, and said, "You know what you ought to do? You ought to go to Russia."

The silence that fell is better described as a vacuum so powerful it threatened to suck the walls in. Even my father woke up on the couch. I asked why I should go to Russia.

"Because in Russia they haven't got anything. Here they got too much. You can't sell anything here any more. You go to Russia and open a chain of clothing stores; you could do a big business. That's a new country, Russia."

"But," I said, "you can't do that there."

"Why not?" he said, disbelieving.

"The government owns the stores there."

His face would have put fear into Karl Marx himself. "Them bastards," he said, and went back to his paper.

By this time, of course, inevitable changes had helped to destroy so much that was human and lovely in my neighborhood (although much remains even today)—changes that had nothing to do with the Depression. The woods were gone now and there were houses everywhere, and even the last lot left to play football on was turned into a fenced-in junkyard. Bars had begun to sprout along Gravesend Avenue, and the whole idea of drinking, which the old neighborhood had never known, became quite normal.

An invisible vise seemed to be forever closing tighter and tighter, and the worst, most unimaginable fates became ordinary. The star football player became a shipping clerk, and was glad to have the job; I, who had planned to go to Cornell because they offered a free course in biology—although I had not the slightest interest in the subject—waited around until the fall term began, and seeing that nobody in the house was in possession of the fare, I went to the employment offices for a couple of months and ended up in a warehouse. It was the time Nick appeared on the scene and the time my grandfather decided to die.

About Nick in a moment. One hot afternoon, while the neighborhood and the nation slumbered in the tortured sleep of the Depression and a fiery heat wave in the bargain, my grandfather began to pant. He rarely sat outside his bedroom without his jacket, stiff collar and tie, but that day he gradually took off all but his shirt, and even went for his wire-frame glasses, which were cooler, he believed, than the tortoise-shell ones. Then he lay down on the couch and heaved his chest and looked terrible, and my mother called the doctor and her two sisters and several sisters-in-law, and in half an hour they were all wailing around him and trying to prevent him from speaking, but at last his right arm raised up imperiously, palm out, and they fell silent.

He had been a blunt sort of Germanic businessman all his life; had had a factory of importance for many years, and it is enough to say of his physique that whenever there was a strike in his plant he would pick up two workers and knock their heads together. This was as far as his ideas of labor relations went.

With the Depression his income was gone, and he had been shunted from one daughter's house to another's, and while no one dared cross him, they did manage to palm him off on the next one every six months or so "for his sake." Unfortunately, he could not get sick. He drank gallons of mineral water, panted, and I had often seen him striding down Avenue M with his cane flashing and hardly touching the pavement, but when he turned into our block, he would slow down, pant, lean heavily on the cane and barely make it to the door. Then he would eat the equivalent of a wash basin of thick soup, as many chops as there were, and sit down to listen to Lowell Thomas, and if some fool forgot and asked him how he was feeling, he would shake his head like an ailing emperor and could barely be heard complaining. He was so neat he folded his socks before putting them in the laundry hamper, and it took him five minutes to get his two pillows set exactly where he wanted them on the bed before he lay down, or rather half sat up, to go to sleep. Once a week he went to the barber to have his little Vandyke trimmed, and insisted on being sprayed with toilet water of a certain brand. Even his rubber heels he wore out evenly, and his four hats were kept in their original boxes. Once every week he smoked a cigar.

And now he lay dying. Slowly the last words issued from his lips. Like Lear parceling out the nation he told each daughter what she was to have of his possessions. The trouble was that he only had twenty-six dollars left, and his hats. But it made no difference, each one burst into thankful tears as her bequest was mentioned. And finally, he said, "And don't bury me in the old plot. It's too crowded there. I want a little room. And I don't want to be where people are going to be walking over me all the time." He always liked room and plenty of air. "Put me on the aisle," he concluded, probably feeling at the moment that it would be cooler there.

Having gotten their agreement, he groaned and sat up. After a while they tried to make him lie down but he said he felt better now. The conversation turned to other things, and pretty soon the women were playing rummy and forgot all about him. The next they knew he was coming down the stairs, cane, jacket, felt hat, stiff collar and tie. "Where you going, Papa?" his daughters screamed.

He turned in the doorway, his brows drawn together as though in preparation for a mission of importance. "I gotta go for a fitting," he said.

"A fitting!" they called. "You can't go out in this weather!"

"I'm having a suit made downtown. Beautiful material. Two pairs of pants." With which he walked out and lived ten years longer. The whole thing was just due to the general discouragement, I guess.

Equally unforeseeable, but a sign of the times and the nature of the neighborhood, was the way Nick made out. One day, in the year of especially long bread lines, a man knocked on my aunt's door and asked if he could wash the windows for her. He was built low to the ground, lisped, and was neatly combed and obviously quite poor. In those days strange men were constantly appearing in the neighborhood looking for work or a piece of bread, and we had more than a few who fainted from hunger on our steps and only my mother's chicken soup could revive them. My father, slightly more cynical than some others, said, "Sure, they smell the chicken soup and decide it's a good place to faint," and we spent one whole Sunday morning looking all over the house for any mark or secret sign that seemed to lead these fellows directly to our door.

But my aunt hired Nick and he worked carefully, and when night came she let him sleep in the cellar. Next morning, when the family came down, the dining-room table was set with a tablecloth and napkins standing up stiffly. The breakfast he cooked and the way he served it swept them all away, as well it might, since Nick had been a steward on three great ocean liners for fifteen years. To make a long story short, Nick lived to bury my uncle and my aunt, painted the house three or four times in the nearly twenty years he lived there, and was periodically thrown out never to return because he would wait until my uncle had squeezed all the grapes and made the wine, and then drank it up down in the cellar, gallon after gallon, and had to have his stomach pumped by the ambulance driver, who, after a while, got out the stomach pump the minute he pulled up in front of the house.

It was a village, and the people died like the elms did, and I do not know those who live in their houses now. I go back there now and then, but whether it is I that am no longer young or the people who have changed, I know only that things are alien to me there and I am as strange to the place as if I had never known it. The cars, for one thing, jam bumper to bumper along the curbs on streets where there was so much clear space we could have bumping matches with our first jalopies, and ride backwards and forwards and up on the sidewalks and never find an obstruction anywhere. And people seem to move in and out more often than they did, and there are many who have lived there five or six years now and the people next door still don't know what they do for a living, or anything more than their names. The drugstore has a chromium front now and fluorescent lighting, and young Mr. Dozik is a gray-haired man. A lot of picture windows are being put in to get a better view of the wall of the next house a driveway's width away. And when anyone looks out the picture window all the people next door are there watching television anyway.

But there is still the smell of the leaves being burned in the fall, and I imagine some boy is delivering the rolls, and all these strangers must be close to somebody, although I would swear they are more formal toward each other than we used to be, and there is an indifference in their eyes, even the ones who sit out in front of their houses in the cool of the evening. My father sits out there waiting for a friendly conversation, and usually ends up, after an hour or so, going up to bed without having talked to anyone. There has been a scandal or two and amorous conflicts the like of which were rare before, but the children still wonder if my father is really the mayor, as he claims to be in such dead earnest, and now and again a few who have not yet caught on will come to the house leading a cat by a rope because, in a sudden fit of ennui, a few weeks ago, he said to a little boy passing by, "I buy all kinds of cats," or a child will stop a stranger to ask what his business might be because my father, what with all the casino games dead and gone, has persuaded the five-year-olds to "stand guard and watch the block."

But I think, as I watch him sitting there, that the smell of the burning leaves and autumn will never be enough to make those few, once space-filled blocks the center of the world again, the way they used to seem. Instead of the pies and cakes being trafficked back and forth across the street, and much visiting from house to house and the late card games and a certain energetic noisiness that was full of heat, there is now an order, and more politeness, and even when people do live there a long time now, they always have the feeling that someday they might not, and that changes things.

Still, as my father said the other night, "It's a different kind of people, but so is the world. They'll make out all right." And he stared down the street at the unbroken line of cars, at the old houses ludicrously changed to look more ranchy, at the tall apartment houses beyond the corner, and the metallic sound such buildings seem to make, and he got up and folded his chair and carried it into the house.

Brooklyn is a lot of villages. And this was one of them.

1955

University of Michigan

My first affection for the University of Michigan was due, simply, to their accepting me. They had already turned me down twice because my academic record (I had flunked algebra three times in my Brooklyn high school) was so low as to be practically invisible, but the dean reversed himself after two letters in which I wrote that since working for two years—in a warehouse at fifteen dollars a week—I had turned into a much more serious fellow. He said he would give me a try, but I had better make some grades. I could not conceive of a dean at Columbia or Harvard doing that.

When I arrived in 1934, at the bottom of the Depression, I fell in love with the place, groggy as I was from the bus ride, because I was out of the warehouse at last and at least formally a part of a beautiful town, the college town of Ann Arbor. I resolved to make good for the dean and studied so hard my first semester that in the history exam my mind went completely blank and the professor led me out of the class and told me to go to sleep and to come back and take the exam again.

I loved it also because of the surprises. Elmo Hamm, the son of a potato farmer in Upper Michigan, turned out to be as sharp a student as any of the myopic drudges who got the best grades in New York. I loved it because Harmon Remmel, the son of an Arkansas banker, lived in the room next to mine, and from him I got a first glimpse of what the South meant to a Southerner, a Southerner who kept five rifles racked on the wall, and two .38's in his valise, and poured himself bullets in a little mold he kept on his desk. (In his sophomore year he disappeared, and I found out he had been unable to bear it any longer once duck-hunting time had rolled around again.)

I loved the idea of being separated from the nation, because the spirit of the nation, like its soil, was being blown by crazy winds. Friends of mine in New York, one of them a cum laude from Columbia, were aspiring to the city fireman's exam, but in Ann Arbor I saw that if it came to the worst a man could live on nothing for a long time. I earned fifteen dollars a month for feeding a building full of mice—the National Youth Administration footing the bill—and out of it I paid $1.75 a week for my room and squeezed the rest for my Granger tobacco (two packs for thirteen cents), my books, laundry, and movies. For my meals I washed dishes in the co-op cafeteria. My eyeglasses were supplied by the health service, and my teeth were fixed for the cost of materials. The girls paid for themselves, including the one I married.

I think I sent more students to Michigan than anybody else who ever went there.

It was a great place for anybody who wanted to write. The Hopwood Awards, with prizes ranging from $250 to $1500, were an incentive, but there was something more. The English Department had, and still has, a serious respect for undergraduate writing efforts. Professor Kenneth Rowe, who teaches playwriting, may not have created a playwright (no teacher ever did), but he surely read what we wrote with the urgency of one who actually had the power to produce the play. I loved the place, too, because it was just big enough to give one the feeling that his relative excellence or mediocrity had real meaning, and yet not so big as to drown one in numbers.

I remember the June of each year when the Hopwood Awards were announced, and the crowds would form to hear the featured speaker—some literary light from the book world—after which the presentations were made. How I hated those speakers for holding up the awards! And those prizes meant more than recognition. In my case at least, they meant the end of mouse-feeding and room-sharing and the beginning of a serious plan to become a playwright. Avery Hopwood made millions by writing bedroom farces like *Getting Gertie's Garter* and *Up in Mabel's Room;* if my sense of it is correct, never was so much hope created in so many people by so modest an accomplishment. I have never sweated on an opening night the way I did at Hopwood time.

I do not know whether the same thing happened at Harvard or Columbia or Yale, but when I was at Ann Arbor I felt I was at home. It was a little world, and it was man-sized. My friends were the sons of diemakers, farmers, ranchers, bankers, lawyers, doctors, clothing workers and unemployed relief recipients. They came from every part of the country and brought all their prejudices and special wisdoms. It was always so wonderful to get up in the morning. There was a lot learned every day. I recall going to hear Kagawa, the Japanese philosopher, and how, suddenly, half the audience stood up and walked out because he had used the word Manchukuo, which is Japanese, for the Chinese province of Manchuria. As I watched the Chinese students excitedly talking outside on the steps of Hill Auditorium, I felt something about the Japanese attack on China that I had not felt before.

It was a time when the fraternities, like the football team, were losing their glamour. Life was too earnest. But I remember glancing with sadness at the photographs of Newman, Oosterbaan, and the other gridiron heroes and secretly wishing that the gladiatorial age had not so completely disappeared. Instead, my generation thirsted for another kind of action, and we took great pleasure in the sit-down strikes that burst loose in Flint and Detroit, and we gasped when Roosevelt went over the line with the TVA, and we saw a new world coming every third morning, and some of the old residents thought we had gone stark raving mad.

I tell you true, when I think of the library I think of the sound of a stump speaker on the lawn outside, because so many times I looked up from what I was reading to try to hear what issue they were debating now. The place was full of speeches, meetings, and leaflets. It was jumping with Issues.

But political facts of life were not all I learned. I learned that under certain atmospheric conditions you could ice-skate up and down all the streets in Ann Arbor at night. I learned that toward June you could swim in a certain place without a suit on and that the Arboretum, a tract of land where the botanists studied plants and trees, was also good for anatomical studies, especially in spring under a moon. I had come to school believing that professors were objective repositories of factual knowledge; I found that they were not only fallible but some of them were damn fools and enough of them seekers and questioners to make talking with them a long-lasting memory.

I left Ann Arbor in the spring of 1938 and in two months was on relief. But, whether the measurement was false or not, I felt I had accomplished something there. I knew at least how much I did not know. I had found many friends and had the respect of the ones that mattered to me. It had been a small world, gentler than the real one but tough enough. It was my idea of what a university ought to be.

What is it now? You can see at once, I hope, that my judgment is not objective, if only because my memories of the place are sweet and so many things that formed those memories have been altered. There are buildings now where I remembered lawn and trees. And yet, I told myself as I resented these intrusions, in the Thirties we were all the time calling for these dormitories and they are finally built. In my day bequests were used for erecting less useful things—the carillon tower whose bells woke us up in the morning, the Rackham Building, a grand mausoleum which seemed to have been designed for sitting around in a wide space.

There are certain facts about the university today that can be disposed of right off. In almost every field of study, a student will probably find no better training anywhere than at Michigan. Some say that in forestry, medicine, creative writing, and many other fields it is really the top. I wouldn't know, I never went to any other school.

The student will need about a thousand dollars a year, which is cheaper than a lot of places. He will get free medical care and hospitalization; he will be able to borrow money from the university if he needs it and may take nearly forever to pay it back; he will use modern laboratories in the sciences and an excellent library in the humanities; as a freshman he will live in new dormitories, and the girls will have to be in bed at ten-thirty; if he flies to school he will land at the Willow Run Airport, the safest in the country, owned now by the university; he will have a radio station and a television station to try his scripts, if he writes, and if he is more literary than that he can try for a Hopwood Award in poetry, drama, the essay and the novel.

He will meet students of many backgrounds. Two thirds will be from Michigan and a large proportion of those from small towns. About nine hundred will be foreign, including Japanese, Turks, Chinese and Europeans. If he is Negro he will find little discrimination, except in a few Greek-letter fraternities. Most of his classes will be large in the first years, but his teachers have regular visiting hours, and with a little push he can get to know them. He will not be permitted to drive a car or to keep liquor in his room.

On many winter mornings he will wake to find great snows, and there will be a serene hush upon the campus and the creaking of branches overhead as he walks to his class. In spring he will glance outside at a blossoming world and resolve to keep his eye away from the girl sitting beside him. By June, the heat of the prairies will threaten to kill him and he will leave just in time.

If he has the talent, he may join the *Michigan Daily* staff, and the *Daily* is as close to a real newspaper as he will find in any school. On its own press, it prints about 7500 copies a day, has the Associated Press wire service and syndicated columnists, and its student staff is paid twelve dollars a month and up. The university athletic plant includes a stadium seating nearly 100,000 people, indoor and outdoor tennis courts, swimming pools, and so on.

If a figure can convey an idea of complexity and size, it costs about $40 million a year to keep the place going. There are now better than 18,000 students and nearly 1200 faculty, and the figures will rise next year and the year after. The school has just bought 347 acres for new buildings. More facts may be had for the asking; but in any case, you couldn't do better for facilities.

Things seem to be getting *done* now. For instance, on the north side of the campus the Phoenix Project is going up, the only thing of its kind in the country. It was conceived by an alumnus in the advertising business who discovered, while traveling through Europe, that we were being accused of using the atom for war only. Returning here, he began a campaign for alumni contributions to create an institute which will accept no government money, do no war work, and instead of operating in secrecy will attempt to discover and disperse the knowledge of the atom that will, some say, revolutionize human life. Research projects are under way, although the scientists are not yet housed in one building, and already a method has been found by which the dreaded trichina, often found in pork, is destroyed. One of the men in charge of the project told me that the implications of Phoenix will reach into every science, that it has already moved into botany, medicine, dentistry, and eventually will span them all.

There is an enormous growth in all kinds of theater since I was at Michigan. Somewhere, sometime this year on campus, you could have seen *Brigadoon*, Gilbert and Sullivan, a German play, a French play, Aristophanes, Pirandello, *Deep Are the Roots, Faust, Madame Butterfly, Mister Roberts*, and more, all acted by students. A professional theater has done Camus, Bridie, Shakespeare, Saroyan, Yeats, Gertrude Stein, Sophocles, Synge and the Norwegian Krog. A symphony orchestra and a jazz band play student compositions frequently; there is a practically continuous art show going on, with both traveling and local exhibitions on view; the best foreign and art films are shown once a week, and the joint is jumping with concerts. All this is proof that a considerable number of people in Ann Arbor are looking for more than technology and are eager to feed their souls—a fact sometimes doubted by many in and out of the university.

The increase in students goes far to explain the impression of great activity, of building, of research, the scores of research projects, and of course the great increases in the faculty, especially in the English and Psychology Departments. But the changes are also qualitative. As one small sign, the music school has a few teachers who actually compose. The old idea of the university is not passing away, it is being worked away, it seems; the study of phenomena is giving way to the creation of useful things. *Generation*, the literary magazine, does not merely publish essays on music but new scores, as well as poetry, photographs and stories.

The university has the feel of a practical workshop these days. In my time a great deal of research and thesis writing was carried on by people who were simply hiding from the Depression. When you asked undergraduates what they intended to major in, and what career they meant to follow, you saw an oblong blur float across their eyes. These days nearly everybody seems to be quite sure. I knew graduate students who lived in an abandoned house with no electricity or heat and never took the boardings off the windows for fear of discovery, and one of them had been around so long he had gone through every course in the lit school but Roman Band instruments. The lucky ones got an assistantship at $600 a year and even so looked like they had dropped out of a novel by Dostoyevski. Now, in some departments, a man doing his dissertation hooks into a research project and earns $2400 a year and sometimes gets secretarial help in the bargain.

The Psychology Department, for instance, which used to have about a half-dozen members, and was year in year out trying to discover the learning processes of rats put through an enormous maze, now spreads out over a whole floor of offices, and spends tens of thousands investigating mass behavior of *people*, of all things, problems of industrial psychology, and in the words of one troubled researcher, "how to make people do what you want them to while thinking they are doing it because *they* want to."

From the physical, quantitative point of view, it seems to me that if by some magic this university of 1953 had suddenly materialized on a morning in 1935, let's say, we would have decided that the millennium had arrived. The mere fact that every morning the Michigan *Daily* displays two columns of invitations from corporations and government bureaus to students to apply for positions would have been enough.

The millennium is here, and yet it isn't here. What's wrong, then? I have no proof for this, but I felt it many times in my stay and I'll say it: I did not feel any love around the place. I suspect that I resent the Detroit Modern architecture of the new administration building and the new Haven and Mason Halls, and the fluorescent lighting and the gray steel furniture in the teachers' office cubicles. Can steel furniture ever belong to anybody, or can anybody ever belong to steel furniture? Is it all right to need so much administration that you have to put up an office building with nothing but administrators in it? Maybe it's all right, but God, it's not a university, is it? Why not? I don't know why not, it just feels like an insurance company, that's all. And yet, with eighteen to twenty thousand students, I suppose you've got to have it. Somebody's got to count them. But there is no love in it.

There is a certain propriety around the place that I found quite strange. Or was it always that way and I didn't notice? I do not remember teachers lowering their voices when they spoke to you in the corridors, but they do that now. At first I thought it was my imagination, and I asked a few men about it, but they denied that they do it. Still, they are doing it. The place is full of comportment. Maybe I have been around theatrical folk too long but it seemed to me that everybody had turned into engineers—in my day all engineers wore black suits and short, antiseptic haircuts. The curious thing is that now the engineers affect buckskin shoes and dungarees or tan chino work pants.

The lists of help-wanted notices alone would have solved the problem of my generation. And yet in talking with a certain high administrative official, it quickly became evident that the millennium had not yet arrived. I found it hard to believe that this gentleman had been elevated to administration, because when he was my teacher several hundred years ago he used to drop his coat on the floor sometimes and forget about tying his tie correctly, and his suits were usually rumpled. He just wasn't executive. Now his suits are pressed and finished worsted not tweed, but the smile is still warm and the eyes crinkle with a great love for humanity. He is very proud of the school, but there is a cloud. There is a cloud over the whole place which is hard to define, and here is part of it. I do not quote him but summarize what he said:

There is less hanging around the lamppost than there used to be. The student now is very young and he has little background. He generally comes with high respect for Michigan's academic standards. The school takes the top half of the in-state students and the top twenty percent of the out-staters. Fear of the competition is one reason why they absorb themselves in the pursuit of grades. Another is that they do not want to lose their Army deferments. Finally, in the old days a corporation would interview a C student because he might have other valuable qualities, while today the selections are almost statistical—they see the very top of the class and no others. The students know this and are more methodical about grades to the neglect of other interests.

The implication seemed to be that they are more machinelike and perhaps even duller. Or perhaps he meant only that some spirit had departed.

What spirit was he referring to? I think I know. The word university used to imply a place of gentle inquiry, an absorbing waste of time from the money point of view, a place where one "broadened" oneself. And I think he meant that everything is being *defined* now, it is all becoming so purposeful in the narrow sense of the trade school that some of the old separation between university and commerce, university and vocation, university and practicality in the narrow sense, is disappearing.

One symptom of this is the growing and dangerous rivalry with Michigan State College. In my day State was an agricultural college, and the University of Michigan was "The Harvard of the West." Today State is challenging the university for supremacy in all departments, even threatening to rename itself Michigan State *University*. Dr. John A. Hannah, State's vigorous president, has been able to raise enough funds to build a row of impressive dormitories along the main road. The public can see and count the things it is getting for its money. The university cannot compete for the public's appreciation—and support—on the basis of invisible accomplishments like culture and broadening. Consequently, a new and in my time unheard-of slogan is going around the faculty gatherings. Service to the state is the idea. Do things they can *see*. My friend spoke with startlingly serious irritation, real misgivings, about State's victories over Michigan in football. It has come even to that.

As in everything else, therefore, the competition must be carried through on the level of the lowest bidder. Michigan State has always been able to show that where one blade of corn had grown now there were two because of its new insecticides, and the cows were happier for its vaccines. Michigan State went on television, got its own station, so the university decided to win friends and acquire *its* station.

A professor of English was speaking to me in his office. I must note the incongruity of this particular man sitting in this particular office. In my time this man was, how shall I say, dusty. We were all afraid of him because in his classes you either knew your stuff or you didn't. His subject had made him pale and austerely exact. A great poem was a structure that had to be turned and turned until you understood its time, its place, its rhythms, and the telling reference in every line. Only a powerful love for the poem itself could have generated his kind of energy in teaching it. He is the kind of man who just does not go with fluorescent lighting and long hallways with little cubicles opening off them, and rivalry toward Michigan State. Or so it seemed long ago.

I asked if he noticed any difference between the present student and school, and the student and school of fifteen years ago. A repressed anger crackled in his eyes.

"It's *all* different. Take the study of literature. Who are its judges? The psychologist is looked to for an analysis of motivations. But even that isn't as bad as looking at a book or a play to discover what kind of Oedipus complex the author had. The sociologists are deferred to as the only men who can really say how typical the situation is in society, and the anthropologist also has a few words handy. Now, I am only an amateur in these disciplines. They are the experts. And what about the literary people? They are becoming experts in their own way. We have what are called The New Critics. The poem to them is a thing in itself. If the diction is exact, the imagery consistent, the writing original and the form consonant with the breadth of the matter, that's the end of it. It is as though the values of humanity——"

The Values. A certain few themes kept coming up wherever I went, and The Values were in the center. The impression gained from certain quarters is that, in 1953, it is thought sufficient to have described a piece of existence, whether it is a book or an isotope. The conflict is being played around certain connected themes. One is The Values. Another is Apathy.

Another English teacher told me: "The student today has no spine. He thinks he is here to receive something that is wrapped up, easily digestible and complete. He is not really working anything *out*."

The *Michigan Daily* keeps bewailing "apathy" among the students. One reason is that it cannot find enough men to man its positions. The Values and Apathy.

I went back to the *Daily* building and looked up the papers of my day, '34 to '38. I was surprised and amused to read that the Michigan student was a lizard, apathetic, uninterested in campus affairs.

So it gets more complicated. The student is apathetic, but the *Daily* thought he was apathetic in 1936. In those days we laughed at research-for-its-own-sake and now people are disturbed because everything has got so practical, provable and dangerously unvague.

A psychology professor told me: "The student *is* different. The back-talk is feeble. They *are* passive. Imagine a graduate student asking me to tell him what his dissertation subject should be. I couldn't believe my ears at first, but it is happening regularly now. And more than that, they expect me to lay out the lines of their research, and when I try not to do it, they are astonished. They regard themselves as instruments. It is as though they thought it a waste of time to speculate, to move into unknown territory, which is just what they should be doing."

Another psychologist said: "The most embarrassing question you can ask a researcher is, 'Why are you doing this?' He can tell you its immediate application, but whether it is good or bad to apply it or whether it could be a disastrous power to put in the wrong hands either is not his business or else he is just hoping for the best."

I began to feel after a while that something was chasing everybody here. The Necessity to Keep Doing. A fantastic number of discoveries being made and a gnawing worry about What it is All For. I think the Phoenix Project is one answer, a statement of the university's conscience.

One example of this atmosphere of pursuit is the television question.

A professor of English: "Now we are going on television. Why? Allegedly to spread education among the people. But is that really why? It is not. It is because Michigan State is winning friends and influencing people, so we must. Did you know that they send out calendars reading, 'Come to Michigan State, The Friendly College'? We are now going to be 'friendly'! Can you really teach people on a university level through TV? My subject is hard. It requires that a student work to understand it. Isn't it inevitable that we will have to make it easier and easier and lower our standards in order to compete? The TV audience is profoundly passive. It is looking for a massage, not a message. And in addition my subject has 'controversial' aspects. Can a teacher maintain the courage to speak his heart in the face of the pressure groups and the mass ignorance they can arouse against him? I don't believe it. We are being asked to become entertainers, and the time will come when a professor will be cast for voice, looks and camera manners. Oh, you can laugh, but it is absolutely in the cards. We are going to have to put ourselves over, we are going to have to sell Michigan. The neon age of education is upon us. And don't confuse this with democracy. It is the triumph of the leveler, and the man in charge is an advertising man."

I could go on endlessly because in nearly every conversation these themes kept cropping up. But there are many who deny their validity.

A physicist: "I know they are all beefing about passivity, but I don't find it in my field. They are as hep and alive as they ever were. Some of this 'apathy' is really a kind of maturity. Kids don't join things so much now, because they are more serious. There is, of course, the problem of values. The atomic boys found that out with a jolt. It is not enough to discover something, one must work on the problem of its use. And you can be sure that a scientist who has the brains to work in nuclear physics is intelligent enough to worry about values. So much so that some people risked a great deal and went to the government to implore them to understand what the atom implied. Don't think for a minute that we are automatons without conscience. Nothing is farther from the truth."

Another English professor: "I can't tell any great difference between these kids and any peacetime class. I think what some of the others are complaining about is really based on our experience with the veterans who left here about 1948. It's true, they were thrilling people to teach. They were serious but inquisitive, they were after the facts, but they knew that a philosophy, a standard of values, was of first importance. But the prewar classes didn't measure up to the veterans either."

I met students in the restaurants, in dormitories, classrooms, hallways, and in the union, the center for nonfraternity students. If there were no two alike, they nevertheless had certain common feelings that came up to the surface very quickly. Michigan means freedom to them. It has nothing to do with academic freedom but a release from home and the neighborhood or town they came from. This is as it always was, but I had forgotten what an adventure it was to leave home. One afternoon I sat with the girls on the veranda of the Martha Cook dormitory. Martha Cook is brick and ivy, lawns and old trees, and windows you remember as leaded but which are not, mellow wood, and an outline of Tudor-out-of-Yale.

The Girl From Massachusetts: "Oh, gosh, yes. I would never dare do at home what I think nothing of doing here. What, exactly? Well, I don't know, but I go out with fellows my parents wouldn't approve of. You couldn't be friendly, really, with a Chinese or a Negro in my town. Not really, you couldn't. You can here."

The Girl From New York (the intellectual): "Well, that's not quite true. It's very complicated."

The Girl From Ohio (who will marry a law student after graduation and settle in Rio, where he will practice): "I think it's enormously freer. It's like, well, it's an explosion, almost. I started in literature, then I went to botany, and now I'm in music." And brother, she was. As they used to say, she was bursting with life, sitting there in blue jeans, her heels tucked against her buttocks, her knees up around her cheeks, and a sunburned face sucking in everything that was said and ever would be said. But the others thought she was hasty in planning to settle outside the country. I was surprised. I had thought they would all be thrilled at the prospect of foreign lands. It took a minute for them to say exactly why they thought her hasty.

"There might be a revolution there," they finally agreed. It would be better to stay home.

Maybe they were just envious. But they weren't apathetic, if that means dull, without thought. The Depression means to them what World War I meant to us; that is, an old-fashioned thing. Time after time I got the same image—"It couldn't happen that way again. The government wouldn't let it, I don't think." They seem to feel that society is under control; it is so enormous, and it *is* operating, that there is just nothing to think about in that department. They feel there is enormous opportunity for anybody; that men are rewarded pretty much according to their abilities, and time and time again said the same line, "It's up to me."

The famous panty raids that swept the country started at Michigan last year and these girls had witnessed that strange crusade. It seems that some guy was blowing a trumpet in one of the men's dorms, and somebody else yelled at him to stop, and the trumpet player dared the other guy to make him stop, but instead of fighting they decided to invade the women's dormitories and steal panties. A crowd gathered and kept getting bigger all night as one dormitory after another was entered. Martha Cook was among those that "fell." The girls were quite gay about it and told the story as though they kind of wished more of the same would happen now and then.

The story sounded as though it might well have happened at any time, the Thirties included, but to my ear there was nevertheless a strange note in it. It did not sound like a simple sexual outburst. As the girls spoke, I had the feeling that the panty raids were one of those phenomena which are only superficially sexual and were directed more as a challenge to the atmosphere of paternal repression which is, and always was, quite strong at Michigan.

An administrative official arranged a luncheon for me with a dozen or so student leaders. I feared this would be a polite waste of time and it is no reflection on the man to say that they were under wraps in his presence. As they themselves told me later, the paternalism of the administration is not conducive to student expression. It was always a rather heavily administration-dominated school, but in the old days they had a fight for their money. I remember one hell of a racket when Fred Warner Neal, probably the most prolific reporter the paper ever had, resigned from the *Daily*—which gave him a full column on Page 1 to write his resignation— because the administration had forbidden him to write some story or other. And I remember he was reinstated. I remember committees demanding to see the president whenever they didn't like something, and I remember a few times when they won the argument, or half won it.

These dozen, being interested enough to head up the student legislature, the interfraternity council and so on, were the contemporary equivalents of the people who made the noise in my time. While the official was with us they weren't very noisy; it might have been a meeting of young bankers. But he had to leave soon and we were alone and it started coming.

"People are afraid to say anything."

Afraid of what?

"Well, for instance, a lot of people are tired of paying high prices for books. We want a university bookstore, but we know we'll never get one because the bookstores will raise hell and, besides, the administration won't pay any attention to us."

But you're evidently not afraid to make the demand.

"No, not exactly afraid——"

What do you think would happen if you tried to rally support on campus for a demand like that?

"You mean, like to have a meeting or demonstrate?"

They all looked uncomfortable. Some laughed nervously.

One boy said, "We'd be called communists."

You mean that truly?

"Sure. But the worst thing would be that back home the papers would pick up our names and there might be trouble."

You mean they'd think you'd been turned into Reds here?

"Some people would think so, but it's not exactly being called communists, it's different."

What exactly is it?

"Well, it's that when you went to, let's say, the local plant for a job, and if they found out about it they would—well, they wouldn't like you."

Oh.

A girl: "I live in a cooperative house." And really, she blushed. "I'm getting ashamed to mention it because people on campus ask me why do you live with those collectivists? But it's cheaper, and anyway they're not collectivists." They all laughed but they knew that what she was saying was true.

A boy hitherto silent: "I know for a fact that everything you do is being written down and sent to the authorities."

Like what?

"Never mind, I just know it."

I had, the day before, been sitting in the *Daily* building going through the 1934–38 papers. A middle-aged man with eyeglasses and a thick neck took out a file and after a while began noting things down. A reporter came over to me and whispered that this man was a state policeman, and his job was to check up on subversives in the school. The reporter said that he and the others on the paper were always trying to tell the man that the people he was listing were not Reds, but he went right on, in a very affable way, listing anyone who was connected with anything "controversial."

It is necessary to add that at the luncheon, the very broaching of this subject reddened some faces. They were bravely willing to discuss it, and really quite eager to, but if they were not in fear I do not understand anything.

"That's why everybody wants to get into Intelligence."

What's that?

"I'm telling you the facts."

"Oh, go on, they just feel they won't get shot in Intelligence."

"There's a lot of jobs in the Army where you don't get shot. I swear, they all want to get into Intelligence."

So that they can investigate other people?

"No, they don't want to investigate other people, but they feel once they get in there they won't be bothered any more."

Would you like to get into Intelligence?

Laughter. "Sure, I'd take it."

And he blushes. That is, he blushes, but he would take it although he's against it.

There are more evidences of gumshoeing around the campus, but it would be false to picture the place as being in fear of any specific thing. The important fact to me is that the gumshoeing is disliked, sometimes scorned, but accepted as perfectly natural. Sometimes the old liberalism will crop up, however. Not long ago the university prohibited a communist from speaking on campus, and Professor Slosson went to the hall where the man had to make his address, debated with him, and from all accounts slaughtered him.

Compared to my years at Michigan there does seem to be a blanket over the place now. The tone is more subdued, if one measures tone by the amount of discussion, argument and protest openly indulged in. In my day we were more likely to believe that what we thought and did would have an effect upon events, while the present student sees himself separated from the great engine that is manufacturing his and the country's fate.

But it would be inaccurate to think that these boys and girls are inert. I sat in on a graduate seminar in political science one afternoon at which five students and a professor were discussing the subtlest relationships between political ideologies over a span of three centuries. It is a long time since I witnessed such complete concentration upon essentials, sharpness of mind, and freedom from cant and sloganeering. In the Thirties such a discussion would have verged on partisanship after an hour, but it never did here, and that is a big change, I think.

They know now that the old easy solutions are suspect, and they are examining rather than exhorting each other. In this sense they are more mature than we were, yet they are also more separated and removed from the idea of action. But action is immensely more complicated than it was and more difficult to conceive; for instance, one of the heaviest loads they bear is the Army draft. In my day we could rally and vote against conscription because it was only a threat, while today there is nothing to be done about it, and it makes futile many of their plans and weakens as well the very idea of controlling their own destinies.

I do not know how things will work out at Michigan any more than the next man does. It may be the faculty men are correct who see a profound shift of values which will make of Michigan a place not unintelligent, not overtly browbeaten, but a school of obedient pragmatists where each individual walks in blinders toward his niche in government or giant corporation, his soul unswept by the hot blasts of new ideas and vast social concepts. The very bigness of Michigan, the size of the investment in it, and the mutual suspicion that is gripping so many people are forces that would help such a process along. And there is a deeper, less-noticed frame of mind which goes even farther to create such an atmosphere, and I think of the faculty man-of-goodwill, in this context, who was talking to me about a certain administrator who paid no attention to the students' ideas or complaints or suggestions. "It's a pity," said this faculty man, "that X's public relations are not better." Whether X might in fact have *been* authoritarian and unheeding was evidently beside the point. The fault to remedy was X's inability to put himself over. It is in such remarks and attitudes that one sees the absence of an idealism I clearly remember at Michigan and in its place a kind of pragmatism that threatens to create a race of salesmen in the tawdry sense of that word.

I cannot promise that it will not end this way: a chromium-plated silence, a highly organized, smoothly running factory for the production of conformism. I only know that in my time it was supposed to be a training ground for leftists or, from the opposite viewpoint, a cave of vigilantism, and it turned out to be neither. I know that when I recently sat with individual students they spoke like seekers, their clean, washed faces as avid for truth as I suppose we were so long ago. I know that they do not think of themselves as a "silent generation" or as a generation at all but simply as "me." I know that in their rooming houses and dormitories the old bull sessions go on into the mornings, but I also know that what so many of them really feel—and here, I think, lies the difference between the generations—they are not saying in public nowadays, if it seems to question that this is the best of all possible worlds. It is simply not done in 1953.

When I stood waiting for the plane at Willow Run I tried to summon up the memory of the other time I had left Ann Arbor, in the fall of 1938. I had had a ride to New York with a young salesman of saddles and riding equipment who had just passed through Ann Arbor. He had been in contact only with the upper echelons of the community—certain high officials, industrialists, a regent or two who owned horses. He had sold a lot of saddles in Ann Arbor. He was leaving with the impression of a fairly ritzy school. For myself, I had not known a single soul in four years who had mounted a horse.

As he started the engine I waved to a girl who was standing in front of the Women's League, a girl that I dared not dream I would ever have money enough, or security of soul enough, to marry. As we drove east, through Toledo, Ashtabula, the red-brick roads through the Ohio farmlands, I tried to tell him what Michigan really was. It was the professor who, with selected members of his class, held séances during which the spirits of Erasmus, Luther and other historical figures were summoned and listened to. It was the fraternity boys sitting on the porches of their mansions, singing nostalgic Michigan songs as in a movie, and it was three radicals being expelled. It was, in short, the testing ground for all my prejudices, my beliefs and my ignorance, and it helped to lay out the boundaries of my life. For me it had, above everything else, variety and freedom. It is probably the same today. If it is not, a tragedy is in the making.

1953

Belief in America
(from Situation Normal*)*

Riding away from the camp it became clear for the first time why I had looked so hard for a sign of Belief in the Army. It was, I saw, a personal reason. I had an instinctive fear that millions of men could not be put through the hell of battle and be expected to return to American life as whole men unless they had some basic elementary understanding of why they had had to go through their battle. I had been, I saw now, afraid of what such men would do to America and what their returning to America would do to them. My fear had not been, as I thought all along, that they would not fight well without the Belief, for everything I saw convinced me that our soldiers, for many different and sometimes totally irrelevant reasons, have sufficient faith in their leaders to follow them into battle. Now I saw that the danger lay in the return of the warriors, in the time when they were no longer webbed into the Army organization, no longer under their military leaders commanding them in the pressure of battle and war. Riding away from the camp I wondered for the first time whether I ought not be wandering through St. Paul and Kansas City, New York and Los Angeles, instead of through the camps. For as far as Watson was concerned it was in America as much as in the island where he fought that his wholeness had been wrecked and his mind distracted. It was not only the Japanese who had shaken his wits. We here did our part in that, and with terrible effect.

It is wrong to use a single man as the basis of a statement about all soldiers, but from what I have been able to learn since speaking to him I have come to the conclusion that he represents a nearly classic extreme of a state of mind found in all men who have been in actual battle, hard battle.

For want of a better word—this one has certain sneering connotations—Watson was in love, in love with his comrades in arms. I sensed it as he spoke to me, and I was sure of it when I had left him. Probably his whole conflict consists of his fear of returning to battle, set against his love for his unit. The feeling of guilt that such a dilemma would generate in a man needs no defining. He was not merely letting "the Army" down or his "unit." He was being forced by fear to forsake a group of men whom he had loved. His avowal that he would die for any of them was even truer than I had imagined.

Now what happens to a Watson when he returns to America? It must be remembered that as far as anyone could tell he returned whole, sane, and fit for further training. What happened to him here? What did he see or fail to see here that so shook him?

I can only guess at that. But I am not trying to solve Watson's problem. In the present state of American affairs I do not know how his problem can be solved. But Watson is an extreme. Many hundreds of thousands of men are going to return from terrible battles, and in some degree they will have shared Watson's feeling of love and identity with their particular comrades and units. And in differing degrees they are going to have to transfer that love to other—civilian—"units" or be forever in that restless, aimless state of emotional thirst which in other countries at other times has made veterans the anxious and willing collaborators of any demagogue who joins them together under a common color of shirt, for a common and often violent social purpose. We will dispense with the argument against those who still say it can't happen here. It has begun to happen here too many times for us to argue about it at this late date. But what about Watson, about the millions of Watsons who are even now coming down the gangplanks in American ports . . .

They have fought their battle. Carried forward by faith in an officer, by a feeling of love for their comrades, by an innate sense of honor, by a plain love of adventure and danger, by whatever drive obtained in them at the time of battle, they fought their battle, and now they are home. No man has ever felt identity with a group more deeply and intimately than a soldier in battle. But now their uniforms are off. They walk out of the circle of the imperative order, out of the unity of feeling they had known in the Army. They go home.

Home is many things. Home can be a family well loved or a wife longed for whose love is all-sufficing. Home may be the feverish joy of resuming projects left half finished. Home may give Watson—many of them—a satisfying substitute for the close comradeship of the battlefield. The battlefield and its emotions may quickly fade once the fighter is really home.

But maybe not. Home, to many, perhaps to most, means a town or a city cut into a thousand little disjointed pieces, each one an exclusive class in itself. If on returning home, the veteran should find the town in immediate danger of being inundated by a flood, with every sort of person in it working together toward a common goal, the problem might hardly exist for him. With each citizen protecting his neighbor, as he does in time of danger, and all divisions of race, economic and social position melted away in the face of the peril, the veteran would find himself strangely at home among his people. But a flood is a rare thing. The usual veteran returning to his city or town on the usual day finds no common goal at all. He finds every group in town excluding the proximate group. It is rich and poor again, it is white and black again, it is Jew and Gentile again, it is, above all, a mass of little groups each of whose apparent goals in life conflict with the goals of the next group. Watson must return to his former group. He must reassume its little prejudices, its hates, its tiny aims. He must lop off at once that onetime feeling of exhilaration he got from the knowledge that whatever the insignificance of his job, it was helping an enormous mass of men toward a great and worthy goal. Now he must forget that. Now he must live unto himself, for his own selfish welfare. Half of him, in a sense, must die, and with it must pass away half the thrill he knew in being alive. He must, in short, become a civilian again.

There is a great and deep sense of loss in that. A man who has known the thrill of giving himself does not soon forget it. It leaves him with a thirst. A thirst for a wider life, a more exciting life, a life that demands all he can give. Civilian life in America is private, it is always striving for exclusiveness. Our lifelong boast is that we got ahead of the next guy, excluded him. We have always believed in the fiction—and often damned our own belief—that if every man privately takes care of his own interests, the community and the nation will prosper and be safe. Unless your Watson's attachment to his family or his wife or his girl is so overwhelming that nothing can distract him from it, he is going to feel the loss of a social unit, a group to which he can give himself, a social goal worth his sacrifice. He may find that unit and that goal in his trade union, his club. But most Americans do not belong to unions, and the goals of most American clubs will never make up in vitality and largeness for the goal he left behind.

Watson, then, if he has the average social connections which are slight, is going to wander around his American town, and he is going to find himself severely lonely a great and growing part of the time. America, to him, is not moving in any direction. His life is standing still. And he is alone and dissatisfied.

What could civilian America possibly give Watson that it did not give? There is only one answer to that. The Belief. America tried everything else imaginable, and nothing satisfied your Watson. It tried giving him medals, it tried giving him a parade, it tried big publicity for him, it tried to give him everything within reach of its well-meaning heart. When people met him they tried being sympathetic, and that did not help. They tried being sorry for him and they tried being proud, and he did not seem to react fully to any of it. What did he want from them? They would give him anything he wanted if only he could tell them what it was that would make him feel at home in America.

Knowing it or not Watson wanted to find the Belief in America. It is a very hard concept to nail down; Belief so often means a dogma of some kind to be memorized and bowed down to, and that is not a thing that could satisfy Watson. But say it this way. If when he returned to this shore he walked in the cities and the towns and all about him he sensed and heard evidence that the people were unified in one concept—that he, Watson, had gone forth to rescue something very very precious and that had he not gone forth, and had that thing been lost, the people would have been left in mourning for it the rest of their lives. What Watson wanted in America is equivalent to what the Russian or British soldier must find when he returns home. In Russia or Britain the broken cities and the maimed children and the many civilian dead and missing say in so many words nearly everything the returning soldier needs to hear. It is very clear, there, why he went; it is superlatively clear what a unity of feeling lay behind him while he was gone, and it is bloody well apparent and understood what it was that he accomplished by going. The force of bombs and the horror of rape and destruction has spawned the quantities of a unified Belief there, and when Tommy and Ivan come marching home their people *know* them through the very arterial link of that commonly held Belief, that rock-like understanding. But here the marks of war are different. Watson found a people without scars and without any commonly held understanding of why he had to go and what he accomplished by going. True, his comrades too were not sure of what, in the end, they were accomplishing by their battles, but for them that kind of understanding, that kind of political Belief was compensated for by an emotional unity born of the common danger and the common military goal—they *knew* each other through that and they were one with each other because of it. What links Watson with the civilians at home though? A parade? Sympathy? Pride in him based on the same kind of understanding required for pride in the hometown football team? The only means by which Watson can rejoin himself with America is by sharing with civilian America a well-understood Belief in the rightness, the justness, the necessity of his fight. That is how he will be made to feel at home. It will by no means dissolve his memories and solve all his problems, but without it nothing can be solved in Watson. He will be wondering why he went and why he is alive for the rest of his days. And what could that Belief be?

Since the war began our most brilliant statesmen and writers have been trying—only in America, as far as I know—to frame a statement, a "name" for this war. They have not found it, and they will not find it, because they are looking for something new. It is pretty late now for this kind of talk, but not too late. From the first day of this war we should have understood that the kind of thing we fight for is a very old thing. We fought for it in 1776 and in 1865, and we found the words for it then, and they are perfectly good words, easy to understand and not at all old-fashioned. They are good words because they recur more times in our ordinary conversation and in the historic conversations of our long tradition than any other words. They represent a concept which, to the vast majority of Americans, must not be offended. The words are not "free enterprise," as the well-known ads of our big industries maintain. Nor are the words, "Keep America the Same," as a certain automobile company insists nearly every week in the national magazines. Neither the people of America nor those of any other nation ever fought a war in order to keep everything the same and certainly never for free enterprise or jobs. No man in his right mind would risk his life to get a job. But we did fight two wars for our Belief. And that Belief says, simply, that we believe all men are equal. We really believe it, most of us, and because a powerful force has arisen in the world dedicated to making the people of the world—us included—unequal, we have therefore decided to fight. We insist upon a state of affairs in which all men will be regarded as equal. There is no nonsense about it. We believe that everything will rot and decline and go backwards if we are forced to live under laws that hold certain nations and peoples to be inferior and without rights. We are thinking primarily of ourselves and our own rights, naturally, but that is perfectly all right, for once our right to be equal is assured we will want nothing better than to see every nation on our level. I believe the majority of Americans agree to this.

Now, if the implications of "all men are equal" were drilled into our men and women, in the Army and out, with at least the assiduousness that the brand names of certain toothpastes are, we would have, I maintain, many fewer Watsons with us now and after the war is over. The concept of equality of man is very easy for a soldier, especially, to take. It is in our tradition quite as firmly as is blueberry pie, for which our radio programs seem to feel most adult Americans are fighting, and sheds considerably more light on the meaning of this war. Its ramifications could be explained in the five-minute orientation periods in the camps quite as easily as the nature of the millimeter. And finally, it happens to be the one idea which Hitler and the Japanese deny most completely and with the heaviest use of force. They, at bottom, demand that this world be fixed into a pattern of inequality of man against man. As Americans we were marked for a secondary status in that world. We refuse to accept it. We are as good as they are, and in time, perhaps, we will help them to be as good as we are. But first we must beat hell out of them until they no longer can dictate our status. Then we will go about making them understand about equality. Again, if this concept of the war, oversimplified as it is, lacking in economic factors as it is, were "sold" across America on even half the advertising budget of our best-selling mouthwash, perhaps—I too am willing to wait and see, but perhaps—the chaos of mind that is America today would be put somewhat in order and many of our returning soldiers made to feel at home.

Watson—the real Watson, the Watson whose story you have just read—is alone in America today. He in particular is alone and lonely because his comrades are not with him, the men he loves. But he is alone and misfitted here also—and more tragically—because America offers him no great social goal. Were we conscious of our Belief, were we *here in America* acting and working and fighting as civilians for the attainment of that goal, Watson would feel it, he would have a place fighting for it, and it would demand of him that part of his character which requires sharing. As it is, the company is gone and all that the company meant. He must wall himself in from his fellow man, he must live only his own little life and do his own unimportant, unsatisfying job when he gets out of the Army. He must begin again the stale and deadly competition with his fellow men for rewards that now seem colorless, even if necessary to his survival. He is alone. Cut off from mankind and that great movement of mankind he once was part of. And the world is alien, and battle . . . It keeps coming back to me with what apparent suddenness Watson came to fear returning to battle. Is it not possible, as Watson's captain implied, that battle is ten thousand times more horrible to him now than it actually was when he was in it, because he is looking at it now as a man cut off, as a man alone with a lonely man's fears, while at the front he saw it as a joined and united part of the race, as a man who is fighting with and for those he loved? Danger breeds understanding, it breeds a growth of common unity among men. And so does Belief. Not as suddenly, perhaps, and without the bottomless emotional depths that danger plumbs, but understanding and love are bred by a commonality of Belief. We have the Belief. We have always had it, but we have stowed it away like a relic, an heirloom to be taken down from the attic on a Sunday afternoon when visitors come and then hidden away. We need it every day now. For Belief is not a bullet, as has been said. Belief is a shield. When will we start the mills that roll such armament? And who will wither away because he went and returned, unarmed?

1944

A Modest Proposal for the Pacification of the Public Temper

There being in existence at the present time a universally held belief in the probability of treasonous actions;

And at the same time no certain method of obtaining final assurance in the faithfulness of any citizen toward his country, now that outright Treason, dallying with the Enemy, and other forms of public and private perfidy have been abundantly demonstrated in and among persons even of the highest office;

I herewith submit a Proposal for the Pacification of the Public Temper, and the Institution among the People of Mutual Faith and Confidence;

Having clearly in mind the Damages, both financial and Spiritual, which have already accrued due to the spread of Suspicion among Citizens, the said Proposal follows, namely:

The Proposal

1. That upon arriving at his eighteenth (18th) birthday, and every second year thereafter so long as he lives, providing said day does not fall upon a Sunday or nationally proclaimed Legal Holiday; in which case performance shall take place on the first regular day of business following, every Citizen of the United States of America shall present himself at the office of the United States Marshal nearest his place of residence;

Duties of Marshal

1. That said Marshal shall immediately place the Citizen under what is hereby officially described and determined as Patriotic Arrest or National Detention, which shall in every way conform to regular and ordinary incarceration in the prison, jail, or other Federal Detention Facility normally used in that locality;

Duties of Incarcerated Citizen

1. That without undue delay the citizen shall be informed that he may avail himself of all subpoena powers of the Government in order to secure for himself all documents, papers, manifolds, records, recorded tapes or discs, witnesses and/or other paraphernalia which he requires to prove his Absolute and steady Allegiance to this Country, its Government, Army and Navy, Congress, and the Structure, Aims, and History of its Institutions;
2. That upon assembling such documents and/or witnesses in support, he shall be brought before a Judge of the United States Court of Clearance, which Court to be established herewith;

Duties of Judge in Court of Clearance

1. That said Judge shall hear all of the defendant's witnesses and examine faithfully all evidence submitted;
2. That said Judge shall, if he deems it necessary, call upon the Federal Bureau of Investigation to refute or corroborate any or all claims submitted by the Citizen in defense of his Loyalty;
3. That if said proofs then be found invalid, untruthful, immaterial, irrelevant, or inconclusive, the Citizen shall be so notified and may thereupon at his option demand a Second Hearing meanwhile being consigned by Warrant and Seal of said Judge within one of the three Classifications hereunder described as Class CT, Class AT, or Class U.

Classifications

Classification CT (Class CT)

1. Classification or Class CT shall be deemed to signify Conceptual Traitor;

Classification CT (Class CT) Defined

1. Class CT signifying Conceptual Traitor is herewith defined as including, but not exclusively,

    a. Any person otherwise of good character, without police record of felony, who has been adjudged at his or her Clearance Trial and/or Second Hearing as having engaged in Conversations, talks, public or private meetings, lectures, visits, or communications the nature of which is not illegal but on the other hand not Positively Conducive to the Defense of the Nation against the Enemy;

    b. Any person who, on evidence submitted by the FBI, or in the Absence of Evidence to the Contrary, has shown himself to have actually expressed concepts, parts of concepts, or complete ideas or sentiments Inimical to the Defense of the Nation against the Enemy;

    c. Persons who have not actually expressed such concepts in whole or part, but have demonstrated a receptivity to such concepts as expressed by others;

    d. Persons who have neither expressed themselves, nor shown a receptivity to expressions by others of concepts or sentiments Inimical to the Defense of the Nation against the Enemy, but on the other hand have failed to demonstrate a lively, visible, or audible resentment against such concepts or sentiments as orally expressed or written by others;

    All the above described, but not exclusively, shall be classified Conceptual Traitors by the duly constituted Court of Clearance.

Classification AT (Class AT)

1. Classification or Class AT shall be deemed to signify Action Traitor;

Classification AT (Class AT) Defined

1. Class AT signifying Action Traitor is herewith defined as including, but not exclusively,

   a. Any person who has been proved to have actually attended meetings of any group, organization, incorporated or unincorporated body, secretly or publicly, whose title is to be found upon the Attorney General's list of proscribed organizations;
   b. Any person who has committed any of the acts attributable to Conceptual Traitor as above defined, but in addition, and within hearing of at least one witness, has spoken in praise of such groups or affiliates or members thereof, or of non-members who have themselves spoken in praise of said groups or organizations so listed;
   c. Any and all persons not falling under the categories above described who nevertheless have been summoned to testify before any Committee of Congress and have failed to testify to the Expressed Satisfaction of said Committee or any two members thereof in quorum constituted;

Penalties

1. Penalties shall be laid upon those classified as Conceptual Traitors, as follows, namely:

   a. The Judge of the Court of Clearance shall cause to be issued Identity Card CT. Upon all correspondence written by said Class CT Citizen the words Conceptual Traitor or the letters CT shall be prominently displayed in print or in ink; as well upon any and all books, articles, pamphlets or announcements whatsoever written by said Citizen; as well any appearance on radio, television, theatrical or other public medium by said Citizen shall be preceded by the clearly spoken announcement of his Classification; and in addition his calling or business cards shall be so marked as well as any other cards, (Christmas, birthday, New Year's, etc., but not exclusively), which he may mail to anyone beyond his own family so connected by blood;

b. Any organization or person employing said citizen with or without remuneration in money or kind, shall, upon agreeing to such employment, apply to the Federal Bureau of Clearance, to be established herewith, for a Conceptual Traitor Employment Permit;

c. It shall be an infraction of this Act to refuse employment to a citizen Classified as Conceptual Traitor, or to discriminate against said Citizen for having been so Classified, and the employer, upon receiving his Conceptual Traitor's Employment Permit, shall cause to be imprinted upon all his stationery, vouchers, public circulars, and advertisements, the following words or legend—"We Employ A Conceptual Traitor"—or the initials, "WECT."

Release of Incarcerated CT's

1. Conceptual Traitors, upon being duly classified by the Court of Clearance, shall be instantly released and guaranteed all the rights and privileges of American Citizenship as defined in the Constitution of the United States.

a. No Conceptual Traitor duly classified shall be detained in jail or prison more than forty-eight hours (48) beyond the time of his Classification;

b. No person awaiting Classification shall be detained more than one year (1 year).

Penalties for Action Traitors

1. Persons classified Action Traitors shall be fined two thousand dollars and sentenced to serve not more than eight (8) years in a Federal House of Detention, nor less than five years (5 years).

Unclassified Persons

1. Persons who are neither Classified as Action Traitor nor Conceptual Traitor shall be classified as Unclassified, or "U."

Unclassified Persons Defined

1. Unclassified persons, (U), shall be defined, although not exclusively, as those persons who are:

   a. Unable to speak or understand the English language or any language for which an accredited Interpreter can be found, or can be reasonably thought to exist within the Continental United States or its Territories, Possessions, or Territories held in Trust;

   b. Able to speak the English language or any of the languages for which an Interpreter may be found, but unable to understand the English language or any of the languages for which an Interpreter may be found;

   c. Committed to institutions for the Insane or Homes for the Aged and Infirm;

   d. Accredited members of the Federal Bureau of Investigation;

   e. Accredited members of any Investigating Committee of the Congress of the United States;

   f. Officers of the United States Chamber of Commerce;

   g. Persons who are able to read, write, and understand the English language but have not registered their names in any Public Library as Lenders or Borrowers; and persons who have been registered as Borrowers in Public Libraries, but whose cards have never been stamped;

   h. Listless persons, or persons who cannot keep their minds attentive to the questions asked by the Judge of the Court of Clearance;

   i. All Veterans of the War Between the States;

   j. All citizens who have Contributed to the Walter Winchell Damon Runyon Cancer Fund or who have been favorably mentioned in the newspaper column written by Ed Sullivan;

   k. Most children, providing;

That none of the entities above mentioned be constituted as exclusive; and that no abridgment is made of the right of Congress to lengthen or shorten any of the defining qualifications of any of the above categories.

Release of Unclassified Persons (Class U)

1. All Unclassified Persons shall be instantly released, but with the proviso that any and all Unclassified Persons may be recalled for Classification.

Possible Objections to This Proposal

The author of the above proposal, or Act, is well aware of certain objections which are bound to be made. All argument will inevitably reduce itself to the question of Civil Liberties.

The author wishes to state that, as will soon become apparent, it is only his devotion to Civil Liberties which has prompted creation of this Proposal, and in order to Enlighten those who on these grounds feel a reservation about this Proposal, he states quite simply the most vital argument against it which is that it sends absolutely everybody to jail.

This, unfortunately, is true. However, the corollary to this objection, namely, that this is exactly what the Russians do, is emphatically not true. I insist that no Russian goes to jail excepting under duress, force, and unwillingly; hence, he loses his liberty. But under this Act the American Presents himself to the prison officials, which is a different thing entirely. Moreover, he Presents himself without loss of liberty, his most precious possession, because he Presents himself with Love in his Heart, with the burning desire to Prove to all his fellow-citizens that he Is an American and is eager to let everybody know every action of his Life and its Patriotic Significance. It may as well be said that if an American boy is good enough to fight he is good enough to go to jail for the peace of mind of his Country.

The author can easily Visualize that going to the local Marshal for his Patriotic Arrest will soon become a kind of Proud Initiation for the Young American. He can Visualize the growth among the Citizens of Coming Out Parties when the young member of the family is released, and there is no doubt that the national Radio and Television Networks will do their best to popularize this form of Patriotic Thanksgiving, and the entire process of Waiting, Classification, and ultimate Deliverance will eventually become a hallowed Ritual without which no young man or woman would feel Complete and At Ease. It is, after all, nothing more than the Winning of Citizenship, something we who were given the blessing of American Birth have come to take for granted.

I would go even farther and say that the psychological significance of Arrest is beneficial. At the age of eighteen, or thereabouts, a person is just getting out of his adolescence, a period marked by strong feelings of guilt due to Pimples and so forth. This guilt, or Pimples, leads many an individual of that age to feelings of high idealism at which point he is amazed to discover the presence of Evil in the world. In turn, the recognition of Evil is likely to cause him to scoff at the Pretensions of the Older Generation, his parents and teachers, who in his new and emotional opinion have Failed to make a decent world for him. He is then wide open to the Propaganda of the Enemy.

It is at this very moment, when his spiritual pores, so to speak, are open, that under this Act he is sent immediately to Jail, and then through a Court of Clearance, to which institution he may Open his Heart. Under this Act, in short, every American over the age of eighteen (18) is automatically regarded as technically and momentarily Guilty. This, of course, represents no profound novelty, but instead of making it possible for only Traitors to Be Discovered, as at present, under this Act everyone will have the opportunity of being, so to speak, Discovered, but as a Patriot, which after all is what most Americans are.

The simple and pervasive Logic of this proposal will be completely evident if one reflects on the fact that in almost every other sphere of human activity the Society does in fact "clear" and give its stamp of Approval beforehand rather than afterwards; in most states we have to renew our dog licenses every year, and no dog with, for instance, rabies, is entitled to a license; we inspect cattle, motorists, buildings, railroads, elevators, sprinkler systems, teachers, and fish markets, for instance; nor do we wait until any of these have caused damage to the community. On the contrary, you have no need of suspecting an elevator, for instance, upon entering it because you know that it has been cleared, in effect, Before you arrived and you may therefore repose in it your utmost Confidence, nor do you take a Driver's Test after you have killed a pedestrian, you take it Before.

It is necessary to imagine, or Project, as the psychologists say, the National Situation as it will be after this Act is operative.

When walking down the street, buying in a store, waiting for a street car or bus, getting gas, buying stocks, Meeting Someone hitherto unknown, answering the doorbell, listening to a lecture, seeing a movie or Television Show, the Citizen will automatically know where everybody around him Stands. A sense of Confidence and Mutual Trust will once more flow into the Land. The Citizen will need have no fear of reading anything, attending any meeting, or being introduced to anyone; instead of an atmosphere of innuendo, suspicion, aborted conversations and low vocal tones, we shall have a situation in which you know and I know that you were in jail and I was in jail and that we are therefore good Americans, and if there was anything Wrong one of us, or both of us, would not be out here talking like this. That is, by and large.

Aside from avowed enemies there are, unfortunately, Patriotic people who will unquestionably be found in opposition to this Act. Mothers, for instance, may shudder at the idea of sending their boys to Jail. But they will quickly see that a short stay in Jail will be the Hallmark of every Good American.

To sum up, then, it can be said that the current sensations of Confusion, Ferment, Distrust, and Suspicion are obviously not being dissolved by any present methods of Investigation and Exposure. A Permanent, Regular, and Uniform Clearance Procedure is vitally necessary, therefore. Everyone knows that a Man is Innocent until proved Guilty. All this Act is meant to provide is a means for securing that proof. God Forbid the day when in America a man is guilty without Proof. Once it was a Land that millions of Americans were trekking thousands of miles to find; later it was Gold; recently Uranium has been sought for at great effort and expense. But it is fair to say that with our characteristic energy we are devoting more time, more concentrated effort, and more Patriotic Concern with discovering Proof than any other material in our Nation's History. Now, in a dignified manner, in a Regularized and profoundly American manner, we shall all have it.

1954

Concerning the Boom

I read in the papers that this 1956 Broadway season has been the most exciting in many years, as well as the most successful financially. The pressure for theaters has been so heavy that even the Lunts were forced to hover in the hinterland with *The Great Sebastians* until a show should close (in this case one of mine, as it turned out). We are, in other words, within yards of the millennium for commercial theater.

As always, there are the vehicles, like *The Desk Set* for Shirley Booth, *Janus* for Margaret Sullavan and Claude Dauphin, and the aforementioned Lunts' play. At least one exceptional musical is with us in the shape of *My Fair Lady* with Rex Harrison, and there are several others which, like most musicals, go on and on whether they are any good or not. There are the realistic plays written in deadly earnest just as they could have been twenty years ago, an improvisation called *A Hatful of Rain,* and even what one could call a social documentary with Paul Muni—*Inherit the Wind.*

In a word, it is the usual trendless jumble. Why such a large percentage of the shows that open should be judged by the critics as hits, I certainly cannot say. I am not a first-nighter, and when I go to the theater at all it is because there seems to be promise of something new, some exciting acting or a novel invention of form. Musicals aside, the three plays which seemed to me to possess a genuine creative vitality were Wilder's *The Matchmaker,* Norman Rosten's adaptation of Joyce Cary's novel, *Mister Johnson,* and *The Chalk Garden* by Enid Bagnold.

My private opinion is that the Wilder play would not have found its audience without the astounding performance of Ruth Gordon. I say this not to denigrate the play, although it is not, in my opinion, his best-organized work, but because Miss Gordon translates its metaphysic in sufficiently broad emotional language for it to appear within the realm of the familiar. Without her filling in the spaces between its always threatening—or promising—passages of abstractness, it might well have been gravely saluted and allowed to die by the critics. Yet, the fact remains as a tribute to the eagerness of this audience that it is a rather successful Broadway show in Broadway's terms. It ought not to be overlooked, however, that the problem of survival for the truly serious work remains unsolved here.

I say this because Wilder's play is not turning them away, nor is *Tiger At The Gates* nor *The Lark* (Lillian Hellman's adaptation from Anouilh), nor *Mister Johnson.* In some cases, as with *Tiger* and *The Lark,* more impetus could not have been asked from the critics, yet the pressure of a real hit never developed around these plays. *Will Success Spoil Rock Hunter?,* a much criticized farcical sex-play, is a hit and will probably run on a long time.

I saw *Chalk Garden* on its closing night and was quite astonished, recalling dimly the carping reviews I had read of it. It is the most steadily interesting, deeply felt, and civilized piece of work I have seen in a very long time. Its final audience, as a matter of fact, behaved as though it were the remnant of a dispersed army rallying to a fallen flag. They were mostly young people, I noticed, and like the audience that came to cheer O'Casey's *Red Roses For Me,* which also failed to gain either critical or audience celebration, the stalwarts who came to bury this work with at least a fond gesture of appreciation were obviously a small minority of those who buy tickets on Broadway.

I have been in this work a long time now, and I cannot yet understand the code under which our critics operate. *A Hatful of Rain,* for instance, was slapped together as an exercise in class at the Actors' Studio, taken onto Broadway by Shelley Winters and Ben Gazzara, who play the leads, and greeted with roars of critical approval. Yet, it is so full of illogical behavior, so evasive in its confrontation with its theme, so unevenly finished in almost every department, that had I seen it before its opening I should have thought it hadn't a chance. Perhaps its appearance of unpretentiousness gratified the critics who saw none of its really serious inner contradictions.

At the same time, *Mister Johnson,* which is at times a genuine lyric thrust, and is always a meaningful dramatic and ethical struggle, if theatrically loose-boned, is for the most part decisively defeated by the critics' cautious praise. But perhaps it is not they who are to blame. The majority of the audience is still essentially a party-going, amusement-seeking throng. Confronted with anything that is not directly linked to some aspect of sexuality it cannot be deeply engaged by a serious work excepting in extremely rare instances.

When I say "serious" I do not mean merely that the author has a message or the play some social or ethical significance. I am speaking mainly of a theatrical seriousness which is made of an ethical preoccupation in the first place but must express itself in new terms and forms. *Inherit the Wind* is a sociological drama without any great exploration of interior human forces; it is a big hit, to be sure, but when Paul Muni had to leave the show temporarily the line leading to the Refunds window stretched to the end of the block.

In one way, perhaps, people like myself have been spoiled. It is true our work has to compete with the lowest of the low or we cannot exist, and that was always the case among us; but despite this we have succeeded often enough in achieving runs of a year or even two, so that when we merely go on for three months it comes as a shock. Yet there aren't many places in the world where any play can run that long, let alone a genuinely serious one. My feeling, however, is that when we do make a real hit out of a serious play it is not because it is serious but in some way sensational. *Cat on a Hot Tin Roof,* Tennessee Williams' work of last season, which is still running well, is, I think, one of these. I venture this undermining thought not only because it has occurred to me but because the critics never seem willing or even interested in discussing the real preoccupation of the writers of these plays but only their most evident effects. I doubt that many people in the audience realize what *Cat* is really saying, for if they did they might not "enjoy" it with such self-assurance. For it is really an attack, I think, on nearly everyone who watches it.

Ibsen's *When We Dead Awaken* comes to mind in this context. Recall the leading character, the world-famous, highly successful and admired sculptor who in his old age points to the many heads in his studio and reveals that they were meant not as flattering portraits of his famous clients but as the images of beasts, of wolves, and dogs, and bears. Papa Ibsen was voicing, I think, the complaint of so many artists who succeed with the public—that they knew not what they saw, and the effects which he labored so hard to achieve were only too successful in concealing what lay behind them.

In the case of *Chalk Garden* the woven surface was perhaps too involved for us; perhaps its admirably hard and even brittle shell demanded too much attention of us. We are not yet ready to follow psychology into a higher atmosphere where its aesthetic reflection glows and spits and then grows cool. Our theater is still essentially the theater of realism. There have been more and more assaults upon it—or, more precisely, some attempts at stretching its bonds, but it is still empathy we want to feel, and the simplest sort of identification still carries a play further than any style or magnification of life can hope to do.

What the sudden boom of hits signifies for the future I can't say. I do not believe that anything has been really changed. No acting company has been put together, no genuine new approach to anything has been developed, and it goes without saying that the theaters still take about forty percent of the gross, and one chain is demanding fifty. The price of seats is still astronomical by my standards, and unless people have adopted an entirely new idea of the value of money, which is not impossible, the audience must still be composed of a very small segment of the population. I doubt that anyone else can account for our sudden prosperity, and if they can't it means that we are building nothing for the future but a fond memory of how good it was in 1956. The fact, nevertheless, is that more people than ever seem eager to come to the theater, and that is at least a good beginning, although toward exactly what end I have not the slightest notion. The thing remains, as always, a chaos of a business having only the most incidental tangency with aesthetic preoccupations.

Another reason for my suspicion of the health of this boom is the remarkable consistency with which the authors of our plays are not mentioned in advertising. Even Wilder's name is off the ad for *Matchmaker*, and the only author mentioned at all is Tennessee Williams. It has gone as far as the elimination of authors' names on the theater marquees themselves. I hope I am not speaking merely as a member of the Dramatists Guild when I say that this, among other things, points to the revival of the star's and director's theater, than which, in my opinion, nothing could promise less for the future, not only the future of the author but of the actors and the directors and finally the audience. For when the power to draw the public is too confined to the actors, as it is coming to be if it is not already a fact, the choice of plays to be produced is inevitably weighted toward the individual part. To put it as quickly and as simply as I can, life is not reflected in plays of that kind.

With all my doubts, however, I must confess that a lot of activity, however dubious its purport, is better than too little. I talk occasionally before groups of yet unknown playwrights, and I get a certain amount of mail from some I have never seen, and it does seem to me that lately there is a kind of dramatic questioning which is deeper and less easily satisfied with opportune answers than once was the case. There seems to be a genuine dissatisfaction with the uncourageous play or the ill-made, meandering work whose only justification is its spontaneity and its departure from living room realism. There is an as yet half-conscious but nevertheless growing awareness of the larger social mission of theater among these people which was not there even two years ago, in my estimation. Form is no longer spoken of as though it were a free choice of the writer, but its roots in the play's forces are being investigated. And despite the preoccupation of the daily critics with questions of effect, and effect at almost any cost, I sense in these writers a need to come to an agreement with themselves as to the value and the meaning for man of these effects. Thus, it is possible that two opposing lines of force are burgeoning at the same time. Our theater is striving at any cost for effect, and its new writers who are as yet unknown are casting a suspicious eye on this kind of pragmatism.

I can hardly end this ramble without mentioning the most enthralling dramatic experience I have had since I first read Ibsen. It is Eugene O'Neill's recently published play, *Long Day's Journey Into Night*. I think it his most moving work. It is as true as an oak board, a remorselessly just play, a drama from which all his other plays seem to have sprung. Excepting for a very few passages, when once again the dramatic strategy threatens to leave his people alone with their self-consciousness, or the author's, the work is written on an exactly hewn plane of awareness which is only rarely violated—for his great previous fault, to my mind, was a mawkishness in voicing his themes. It is his most modern play, his most fluidly written. It is as though here his symbol and his action came up out of him intertwined and at one with each other. His pity here, and his justice, lift him as a writer to a genuinely philosophic height. Its only production took place recently in Sweden. I have not heard that there is a line of producers clamoring for it here, but it will surely be done and it must be for all our sakes. It will be good once again to watch a play which holds on to its prey with the teeth of a bulldog.

1956

The Bored and the Violent

If my own small experience is any guide, the main difficulty in approaching the problem of juvenile delinquency is that there is very little evidence about it and very many opinions as to how to deal with it. By evidence I do not mean the news stories telling of gang fights and teenage murders—there are plenty of those. But it is unknown, for instance, what the actual effects are on the delinquent of prison sentences, psychotherapy, slum-clearance projects, settlement-house programs, tougher or more lenient police attitudes, the general employment situation, and so on. Statistics are few and not generally reliable. The narcotics problem alone is an almost closed mystery.

Not that statistical information in itself can solve anything, but it might at least outline the extent of the disease. I have it, for instance, from an old and deservedly respected official—it is his opinion anyway—that there is really no great increase in delinquent acts but a very great intensification of our awareness of them. He feels we are more nervous now about infractions of the social mores than our ancestors, and he likes to point out that Shakespeare, Boccaccio, and other writers never brought on stage a man of wealth or station without his bravos, who were simply his private police force, necessary to him when he ventured out of his house, especially at night. He would have us read *Great Expectations, Oliver Twist, Huckleberry Finn,* and other classics, not in a romantic mood but in the way we read about our own abandoned kids and their depredations. The difference lies mainly in the way we look at the same behavior.

The experts have only a little more to go on than we have. Like the surgeon whose hands are bloody a good part of the day, the social worker is likely to come to accept the permanent existence of the delinquency disease without the shock of the amateur who first encounters it.

A new book on the subject [by Vincent Riccio and Bill Slocum], *All the Way Down,* reports the experience of a social worker—of sorts—who never got used to the experience, and does not accept its inevitability. It is an easy book to attack on superficial grounds because it has no evident sociological method, it rambles and jumps and shouts and curses. But it has a virtue, a very great and rare one, I think, in that it does convey the endless, leaden, mind-destroying boredom of the delinquent life. Its sex is without romance or sexuality, its violence is without release or gratification—exactly like the streets—movies and plays about delinquency notwithstanding.

Unlike most problems which sociology takes up, delinquency seems to be immune to the usual sociological analyses or cures. For instance, it appears in all technological societies, whether Latin or Anglo-Saxon or Russian or Japanese. It has a very slippery correlation with unemployment and the presence or absence of housing projects. It exists among the rich in Westchester and the poor in Brooklyn and Chicago. It has spread quickly into the rural areas and the small towns. Now, according to Harrison Salisbury, it is the big problem in the Soviet Union. So that any single key to its causation is nowhere visible. If one wants to believe it to be essentially a symptom of unequal opportunity—and certainly this factor operates—one must wonder about the Russian problem, for the Soviet youngster can, in fact, go right up through the whole school system on his ability alone, as many of ours cannot. Yet the gangs are roaming the Russian streets, just as they do in our relatively permissive society.

So no one knows what "causes" delinquency. Having spent some months in the streets with boys of an American gang, I came away with certain impressions, all of which stemmed from a single, overwhelming conviction—that the problem underneath is boredom. And it is not strange, after all, that this should be so. It is the theme of so many of our novels, our plays, and especially our movies in the past twenty years and is the hallmark of society as a whole. The outcry of Britain's so-called Angry Young Men was against precisely this seemingly universal sense of life's pointlessness, the absence of any apparent aim to it all. So many American books and articles attest to the same awareness here. The stereotype of the man coming home from work and staring dumbly at a television set is an expression of it, and the "New Wave" of movies in France and Italy propound the same fundamental theme. People no longer seem to know why they are alive; existence is simply a string of near experiences marked off by periods of stupefying spiritual and psychological stasis, and the good life is basically an amused one.

Among the delinquents the same kind of mindlessness prevails, but without the style—or stylishness—which art in our time has attempted to give it. The boredom of the delinquent is remarkable mainly because it is so little compensated for, as it may be among the middle classes and the rich who can fly down to the Caribbean or to Europe, or refurnish the house, or have an affair, or at least go shopping. The delinquent is stuck with his boredom, stuck inside it, stuck to it, until for two or three minutes he "lives"; he goes on a raid around the corner and feels the thrill of risking his skin or his life as he smashes a bottle filled with gasoline on some other kid's head. In a sense, it is his trip to Miami. It makes his day. It is his shopping tour. It gives him something to talk about for a week. It is *life*. Standing around with nothing coming up is as close to dying as you can get. Unless one grasps the power of boredom, the threat of it to one's existence, it is impossible to "place" the delinquent as a member of the human race.

With boredom in the forefront, one may find some perspective in the mélange of views which are repeated endlessly about the delinquent. He is a rebel without a cause, or a victim of poverty, or a victim of undue privilege, or an unloved child, or an overloved child, or a child looking for a father, or a child trying to avenge himself on an uncaring society, or whatnot. But face to face with one of them, one finds these criteria useless, if only because no two delinquents are any more alike than other people are. They do share one mood, however. They are drowning in boredom. School bores them, preaching bores them, even television bores them. The word rebel is inexact for them because it must inevitably imply a purpose, an end.

Other people, of course, have known boredom. To get out of it, they go to the movies, or to a bar, or read a book, or go to sleep, or turn on TV or a girl, or make a resolution, or quit a job. Younger persons who are not delinquents may go to their room and weep, or write a poem, or call up a friend until they get tired talking. But note that each of these escapes can only work if the victim is sure somewhere in his mind, or reasonably hopeful, that by so doing he will overthrow his boredom and with luck may come out on the other side where something hopeful or interesting waits. But the delinquent has no such sense of an imminent improvement. Most of the kids in the Riccio and Slocum book have never known a single good day. How can they be expected to project one and restrain themselves in order to experience such joy once more?

The word rebel is wrong, too, in that it implies some sort of social criticism in the delinquent. But that would confuse him with the bourgeois beatnik. The delinquent has only respect, even reverence, for certain allegedly bourgeois values. He implicitly believes that there are good girls and bad girls, for instance. Sex and marriage are two entirely separate things. He is, in my experience anyway, deeply patriotic. Which is simply to say that he respects those values he never experienced, like money and good girls and the Army and Navy. What he has experienced has left him with absolute contempt, or more accurately, an active indifference. Once he does experience decency—as he does sometimes in a wife—he reacts decently to it. For to this date the only known cure for delinquency is marriage.

The delinquent, far from being the rebel, is the conformist par excellence. He is actually incapable of doing anything alone, and a story may indicate how incapable he is. I went along with Riccio and the gang in his book to a YMCA camp outside New York City for an overnight outing. In the afternoon we started a baseball game, and everything proceeded normally until somebody hit a ball to the outfield. I turned to watch the play and saw ten or twelve kids running for the catch. It turned out that not one of them was willing to play the outfield by himself, insisting that the entire group hang around out there together. The reason was that a boy alone might drop a catch and would not be able to bear the humiliation. So they ran around out there in a drove all afternoon, creating a stampede every time a ball was hit.

They are frightened kids, and that is why they are so dangerous. But again, it will not do to say—it is simply not true—that they are therefore unrelated to the rest of the population's frame of mind. Like most of us, the delinquent is simply doing as he was taught. This is often said but rarely understood. Only recently a boy was about to be executed for murder in New York state. Only after he had been in jail for more than a year after sentencing did a campaign develop to persuade the governor to commute his sentence to life imprisonment, for only then was it discovered that he had been deserted by his father in Puerto Rico, left behind when his mother went to New York, wandered about homeless throughout his child-hood, and so on. The sentencing judge learned his background only a week or two before he was to be officially murdered. And then what shock, what pity! I have to ask why the simple facts of his deprivation were not brought out in court, if not before. I am afraid I know the answer. Like most people, it was probably beyond the judge's imagination that small children sometimes can be treated much worse than kittens or puppies in our cities.

It is only in theory that the solution seems purely physical—better housing, enlightened institutions for deserted kids, psychotherapy, and the rest. The visible surfaces of the problem are easy to survey—although we have hardly begun even to do that.

More difficult is the subterranean moral question which every kind of delinquency poses. Not long ago a gang was arrested in a middle-class section of Brooklyn, whose tack was to rob homes and sell the stuff to pro-fessional fences. Many of these boys were top students, and all of them were from good, middle-class backgrounds. Their parents were floored by the news of their secret depredations, and their common cry was that they had always given their sons plenty of money, that the boys were secure at home, that there was no conceivable reason for this kind of aberration. The boys were remorseful and evidently as bewildered as their parents.

Greenwich, Connecticut, is said to be the wealthiest community in the United States. A friend of mine who lives there let his sons throw a party for their friends. In the middle of the festivities a gang of boys arrived—their own acquaintances, who attend the same high school. They tore the house apart, destroyed the furniture, pulled parts off the automobile and left them on the lawn, and split the skulls of two of the guests with beer cans.

Now if it is true that the slum delinquent does as he is taught, it must be true that the Greenwich delinquent does the same. But obviously the lines of force from example to imitation are subtler and less easily traced here. It is doubtful that the parents of this marauding gang rip up the fur-niture in the homes to which they have been invited. So that once again it is necessary to withhold one's cherished theories. Rich delinquency is delinquency, but it is not the same as slum delinquency. But there is one clear common denominator, I think. They do not know how to live when alone. Most boys in Greenwich do not roam in gangs, but a significant frac-tion in both places find that counterfeit sense of existence which the gang life provides.

Again, I think it necessary to raise and reject the idea of rebellion, if one means by that word a thrust of any sort. For perspective's sake it may be wise to remember another kind of youthful reaction to a failed society in a different era. In the Thirties, for instance, we were also contemptuous of the given order. We had been brought up to believe that if you worked hard, saved your money, studied, kept your nose clean, you would end up made. We found ourselves in the Depression, when you could not get a job, when all the studying you might do would get you a chance, at best, to sell ties in Macy's. Our delinquency consisted in joining demonstrations of the unemployed, pouring onto campuses to scream against some injustice by college administrations, and adopting to one degree or another a socialist ideology. This, in fact, was a more dangerous kind of delinquency than the gangs imply, for it was directed against the social structure of capitalism itself. But, curiously, it was at the same time immeasurably more constructive, for the radical youth of the Thirties, contemptuous as he was of the social values he had rejected, was still bent upon instituting human values in their place. He was therefore a conserver, he believed in *some* society.

Gide wrote a story about a man who wanted to get on a train and shoot a passenger. Any train, any passenger. It would be a totally gratuitous act, an act devoid of any purpose whatever, an act of "freedom" from purpose. To kill an unknown man without even anger, without unrequited love, without love at all, with nothing in his heart but the sheerly physical contemplation of the gun barrel and the target. In doing this one would partake of death's irreproachable identity and commit an act in revolt against meaning itself, just as death is, in the last analysis, beyond analysis.

To think of contemporary delinquency in the vein of the Thirties, as a rebellion toward something, is to add a value to it which it does not have. To give it even the dignity of cynicism run rampant is also overelaborate. For the essence is not the individual at all; it is the gang, the herd, and we should be able to understand its attractions ourselves. It is not the thrust toward individual expression but a flight from self in any defined form. Therefore, to see it simply as a protest against conformism is to stand it on its head; it is profoundly conformist but without the mottoes, the entablature of recognizable, "safe" conformism and its liturgy of religious, patriotic, socially conservative credos.

The Greenwich gang, therefore, is also doing as it was taught, just as the slum gang does, but more subtly. The Greenwich gang is conforming to the hidden inhumanity of conformism, to the herd quality in conformism; it is acting out the terror-fury that lies hidden under Father's acceptable conformism. It is simply conformity sincere, conformity revealing its true content, which is hatred of others, a stunted wish for omnipotence, and the conformist's secret belief that nothing outside his skin is real or true. For which reason he must redouble his obeisance to institutions lest, if the acts of obeisance be withheld, the whole external world will vanish, leaving him alone. And to be left alone when you do not sense any existence in yourself is the ultimate terror. But this loneliness is not the poet's, not the thinker's, not the loneliness that is filled with incommunicable feeling, insufficiently formed thought. It is nonexistence and must not be romanticized, as it has been in movies and some of the wishful Beat literature. It is a withdrawal not from the world but from oneself. It is boredom, the subsidence of inner impulse, and it threatens true death unless it is overthrown.

All of which is said in order to indicate that delinquency is not the kind of "social problem" it is generally thought to be. That is, it transcends even as it includes the need for better housing, medical care, and the rest. It is our most notable and violent manifestation of social nihilism. In saying this, however, it is necessary to short-circuit any notion that it is an attempt by the youth to live "sincerely." The air of "sincerity" which so many writers have given the delinquent is not to be mistaken as his "purpose." This is romanticism and solves nothing except to sentimentalize brutality. The gang kid can be sincere; he can extend himself for a buddy and risk himself for others; but he is just as liable, if not more so than others, to desert his buddies in need and to treat his friends disloyally. Gang boys rarely go to visit a buddy in jail excepting in the movies. They forget about him. The cult of sincerity, of true human relations uncontaminated by money and the social rat race, is not the hallmark of the gang. The only moment of truth comes when the war starts. Then the brave show themselves, but few of these boys know how to fight alone and hardly any without a knife or a gun. They are not to be equated with matadors or boxers or Hemingway heroes. They are dangerous pack hounds who will not even expose themselves singly in the outfield.

If, then, one begins to put together all the elements, this "social problem" takes on not merely its superficial welfare aspects but its philosophical depths, which I think are the controlling ones. It is not a problem of big cities alone but of rural areas too; not of capitalism alone but of socialism as well; not restricted to the physically deprived but shared by the affluent; not a racial problem alone or a problem of recent immigrants, or a purely American problem. I believe it is in its present form the product of technology destroying the very concept of man as a value in himself.

I hesitate to say what I think the cure might be, if only because I cannot prove it. But I have heard most of the solutions men have offered, and they are spiritless, they do not assume that the wrong is deep and terrible and general among us all. There is, in a word, a spirit gone. Perhaps two world wars, brutality immeasurable, have blown it off the earth; perhaps the very processes of technology have sucked it out of man's soul; but it is gone. Many men rarely relate to one another excepting as customer to seller, worker to boss, the affluent to the deprived and vice versa—in short, as factors to be somehow manipulated and not as intrinsically valuable persons.

Power was always in the world, to be sure, and its evils, but with us now it is strangely, surrealistically masked and distorted. Time was, for example, when the wealthy and the politically powerful flaunted themselves, used power openly as power, and were often cruel. But this openness had the advantage for man of clarity; it created a certain reality in the world, an environment that was defined, with hard but touchable barriers. Today power would have us believe—everywhere—that it is purely beneficent. The bank is not a place which makes more money with your deposits than it returns to you in the form of interest; it is not a sheer economic necessity, it is not a business at all. It is "Your Friendly Bank," a kind of welfare institution whose one prayer, day and night, is to serve your whims or needs. A school is no longer a place of mental discipline but a kind of day-care center, a social gathering where you go through a ritual of games and entertainments which insinuate knowledge and the crafts of the outside world. Business is not the practice of buying low and selling high, it is a species of public service. The good life itself is not the life of struggle for meaning, not the quest for union with the past, with God, with man that it traditionally was. The good life is the life of ceaseless entertainment, effortless joys, the air-conditioned, dust-free languor beyond the Mussulman's most supine dream. Freedom is, after all, comfort; sexuality is a photograph. The enemy of it all is the real. The enemy is conflict. The enemy, in a word, is life.

My own view is that delinquency is related to this dreamworld from two opposing sides. There are the deprived who cannot take part in the dream; poverty bars them. There are the oversated who are caught in its indefiniteness, its unreality, its boring hum, and strike for the real now and then—they rob, they hurt, they kill. In flight from the nothingness of this comfort they have inherited, they butt against its rubber walls in order to feel a real pain, a genuine consequence. For the world in which comfort rules is a delusion, whether one is within it or deprived of it.

There are a few social theorists who look beyond poverty and wealth, beyond the time when men will orient themselves to the world as bread-winners, as accruers of money-power. They look to the triumph of technology, when at least in some countries the physical struggle to survive will no longer be the spine of existence. Then, they say, men will define themselves through varying "styles of life." With struggles solved, nature tamed and abundant, all that will be left to do will be the adornment of existence, a novel-shaped swimming pool, I take it, or an outburst of artistic work.

It is not impossible, I suppose. Certainly a lot of people are already living that way—when they are not at their psychiatrists'. But there is still a distance to go before life's style matters very much to most of humanity in comparison with next month's rent. I do not know how we ought to reach for the spirit again, but it seems to me we must flounder without it. It is the spirit which does not accept injustice complacently and yet does not betray the poor with sentimentality. It is the spirit which seeks not to flee the tragedy which life must always be but seeks to enter into it, thereby to be strengthened by the fullest awareness of its pain, its ultimate non sequitur. It is the spirit which does not mask but unmasks the true function of a thing, be it business, unionism, architecture, or love.

Riccio and Slocum's book, with all its ugliness, its crudeness, its lack of polish and design, is good because it delivers up the real. It is only as hopeless as the situation is. Its implied solutions are good ones: reform of idiotic narcotics laws, a real attempt to put trained people at the service of bewildered, desperate families, job-training programs, medical care, reading clinics—all of it is necessary, and none of it would so much as strain this economy. But none of it will matter, none of it will reach further than the spirit in which it is done. Not the spirit of fear with which so many face delinquency, nor the spirit of sentimentality which sees in it some virtue of rebellion against a false and lying society. The spirit has to be that of those people who know that delinquents are a living expression of our universal ignorance of what life ought to be, even of what it is, and of what it truly means to live. Bad pupils they surely are. But who from his own life, from his personal thought, has come up with the good teaching, the way of life that is joy? This book shows how difficult it is to reach these boys; what the country has to decide is what it is going to say if these kids should decide to listen.

1962

The Nazi Trials and the German Heart

There is an unanswerable question hovering over the courtroom at Frankfurt, where twenty-two Hitler SS men are on trial for murdering inmates in the Auschwitz concentration camp during World War II. Can the kind of movement which gave life-and-death power to such men ever again rise in Germany?

It seemed to me, sitting at one side of the courtroom one day last week, that as in all murder trials the accused here were becoming more and more abstract. Once the jackbooted masters of a barbed-wire world, they are now middle-aged Germans in business suits, nearsighted some of them, laboriously taking notes, facing the high tribunal with a blue-uniformed policeman at each one's elbow. The two exceptions are indeed extraordinary. One has an imbecile stupidity written on his face, the other shifts constantly in his chair, a free-floating violence so clear in his eyes that one would find him frightening if met on a train, let alone on trial for murder.

But the others could pass for anybody's German uncle. In fact, the lives most of them have lived since they scooted into oblivion before the allied advance show them entirely capable of staying out of trouble. Some have turned into successful business men, professionals and ordinary workers. They have reared families and even became civic leaders in their communities. When arrested they were not picked up drunk or disorderly, but at work or at rest in the bosom of their families.

For example, the one whose violence seemed to show in his quick roving eyes was, in fact, a real sadist. He was almost constantly drunk in the camp and liked to walk into a barracks and fire his pistol at random into the sleeping prisoners. If he didn't like the look of a passing inmate he would blow his head off.

But after the war this man got a job in a hospital as a nurse, and his patients have written to the court saying that he was an especially tender helper, an unusually warm person. "Papa Kaduk," they called him. No one knows anymore exactly how many defenseless people Papa Kaduk murdered in his four years at Auschwitz. A massive man, overweight now, his small eyes blaze with mocking victory whenever a witness sounds uncertain of a date or a fact, and he reaches over to nudge his black-robed lawyer who then rises to protest hearsay evidence. He seems, in short, to be quite convinced that he is indeed Papa Kaduk and not at all the monster being painfully described from the witness chair.

Another is a pharmacist who helped select prisoners for the gas chambers. He has become an important man in his town; the arresting officer had had to wait for him to return from a hunting expedition in Africa, and the local gentry showed real surprise on learning of the charges against him. Especially since it had been he who suggested that whenever the town leaders met to discuss civic affairs they wear tuxedos. How, it was actually asked, could a gentleman of such sensibility have done such awful things?

Yet, the doctor testifying hour after hour this day leaves no doubt about the facts. He was himself an inmate, but since he did get more food than the others he is here to tell the tale. And as he describes babies ripped from their mothers' arms, bed linen changed twice a year, the almost total absence of medicine, Red Cross trucks being used to transport prisoners to their deaths, tortures and beatings, and names one of the defendants after the other as the actual perpetrators, the German housewives who comprise most of the jury burst into tears or sit with open horror in their faces. And they are of an age which indicates they lived in Nazi Germany while this was happening: they were shopping, putting their children to bed, going on picnics on sunny days, worrying about a daughter's wedding dress or a son's well-being in the army while mothers like themselves and children no different from their own were forced to undress, to walk into a barren hall, and breathe the gas which some of the defendants now sitting here carefully administered.

Yet, lawyers on the tiny prosecution staff believe that ninety percent of the German people are opposed to this and other trials like it. They base their judgment on the mail they receive and on their own difficulties in

getting local cooperation for some of the arrests they have made, and finally, on the absence of any clear voice or movement from among the Germans demanding that the country's honor be cleared by bringing such
murderers to justice.

On the contrary, it is widely felt, according to these lawyers, that trials
like this only give Germany a bad name; that it all happened so long ago
why pluck men out of their lives at this late date, and so on. Time and
again these lawyers have had to escort arrested men across Germany to the
Frankfurt jail because they could not find a police officer to help. And the
government has given them twenty-five marks a day for expenses on these
trips; the most common lodging for a night costs eleven marks. This handful of Germans nevertheless intends to go on searching for every last man
down to the truck drivers who drove prisoners to the gas chambers, until
justice is done.

But is there really any long-range point in all this? They do not know.
Some of them have been on these cases since 1959 when the first arrests
were made in this particular group of cases. They have read through millions of words of testimony, stared at photographs of the camps taken by an
SS man with a penchant for photography, showing the defendants actually
at work separating the doomed from those temporarily spared for labor in
the camp. By this they have lost any sensitivity about what others might
think and are doggedly pursuing the goal.

And what is the goal? These lawyers are in their middle thirties, veterans of the Wehrmacht themselves, German through and through. They
know their people and they know that even if every last SS man were convicted for his particular crime, it would not in itself prevent a new recrudescence of brutal nationalism which could once again confront the
world with a German problem. It is something else they are after.

Imbedded in every word of testimony, and in the very existence of this
trial, is a dilemma which is first of all a German dilemma, given the history of concentration camps, but is actually an unresolved problem for all
mankind. For the final defense of these accused is that they acted under
government orders.

When so many Germans oppose this trial, it is not simply an insensi-
tivity to suffering, or even an immunity to the question of justice. Germans
too weep for their dead and help the sick and care very much about their
children. As for a respect for law, they have that even to an inordinate de-

gree. What scares some Germans, however, and makes the German to this day an enigma to many foreigners, is his capacity for moral and psychological collapse in the face of a higher command.

Several times during the course of this trial, newsmen covering it were ordered to leave, for one reason or another, and the dozen or so police who sit below the judges' tribunal are in charge of carrying out such orders. Not long ago three policemen were asked what they would do if ordered to shoot a newsman who disobeyed the court's command. One replied that he could not do that; the other two said they would carry out orders.

The point which the prosecution is trying to open up first to Germany, and then to the world, is individual conscience and responsibility in the face of inhuman orders. A judge (who has no connection with this trial) told me that his fears for Germany stemmed from precisely this profound tendency to abjure freedom of choice, to fall into line on orders from above. Another man of the law, a high official in this court, feels that the day is far off, but that his duty is to work for its coming when the Germans would question authority. He sees the root of the difficulty in the especially authoritarian role of the father in the German family, which is the microcosm reflected in the authoritarian state. The underlying point of these trials is that there can be no mitigating excuse for the conscious and planned murder of six million men, women and children, orders or no orders. Some six thousand SS men did duty in Auschwitz during its four years of operation, and not one is known to have refused to do what he was told. And it is no mean irony that the Jew, whose skepticism once leavened the authoritarian character of German culture, is not around any more to help humanize the pompous general with a little healthy doubt as to his real importance.

All of which sounds hopeless and dangerous, and perhaps that is all that should be said. But there are a few unknowns which some Germans would point to with some small and uncertain hopefulness. The young, they say, are less hermetically sealed in the old German ways than any younger generation of the past. Movies, television, books and plays from abroad flood Germany. Germans travel more than they used to, and tourists from abroad come in greater numbers than ever, and there are over one million foreign workers employed in the country now.

So that a German youth is perhaps more internationally minded than his parents and not as contemptuous of strangers and ways of life that are not German. Finally there is the more impressive fact that Germany for the first time in modern history is not flanked by a line of backward peasant countries whose defenselessness was all too tempting in the past. The equalization of industrial and hence military strength through the whole of Europe makes expansion by force a good deal less possible than before.

It is in this context, a context of much distrust and some hopefulness, that the prosecution presses for a German verdict of guilty upon members of the German armed forces. Thus far none of the accused has suggested he may have done something wrong; there is no sign of remorse, and they appear to maintain a certain unity among themselves even now. Some have been in jail two, three and four years awaiting trial and have undoubtedly read what the world press has had to say about their deeds, but no sign shows of any change of attitude toward the past.

In fact, one defendant carries out his familial duties from prison, and his authority and racial ideas are still so powerful (he dropped the gas cartridges into the gas chambers full of people) that his daughter broke off with her betrothed because he, the defendant, believes that no good German girl can possibly marry an Italian.

This trial will go on for about a year, during which time some three hundred psychologically and physically scarred survivors will face the high tribunal in Frankfurt, living evidence of how one of the most educated, technically developed, and artistic nations in the world gave itself over to the absolute will of beings it is difficult to call human. And while that testimony fills the silent courtroom, and the world press prints its highlights, German industry will pour out its excellent automobiles, machine tools, electronic equipment, German theaters will excellently produce operas and plays, German publishers will put out beautifully designed books—all the visible signs and tokens of civilization will multiply and make even more abstract, more bewildering the answer to the riddle which the impassive faces of the accused must surely present to any one who looks at them. How was it possible in a civilized country?

It is the same question to which Cain gave his endlessly echoed answer, and I have often thought that this is why it is the first drama in the Bible, for it provides the threat, the energy for all that comes after. If man can murder his fellows, not in passion but calmly, even as an "honorable" duty leading to a "higher" end—can any civilization be called safe from the ravages of what lies waiting in the heart of man? The German government which Hitler destroyed had some of the most intelligent and advanced legislation in the world. The present republic also is buttressed by excellent laws.

What is in the German heart, though? Does the rule of law reach into that heart or the rule of conformity and absolute obedience? Surely, if the German police had picked up a twenty-two-man gang that had tortured and killed merely for money, or even for kicks, an outcry would go up from the Germans, a demand that justice be done. Why is there this uneasy silence at best, and this resentment at worst, excepting that in the Frankfurt cases these accused worked for a state under its orders? Perhaps the problem becomes clearer now, and not only for the Germans.

The disquieting, nagging truth which I think dilutes the otherwise clear line this trial is taking is that the human mind does in fact accept one kind of murder. It is the murder done under the guise of social necessity. War is one example of this, and all peoples reject the idea of calling soldiers murderers. In fact, the entire nation so deeply shares in this kind of killing that it must reject any condemnation of the individuals who actually do the killing, lest they have to condemn themselves.

The problem for the Germans is that they are being called upon to identify themselves with the victims when their every instinct would lead them to identify with the uniformed, disciplined, killers. In short, they are being called on to be free, to rebel in their spirit against the age-old respect for authority which has plagued their history.

This, I think, is why it is perfectly logical for the German housewife on the jury to weep as any human being would at the horrors she hears, even as she and her millions of counterparts have, for at least a decade now, heard just such evidence a hundred times with no sign of public protest against Nazism. It is why the officers who tried to assassinate Hitler in 1944 have never been celebrated in Germany either: for they did the unthinkable, they took a moral decision against their obedience to authority.

So that the German looking at these twenty-two men may well be revolted by their crimes and yet feel paralyzed at the thought of truly taking sides against them. For part of his soul is caught in the same airtight room with theirs—the part that finds honor and goodness and decency in obedience.

But who, in what country, has not heard men say, "If I did not do this someone else would, so I might as well go along?"

So the question in the Frankfurt courtroom spreads out beyond the defendants and spirals around the world and into the heart of every man. It is his own complicity with murder, even the murders he did not perform himself with his own hands. The murders, however, from which he profited if only by having survived.

It is this profound complicity which the Frankfurt prosecution is trying to open up by sticking to its seemingly simple contention that all murder is murder. With the atomic bomb in so many different hands now it might be well to take a good look at the ordinariness of most of the defendants in Frankfurt. The thought is hateful, to be sure, and no one would willingly think it, but we do, after all, live in the century when more people have been killed by other people than at any other period. Perhaps the deepest respect we can pay the millions of innocent dead is to examine what we believe about murder, and our responsibility as survivors for the future.

1964

Guilt and Incident at Vichy

About ten years ago a European friend of mine told me a story. In 1942, said he, a man he knew was picked up on the street in Vichy, France, during a sudden roundup of Jews, taken to a police station, and simply told to wait. Refugees of all sorts had been living in Vichy since the invasion of France because the relatively milder regime of Marshal Pétain had fended off some of the more brutal aspects of German occupation. With false papers, which were not hard to buy, a Jew or a politically suspect person could stay alive in the so-called Unoccupied Zone, which covered the southern half of the country. The racial laws, for one thing, had not been applied by Pétain.

In the police station the arrested man found others waiting to be questioned, and he took his place on line. A door at the front of the line would open, a Vichy policeman would beckon, a suspect would go in. Some soon came out again and walked free into the street. Most did not reappear. The rumor moved down the line that this was a Gestapo operation and that the circumcised would have to produce immaculate proof of their Gentileness, while the uncircumcised would of course go free.

The friend of my friend was a Jew. As he got closer and closer to the fatal door he became more and more certain that his death was near. Finally, there was only one man between him and that door. Presently, this last man was ordered into the office. Nothing stood between the Jew and a meaningless, abrupt slaughter.

The door opened. The man who had been the last to go in came out. My friend's friend stood paralyzed, waiting for the policeman to appear and beckon him into the office. But instead of walking past him with his pass to freedom, the Gentile who had just come out stopped in front of my friend's friend, thrust his pass into his hand, and whispered for him to go. He went.

He had never before laid eyes on his saviour. He never saw him again.

In the ten years after hearing it, the story kept changing its meaning for me. It never occurred to me that it could be a play until this spring when *Incident at Vichy* suddenly burst open complete in almost all its details. Before that it had been simply a fact, a feature of existence which sometimes brought exhilaration with it, sometimes a vacant wonder, and sometimes even resentment. In any case, I realize that it was a counterpoint to many happenings around me in this past decade.

That faceless, unknown man would pop up in my mind when I read about the people in Queens refusing to call the police while a woman was being stabbed to death on the street outside their windows. He would form himself in the air when I listened to delinquent boys whose many different distortions of character seemed to spring from a common want of human solidarity. Friends troubled by having to do things they disapproved of brought him to mind, people for whom the very concept of choosing their actions was a long forgotten thing. Wherever I felt the seemingly implacable tide of human drift and the withering of will in myself and in others, this faceless person came to mind. And he appears most clearly and imperatively amid the jumble of emotions surrounding the Negro in this country and the whole unsettled moral problem of the destruction of the Jews in Europe.

At this point I must say that I think most people seeing this play are quite aware it is not "about Nazism" or a wartime horror tale; they do understand that the underlying issue concerns us now and that it has to do with our individual relationships with injustice and violence. But since a few critics persist in their inability to differentiate between a play's story and its theme, it is just as well to make those differences plain.

The story as I heard it never presented a "problem": everyone believes that there are some few heroes among us at all times. In the words of Hermann Broch, "And even if all that is created in this world were to be annihilated, if all its aesthetic values were abolished . . . dissolved in skepticism of all law . . . there would yet survive untouched the unity of thought, the ethical postulate." In short, the birth of each man is the rebirth of a claim to justice and requires neither drama nor proof to make it known to us.

What is dark if not unknown is the relationship between those who side with justice and their implication in the evils they oppose. So unknown is it that today in Germany it is still truly incomprehensible to many people how the crude horrors of the Nazi regime could have come to pass, let alone have been tolerated by what had for generations been regarded as one of the genuinely cultured nations of the world. So unknown that here in America, where violent crime rises at incredible rates—and, for example, the United Nations has to provide escorts for people leaving the building after dark in the world's greatest city—few people even begin to imagine that they might have some symbolic or even personal connection with this violence.

Without for an instant intending to lift the weight of condemnation Nazism must bear, does its power not become more comprehensible when we see our own helplessness toward the violence in our own streets? How many of us have looked into ourselves for even a grain of its cause? Is it not for us—as it is for the Germans—the others who are doing evil?

The other day on a news broadcast I heard that Edward R. Murrow had been operated on for lung cancer. The fact was hardly announced when the commercial came on—"Kent satisfies best!" We smile, even laugh; we must, lest we scream. And in the laughter, in the smile, we dissolve by that much. Is it possible to say convincingly that this destruction of an ethic also destroys my will to oppose violence in the streets? We do not have many wills, but only one: it cannot be continuously compromised without atrophy setting in altogether.

The first problem is not what to do about it but to discover our own relationship to evil, its reflection of ourselves. Is it too much to say that those who do not suffer injustice have a vested interest in injustice?

Does any of us know how much of his savings-bank interest is coming from investments in Harlem and Bedford-Stuyvesant real estate, those hovels from which super profits are made by jamming human beings together as no brute animals could be jammed without their dying? Does anyone know how much of his church's income is derived from such sources?

Let the South alone for a moment—who among us has asked himself how much of his own sense of personal value, how much of his pride in himself is there by virtue of his not being black? And how much of our fear of the Negro comes from the subterranean knowledge that his lowliness has found our consent and that he is demanding from us what we have taken from him and keep taking from him through our pride?

It was not to set forth a hero, either as a fact of history or as an example for us now, that I wrote this play but to throw some light on evil. The good and the evil are not compartments but two elements of a transaction. The hero of the play, Prince Von Berg, is mistakenly arrested by a Nazi race "expert." He comes into the detention room with his pride of being on the humane side, the right side, for he has fled his Austria and his rank and privilege rather than be part of a class which oppresses people.

None of the horrors he witnesses are really surprising to him here, nothing is forbidden any more, as he has long known. What he discovers in this place is his own complicity with the force he despises, his own inherited love for a cousin who, in fact, is a Nazi and an oppressor, the material cause, in short, for what before was a general sense of guilt, namely, his own secret joy and relief that, after all, he is not a Jew and will not be destroyed.

Much is made of guilt these days, even some good jokes. Liberalism is seen now as a response to guilt; much of psychiatry has made a business of evaporating guilt; the churches are no longer sure if their age-old insistence on man's guilt is not an unwitting spur to neurosis and even the acting-out of violence; the Roman Catholic church has only recently decided to lift the Crucifixion guilt from the Jews alone and to spread it evenly over mankind.

I have no "solution" to human guilt in this play, only a kind of remark, no more. I cannot conceive of guilt as having an existence without the existence of injustice. And injustice, like death itself, creates two opposing interests—one more or less profits from it, the other more or less is diminished by it. Those who profit, either psychically or materially, seek to even out the scales by the weight of guilt. A "moral" ounce is taken up to weigh down the otherwise too-light heart which contemplates uneasily its relative freedom from injustice's penalty, the guilt of having been spared.

In my play, the hero is that man whose guilt is no longer general but suddenly a clear transaction—he has been, he sees, not so much an opponent of Nazism but a vessel of guilt for its brutalities. As a man of intense sympathy for others he will survive but at a price too great for him to pay— the authenticity of his own self-image and his pride. And here I stop; I do not know why any man actually sacrifices himself any more than I know why people commit suicide. The explanation will always be on the other side of the grave, and even that is doubtful.

If they could speak, could the three boys who were murdered in Mississippi really explain why they had to go to the end? More—if each of them could discover for us in his personal history his motives and the last and most obscure corner of his psychology, would we really be any closer to the mystery of why we first require human sacrifices before our guilt can be transformed into responsibility? Is it not an absurdity that the deaths of three young men should make any difference when hundreds have been lynched and beaten to death before them, and tens of thousands humiliated?

The difference, I think, is that these, including Chaney, the young Negro, were not inevitable victims of Mississippi but volunteers. They had transformed guilt into responsibility and in so doing opened the way to a vision that leaped the pit of remorse and helplessness. And it is no accident that the people of Mississippi at first refused to concede they had been murdered, for they have done everything in their power to deny responsibility for the "character" of the Negro they paternalistically "protect," and here in these three young bodies was the return with interest for their investment in the guilt that does not act.

At the end of *Incident at Vichy*, the Prince suddenly hands his pass to a Jew, a psychiatrist, who accepts it in astonishment, in awe and wonder, and walks out to freedom. With that freedom he must accept the guilt of surviving his benefactor. Is he a "good" man for accepting his life this way or a "bad" one? That will depend on what he makes of his guilt, of his having survived.

In any case, death, when it takes those we have loved, always hands us a pass. From this transaction with the earth the living take this survivor's reproach; consoling it and at turns denying its existence in us, we constantly regenerate Broch's "unity of thought, the ethical postulate"— the debt, in short, which we owe for living, the debt to the wronged.

It is necessary to say something more about Germany in this context of guilt. I cannot read anyone's mind, let alone a nation's, but one can read the drift of things. About a year ago I wrote some thoughts about the current Frankfurt trials of Nazi war criminals, which were published in Germany, among other countries. There was much German mail in response and a good lot of it furious, in part because I asked the question whether a recrudescence of Nazism was possible again in the future. The significant thing in many letters was a resentment based on the idea that the Nazis and the regime were something apart from the German people. In general, I was giving Germany a "bad name."

Apart from the unintended humor, I think this reaction is to be faced by the world and especially by the Germans. It is, in fact, no good telling people they are guilty. A nation, any more than an individual, helps nobody by going about beating its chest. I believe, in truth, that blame and emotional charges of a generalized guilt can only help to energize new frustrations in the Germans and send them striving for dignity through a new, strident, and dangerous nationalism. Again, guilt can become a "morality" in itself if no active path is opened before it, if it is not transformed into responsibility. The fact, unfortunately, is that for too many the destruction of the Jews by Germans has become one of Orwell's non-actions, an event self-propelled and therefore incomprehensible.

But if the darkness that persists over human guilt were to be examined not as an exceptional condition or as illness but as a concomitant of human nature, perhaps some practical good could come of it instead of endless polemic. If the hostility and aggression which lie hidden in every human being could be accepted as a fact rather than as reprehensible sin, perhaps the race could begin to guard against its ravages, which always take us "unawares," as something from "outside," from the hands of "others."

The reader has probably been nodding in agreement with what I have just said about Germany, but who among us knew enough to be shocked, let alone to protest, at the photographs of the Vietnamese torturing Vietcong prisoners, which our press has published? The Vietnamese are wearing United States equipment, are paid by us, and could not torture without us. There is no way around this—the prisoner crying out in agony is *our prisoner.*

It is simply no good saying that the other side probably does the same thing; it is the German's frequent answer when you raise the subject of Nazi atrocities—he begins talking about Mississippi. And more, if he is intelligent he will remind you that the schoolbooks sent to Germany by the United States immediately after the war included the truth about Nazism, but that they were withdrawn soon after when the Cold War began, so that a generation has grown up which has been taught nothing about the bloodiest decade in its country's history.

What is the lesson? It is immensely difficult to be human precisely because we cannot detect our own hostility in our own actions. It is tragic, fatal blindness, so old in us, so ingrained, that it underlies the first story in the Bible, the first personage in that book who can be called human. The rabbis who collected the Old Testament set Cain at its beginning not out of some interest in criminology but because they understood that the sight of his own crimes is the highest agony a man can know and the hardest to relate himself to.

Incident at Vichy has been called a play whose theme is "Am I my brother's keeper?" Not so. "Am I my own keeper?" is more correct.

Guilt, then, is not a featureless mist but the soul's remorse for its own hostility. We punish ourselves to keep from being punished and to keep from having to take part in regenerating that "unity of thought, that ethical postulate," which nevertheless is reborn with every child, again and again forever.

1965

The Battle of Chicago: From the Delegates' Side

There was violence inside the International Amphitheater before violence broke out in the Chicago streets. One knew from the sight of the barbed wire topping the cyclone fence around the vast parking lot, from the emanations of hostility in the credential-inspecting police that something had to happen, but once inside the hall it was not the hippies one thought about anymore, it was the delegates.

Violence in a social system is the sure sign of its incapacity to express formally certain irrepressible needs. The violent have sprung loose from the norms available for that expression. The hippies, the police, the delegates themselves were all sharers in the common breakdown of the form which traditionally has been flexible enough to allow conflicting interests to intermingle and stage meaningful debates and victories. The violence inside the amphitheater, which everyone knew was there and quickly showed itself in the arrests of delegates, the beatings of newsmen on the floor, was the result of the suppression, planned and executed, of any person or viewpoint which conflicted with the president's.

There had to be violence for many reasons, but one fundamental cause was the two opposite ideas of politics in this Democratic party. The professionals—the ordinary senator, congressman, state committeeman, mayor, officeholder—see politics as a sort of game in which you win sometimes and sometimes you lose. Issues are not something you feel, like morality, like good and evil, but something you succeed or fail to make use of. To these men an issue is a segment of public opinion which you either capitalize on or attempt to assuage according to the present interests of the party. To the amateurs—the McCarthy people and some of the Kennedy adherents—an issue is first of all moral and embodies a vision of the country, even of man, and is not a counter in a game. The great majority of the men and women at the convention were delegates from the party to the party.

Nothing else can explain their docility during the speeches of the first two days, speeches of a skull-flattening boredom impossible to endure except by people whose purpose is to demonstrate team spirit. "Vision" is always "forward," "freedom" is always a "burning flame," and "our inheritance," "freedom," "progress," "sacrifices," "long line of great Democratic presidents" fall like drops of water on the head of a tortured Chinese. And nobody listens; few even know who the speaker is. Every once in a while a cheer goes up from some quarter of the hall, and everyone asks his neighbor what was said. For most delegates just to be here is enough, to see Mayor Daley in the life even as the TV cameras are showing him to the folks back home. Just being here is the high point, the honor their fealty has earned them. They are among the chosen, and the boredom of the speeches is in itself a reassurance, their deepening insensibility is proof of their faithfulness and a token of their common suffering and sacrifice for the team. Dinner has been a frankfurter, the hotels are expensive, and on top of everything they have had to chip in around a hundred dollars per man for their delegation's hospitality room.

The tingling sense of aggressive hostility was in the hall from the first moment. There were no Chicago plainclothes men around the Connecticut delegation; we sat freely under the benign smile of John Bailey, the Democratic National Chairman and our own state chairman, who glanced down at us from the platform from time to time. But around the New York delegation there was always a squad of huskies ready to keep order—and indeed they arrested New Yorkers and even got in a couple of shoves against Paul O'Dwyer when he tried to keep them from slugging one of the members. Connecticut, of course, was safely machine, but New York had great McCarthy strength.

The McCarthy people had been warned not to bring posters into the hall, but at the first mention from the platform of Hubert Humphrey's name hundreds of three-by-five-foot Humphrey color photos broke out all over the place. By the third day I could not converse with anybody except by sitting down; a standing conversation would bring inspectors, sometimes every fifteen seconds, asking for my credentials and those of anyone talking to me. We were forbidden to hand out any propaganda on the resolutions, but a nicely printed brochure selling the Administration's majority Vietnam report was on every seat. And the ultimate mockery of the credentials themselves was the flooding of the balconies by Daley ward heelers who carried press passes. On the morning before the convention began, John Bailey had held up twenty-two visitors' tickets, the maximum, he said, allowed any delegation, as precious as gold.

The old-time humor of it all began to sour when one realized that of 7.5 million Democrats who voted in the primaries, eighty percent preferred McCarthy's and/or Robert Kennedy's Vietnam positions. The violence in the hall, let alone on the streets, was the result of this mockery of a vast majority who had so little representation on the floor and on the platform of the great convention. Had there never been a riot on Michigan Avenue the meeting in the amphitheater would still have been the closest thing to a session of the All-Union Soviet that ever took place outside of Russia. And it was not merely the heavy-handed discipline imposed from above but the passionate consent from below that makes the comparison apt.

On the record, some six hundred of these men were selected by state machines and another six hundred elected two years ago, long before the American people had turned against the Vietnam war. If they represent anything it is the America of two years past or the party machine's everlasting resolve to perpetuate the organization. As one professional said to me, "I used to be an idealist, but I learned fast. If you want to play ball you got to come into the park." Still, another of them came over to me during the speech of Senator Pell, who was favoring the bombing halt, and said, "I'd love to vote for that but I can't. I just want to tell you." And he walked away.

Connecticut caucused before casting its vote for the administration plank. We all, forty-four of us, sat in a caucus room outside the great hall itself and listened to Senator Benton defending the bombing position and Paul Newman and Joseph Duffey attacking it. The debate was subdued, routine. The nine McCarthy people and the thirty-five machine people were merely being patient with one another. One McCarthy man, a teacher, stood up and with a cry of outrage in his voice called the war immoral and promised revolution on the campuses if the majority plank was passed. Angels may have nodded, but the caucus remained immovable. Perhaps a few were angry at being called immoral, in effect, but they said nothing to this nut.

But when the roll was called, one machine man voted for the minority plank. I exchanged an astonished look with Joe Duffey. Another followed. Was the incredible about to happen?

We next began voting on the majority plank, the Johnson position. The machine people who had voted "Yes" on the minority plank also voted "Yes" on the majority plank. The greatness of the Democratic party is its ability to embrace conflicting viewpoints, even in the same individuals.

Having disposed of Vietnam, Mr. Bailey then suggested the delegation take this opportunity to poll itself on its preference for a presidential candidate, although nominations had not yet been made on the floor of the convention. This, I said, was premature since President Johnson, for one, might be nominated by some enthusiast and we would then have to poll ourselves all over again. In fact, I knew privately that William vanden Heuvel, among others, was seriously considering putting up the president's name on the grounds that the Vietnam plank was really a rephrasing of his program and that he should be given full credit as its author rather than Humphrey, who was merely standing in for him. But Mr. Bailey merely smiled at me in the rather witty way he has when his opponent is being harmlessly stupid, and Governor Dempsey, standing beside him behind the long table at the front of the room, assured all that as head of the delegation he would see to it that in the event of a nomination on the floor of any candidate other than Humphrey, McCarthy, and McGovern, we would certainly be allowed to change our votes. Immediately a small man leaped to his feet and shouted, "I nominate Governor Dempsey!" The governor instantly pointed at him and yelled, "Good morning, Judge!" This automatic reward of a seat on the bench, especially to a man obviously of no distinction, exploded most of the delegation—excepting the indignant teacher—into a burst of laughter and the governor and his nominator swatted at each other in locker-room style for a moment. Then seriousness returned, and resuming his official mien of gravity, the governor ordered the polling to begin. The nine McCarthy delegates voted for McCarthy and the rest for Humphrey, and there was no doubt of an honest count. It may be a measure of the tragedy in which both factions were caught that when, later on, the governor was handed teletyped reports of the Michigan Avenue riots, his face went white, and he sat with his head in his hands even as it became clearer by the minute that Humphrey and the administration would be victorious.

After two nights on the floor, whatever trends and tides the TV commentators might have been reporting, one felt like a fish floating about in still water. Nothing had been said on either side that aroused the slightest enthusiasm. The water above was dark, and whatever winds might be raising waves on the surface did not disturb the formless chaos, really the interior leaderlessness of the individual delegates. We were the crowd in an opera waiting for our cue to shout in unison when the time for it came. First depression and then anger began moving into the faces of the McCarthy people as the speeches ground on. Some of us had campaigned all over the state and the nation to rouse people to the issues of the war, and in many places we had succeeded. There was no trace of it here and clearly there never could have been. The machine had nailed down the nomination months before. We had not been able even to temper the administration's Vietnam plank, not in the slightest. The team belonged to the president, and the team owned the Democratic party.

As I sat there on the gray steel chair, it was obvious that we could hardly have expected to win. Behind Connecticut sat two rows of Hawaiians. Middle-aged, kindly looking, very polite, eager to return a friendly glance, they never spoke at all. When it came time for any vote, their aisle man picked up his phone, listened, hung up, stood, and turned thumbs up or down. The brown faces watched his hands. So much for deliberation. It was not quite that crude among the others, except for Illinois, but Illinois did not need thumbs. Illinois had somehow located the fact that we McCarthy people of Connecticut were occupying nine seats in the same row, and Illinois stared at us from time to time with open, almost comical, ferocity. Every time I turned to my left, I found the face of a man who might have been a retired hockey player. He sat staring at me through close-set eyes over a strong, broken nose, his powerful hands drooping between his knees, his pointy shoes worn at the heels, his immense neck bound to bursting by a tiny knot in his striped tie. Once I tried to give him a smile of greeting, a recognition of his interest. He gave nothing, like a watchdog trained to move only on signal.

There was this discipline but there was no leadership. None of the Humphrey people ever argued with me when I said they were sinking the party by hanging the Johnson position on the war around Humphrey's neck. None ever had a positive word to say about Humphrey himself. They were beyond—or beneath—discourse, and if by some miracle Humphrey had let it be known he was now in favor of an unconditional halt in the bombing they would have been as perfectly happy to applaud that stand as the opposite. They were lemminglike, clinging to one another in a mass that was moving toward where the leaders had pointed. And then, suddenly, there was a passion.

Representative Wayne Hays of Ohio got to the podium and began, like the others, in a rhetorical vein. Something to the effect that his teacher in school had taught him that history was a revelation of the past, a guide to the present, and a warning of the future. The delegates resumed their private conversations. But suddenly he was talking about hippies in paired contraries. Not long hair, he said, but long thought; not screaming in the streets but cleaning the streets; not . . .

Leadership, quite unannounced, had arrived. All around me men were turning to this clear voice on the platform. His list of mockeries of the errant generation mounted and grew more pointed, more vicious, more mocking, and applause was breaking out all over the floor, men were getting to their feet and yelling encouragement, and for the first time in two days there was electricity in the crowd, a vibrant union of mind, a will to act, a yea-saying from the heart. Men were hitting each other on the back with elation, fists were raised in encouragement, bull roars sounded out, and an ovation swept over Hays as he closed his papers and walked off. It was a congregation of the aged, men locked into a kind of political senility that was roaring its challenge across the six miles of superhighway to the ten thousand children just then gathering for the slaughter opposite the Conrad Hilton Hotel. The old bulls against the young bulls under the overhanging branches of the forest.

Then it struck me that there was no issue cleaving the convention; there was only a split in the attitude toward power, two mutually hostile ways of being human. The Humphrey men were supporting him not basically because he was right but because he was vice president and the candidate of the president. In any ten of them there will only be two or three at most who are themselves convinced that we should be in Vietnam, that if necessary we must fight on for years, that lamentable as the civilian casualties are they are justified by the need to protect democracy and the Thieu–Ky Government, and so on. This minority is passionate, it is deeply afraid that the communist powers, if they win in Vietnam, will flood over into Hawaii and ultimately California. But the others are supporting authority which happens at the moment to be fighting the war. Congressman Don Irwin of Norwalk, for example, is a principled supporter of the war and for him it is righteous, to the point where he openly says his position will probably defeat him the next time he runs. He is a man in his forties who smiles constantly and in a group quickly loses his voice from laughing so much, a common vocal problem with professionals, the accepted social greeting being laughter. They shake hands and laugh. It is not unnecessary, it is not merely a tic but a working out of conflict, for many of them have had terrible political battles against one another and have come close to insulting one another in various log jams, and the quick laugh is a signal of mutual disarmament, a warding-off of violence, for many are physical men quick to take umbrage, like their forefathers who more than once beat each other senseless in the halls of Congress.

There were two Americas in Chicago, but there always are. One is passionately loyal to the present, whatever the present happens to be; the other is in love with what is not yet. Oppressed by the team spirit all around me, I thought of a morning in Moscow when I was passing under the walls of the Kremlin with a young interpreter. I said that there must have been some terrific battles in those offices the day they decided to get rid of Khrushchev. The young man refused to join this idle speculation: "We don't think about what goes on in there. It is not our business. They know what they are doing."

But everywhere I went I also met young—and not so young—Russians who knew it was up to them to make the future of the country, men and women who wanted a hand on the tiller. But there they have no legal means of putting new ideas forward; here we do. Or did. The underlying fright in the Democratic convention, and the basic reason for the violence on Michigan Avenue, was that perhaps the social compact had fallen apart. As one TV correspondent said to me as we stood watching the line of troops facing the hippies across the boulevard from the Hilton, "It lasted two hundred years. What law says it may not be over? Maybe we've come to the end of the string. Those kids," he went on, "are not bohemians. Most of them aren't what you'd call hippies, even. There are a lot of graduate students in that crowd, medical students, too. They haven't dropped out at all. Somebody upstairs had better start asking himself what they're trying to tell the country."

To me, standing there at four in the morning with the arc lights blasting the street and no one knowing when the police and the troops would again go berserk, the strangest irony was that the leader they had come to hate, the president, had months ago removed himself as being too divisive. And yet all the force of the state was in play to give that president what he wanted in the convention. The whole thing might have been understandable if the country were in love with its leader. What, I wondered, was being so stoutly defended on this avenue?

The question itself only added to the general surrealism. In the main CBS workroom behind the auditorium, I watched a row of five TV sets. NBC was showing the attack by the club-swinging police, the swarming squads of helmeted cops, and one heard the appalling screaming. Next to it, CBS was showing the platform speaker inside the auditorium and the applauding delegates. Next to CBS was ABC, with close-ups of bleeding demonstrators being bandaged. Then a local station showing a commercial, Mister Clean having his moustache rubbed off. The last was another local station whose screen showed some sort of ballet.

In one of the corridors a young man stopped me, holding the microphone of a portable tape recorder up to my mouth. He came from the University of Chicago's radio station. We quickly agreed the whole spectacle was a horror. "How can you have anything to do with this?" he asked. My answer, which I found embarrassing at that moment, was that I had hoped to change it and that it might be changed if people like me tried to move into the party in a serious way rather than only during presidential campaigns.

"But how can you have any faith now in this kind of democratic politics?"

He was intelligent and eager and angry, and I thought I had misunderstood him. "What would you put in its place?" I asked.

"Well, I don't know. But not this."

"But what, then? One way or another people have to delegate powers to run the country, don't they? This is one way of delegating them. Right?"

"You mean you believe in this?" he asked, incredulously.

"Not this. Not this gang, no. But. . . ." I broke off, aware now that it was not merely the antics of the convention we were talking about. "Do you mean that the more intelligent should rule? The more idealistic? Is that it?"

"Well, not this," he repeated, his anger mounting.

"But what are you going to substitute for this?" The crowds were pushing us to one side and then another. The announcer on a nearby TV set was yelling a description of the battle on Michigan Avenue. "Are you just going to substitute intelligent people telling the others what to do instead of the others telling the intelligent? Isn't that the same kind of violence we're going through right here? What are you going to put in place of this?"

The look in his eyes amazed me. He seemed never to have considered the problem. It was unbelievable. He was ready, it seemed, for some kind of benevolent dictatorship. If this, this hall full of middle-aged men who had yelled their pleasure at the condemnation of the young—if this was democracy, he hated it, and that hatred was enough for him. We were being torn apart now by the crowd. I called to him as he moved away, "That's the problem, don't you see? What do you want? It's not enough to hate all this!" But he was gone.

Life is always more perfect than art. The endings and codas it provides to experience always tell more of the truth than any construction on the stage or in a book. At about two in the morning, after the fighting on Michigan Avenue had quieted, about five hundred delegates under the impromptu chairmanship of New York's Paul O'Dwyer decided to hold a march past the scene of the carnage. We gathered a few blocks from the Hilton, many of us holding lighted candles, and moved in near silence, some singing softly, toward the battleground. Police, who had been alerted to our plan, sat in squad cars on the avenue, none getting out, for we were official delegates and not to be pushed around, or not yet anyway. The night was lovely; all the stars were out. Chicago looked beautiful. A block from the Hilton we were stopped by a police captain. He was six-and-a-half-feet tall, wearing the blue crash helmet whose edges were lined with gray rubber, a hinged Plexiglas face shield pushed up. I have never seen such eyes or a smile so fixed and hard. The procession halted, and O'Dwyer stepped forward to parley.

"Now, what is it you want to do, gentlemen?" the officer asked.

O'Dwyer said that we intended to walk past the hippies, who were still congregated in the little park across the street from the hotel, past them and the line of soldiers and police facing them.

"I see," said the officer. "All right, then. Just keep it orderly and quiet. We are here to protect lives and property. Keep it orderly and keep moving."

We moved, and as we approached the hippies who had crowded to the edge of the park to see this strange, apparitional procession, they began whistling, and some said, "It's a wake, a funeral for the Democratic party." We kept coming, and some of them began to get the point. Cheers went up. We exchanged the V-for-victory sign. There was laughter and someone began to sing "We Shall Overcome." The line of soldiers stood expressionless, holding their rifles up to bar us from the hotel across the street, some of them looking at our candles as though they were in a hallucination. Nothing happened. In a while, the silence returned to the avenue again. The conversation between us and these kids was neither more nor less interesting than any such conversation on any street anywhere.

Next afternoon, I went to a TV studio to join a telecast being beamed by Telstar to England. I had been told to get there no later than three o'clock because the program was being sent live and the Telstar time was open only from 3:30 to 4. I had had to commandeer a taxi with a Time-Life sticker on the windshield, there being no free taxis or buses because of strikes. Breathless, I ran in at 3:10 to find that the other participants had not arrived. But the moderator, Byran Magee, told me to take it easy. "We are going to tape it and send it by plane to London, so there's time now. You see," he said, raising one eyebrow, "the United States Government has preempted the Telstar, due to the Czech crisis. No one believes it, of course."

In a few minutes, Pierre Salinger and former ambassador to Poland John Gronouski arrived. They knew nothing of the preemption. Once again Byran Magee said he did not believe the excuse for the preemption. Gronouski had no opinion, but he did not look happy. We proceeded to discuss the convention, the riots and Chicago, but someone had turned out our star just as someone had made it impossible for the TV people to shoot outside the International Amphitheater on simultaneous hookups.

Checking into this scandalous censorship, this heavenly blackout, I discovered later that it was not true. According to BBC in London, there had been no interruption in Telstar's availability. How and why Byran Magee had been misinformed I do not know, but the interesting fact remains that he, Salinger, Ambassador Gronouski and I never questioned that the government had indeed tried to block this telecast. The point is, that I remember quite clearly a time when something like this would not have been credible. Now everything is possible, anything at all, and that is where we're at.

I left Chicago while the final session was going on. What the new candidate might or might not say seemed the last thing in the world to concern oneself about. And this, because the authority, the leadership was not in him. It was not in anyone whose face was visible in Chicago. It was in the president, and he was only an unseen presence whom no majority man on that platform dared contradict or too openly obey. I wondered who would eat the president's birthday cake, now that he had decided it was too dangerous to appear—in one of his own cities, and in his own convention. I stood in the airport with thirty or so other passengers waiting to board the plane, which, quite symbolically, had had to be replaced with another because of a faulty oil warning light. We waited an hour.

A long line of draftees appeared, kids in shirtsleeves, carrying valises, chattering like campers, walking five abreast down the corridor. A few Negro boys were scattered in among them, and as one Negro passed he turned to the watching passengers and called out, "We're off to defend your country. Your country!" And another Negro boy just behind him held out his hand: "Got some pennies, anybody?" The passengers said nothing, their faces registered nothing.

During our telecast, Ambassador Gronouski had said that Hubert Humphrey could not be blamed for what had happened in Chicago. Pierre Salinger said he could be, that he was the leader and could at least have dissociated himself from a riot of police. Ambassador Gronouski said Hubert Humphrey had a good rapport with youngsters. I said it was time to stop talking like this. Mrs. Humphrey had announced she was going to visit all the new youth-aid projects, including the Junior Chamber of Commerce. Where had these people been living? What had to happen before the powers realized they were not living in this time and in this place?

On the wide lawn behind my house at five o'clock in the morning the stars hung as bright and orderly as they had over Michigan Avenue. The sun rose on time. The morning paper said that a poll showed that the majority of Americans sympathized with the police. It was not a surprise. Not in the least. The voice that might have spoken both with authority, respectability, and confidence about the honest despair of a generation of Americans had never been heard in Chicago. Within a day I was being asked from London to organize a protest against the jailing of writers by the Russians in Prague. Prague, perhaps the freest city, the most hopeful and experimental in Eastern Europe, was being cleansed of the enemies of the people.

1968

Kidnapped?

Even as I walked toward the turnstiles the light inside the massive airport building was rapidly turning blue, and through the tall columns of the portico outside the orange sunset sky was swiftly transforming to violet, and the surprising silence in such a place gave off a sudden sensation of a ruin. It must have been one of those statistically odd hours when for a few minutes no passengers were arriving for takeoffs and no planes discharging. My Caravelle from Paris had been two-thirds empty and the other passengers had somehow vanished by this time. I looked in every direction, out onto the portico and behind me toward the interior of the building, and to right and left down the block-long marble entrance hall, but the chauffeur was not there, only two women soundlessly mopping in the distance.

Outside on the stone steps, perhaps. I walked out under the portico and saw the sea of parked cars, but even here nothing moved. The soft Los Angeles air of Rome, the sexual damp. In the dusk, silver flecks of light flashed in the sky. The continuing silence—in an airport—was incredible, like a hole in all the schedules. I was caught in a vacuum and longed for a sound that would show the world had not died. Baldo's failure to send someone to meet me was angering; I had a good mind to catch the next plane back to Paris. Then there was someone running between the cars, toward me surely. A short man in a black suit. Yes, it could be a chauffeur's suit, although he had no cap. His arm was rising, his finger pointing at me. An embarrassed way of running, and quite properly so, I thought, since Baldo must be a tough boss to work for, rich as he was and in the line of spoiled princes.

"Signor Miller!" the man declared and asked, nearly skidding to a halt before me. I nodded down to him. He lowered his finger, and his eyes filled with excited relief. Had my plane been late, and he on the verge of returning to a furious Baldo with an empty car? As though to make up for the indignity of my few minutes' uncertainty, he held up a beseeching palm. *"Aspett', aspett'."* He already knew I could not speak Italian. Baldo had briefed him, no doubt. He turned and ran sideways, still holding up his palm. I followed his form as it entered the ranks of cars, my eyes alert for the Rolls, the Mercedes, the Ferrari, perhaps. The man disappeared. Then I could see an ordinary black Fiat sedan threading through the aisles of cars.

The man drove fast and in silence as though trying to make up for his failure to meet me promptly. Night had fallen but the headlights flashed among the old trees beside the highway. Twenty (*twenty?*) years ago there had been sunshine. The old green taxi had had a meter one ignored because it was still on the Fascist money scale, and I had paid seventeen dollars to get into Rome, the price of not being able to bargain in Italian. The driver then was thin, like most Italians, and his taxi a slope-nosed Fiat built in the Twenties. This Fiat now was tight and quiet; this driver had a filled-out face. I had not known a soul in Rome then. I soon met Emilio, an anarchist novelist just freed after fourteen years in jail. We met on the face of a cliff in front of one of the hundreds of holes bored into the earth where families lived. A ring of caves around Rome smelling of sewage. Emilio's hair grew straight out sideways from his temples, and he wore a brown overcoat, shoes and trousers but no socks, underwear or shirt. He was round and jolly, like a friar, but he had shot and killed two *Fascisti* the day of his release. He lived in a *palazzo* on a kind of balcony open to the air. On it he had a bed and a desk. Six or seven families shared the balcony, but the children never touched his papers because he was The Poet. I gave him razor blades and a shirt, but he gave them to "the poor." In the afternoons he went to a bordello and wrote at a marble table in a vast ballroom where a dozen women stood on display against a wall facing him, and customers sat on long padded benches, playing chess or reading newspapers or answering mail while their senses awoke. It was one of the few warm buildings in Rome then. Occasionally one would finish a letter or fold up his newspaper and go to the line of women and make a selection and disappear upstairs. Emilio died in the bordello one February afternoon.

The driver turned his head toward me and said something. I said, *"Non capisco."* He looked ahead again. After a moment he turned back and said simply, "Hotel?"

I had a flush of confusion. Surely Baldo had told him where to take me. He was holding a business conference in his home which would last into the late evening, and I had not wanted to hang around waiting for it to finish, so he had reserved a room for me at the Hotel d'Inghilterra. We would meet next morning and discuss my play, and I would return to Paris around noon. I said, "Hotel d'Inghilterra," and the driver nodded and said, "Ah, *sì, sì*," and seemed more content now as he drove.

It was time to say something. I formed an Italian sentence in my mind and corrected it two or three times, then said, "How is Mr. di Castello?"

"Di Castello?"

"Yes." Possibly I was not pronouncing the name correctly, and I repeated it.

The driver shook his head. He did not know a Mr. di Castello, and it obviously was an embarrassment to him.

"The director of plays and films. Baldo di Castello," I reminded him.

Quite as though it were not of any importance, the driver shook his head again—then suddenly recalled. "Oh yes, the film director. I have heard of him. Baldo di Castello. Yes." Again his contentment returned, and he drove on in silence.

I stared out at the darkness. What was the word for "who"? And "sent"? And "meet"? Anger was breaking apart my attempt to translate French and Latin equivalents into Italian. I leaned forward and touched the driver's shoulder. He slowed the car. In the segment of his right eye that I could see there was undoubtedly an abnormal excitement. For the first time I noticed he had a wide, thick jaw. *"Qui,"* I said, hoping it was the same in Italian as in French, but then there was nothing. I sat back in the seat again. Possibly Baldo had hired the car through a secretary—he had a Mafia of boys and girls around him—and no one at the garage had bothered to tell this driver in whose name the car had been sent.

"Agenzia" sounded good for a car-rental place. I leaned forward again, touched the driver's shoulder and pointed at him. *"Auto agenzia?"*

He glanced at me with sweat shining on his forehead. "No, no," he said. A denial. The sting of accusation was in the air between us. Clearly now there was a commercial proposition somewhere in the car with us. I pointed beside him at the front seat. "Taxi?"

"No taxi. No, no. No taxi," he said.

I sat back again. In other words, I had been captured; he was just a private gangster preying on foreigners who looked as though they didn't know where they were going. I leaned forward again. *"Quanto"*—thank God for "quanto"—and then, *"per . . ."*

He looked at me again but this time real shock exploded on his face. He had met his match. This was not the Forties, not this time. This was the Sixties and the sentimental game was over. He would get exactly what such a trip was normally worth, and no tip. Christ's sake, Baldo's chauffeur was probably looking for me back at the airport this minute. *"Signor, il chauffeur—capisco?—il auto di Signor di Castello es (es? Spanish?) aspettar (possible?) por me a aeroporto."*

The driver, from the rear, seemed stabbed. It was unlooked for, his sinking into his suit like this, an encouragingly introverted sensitivity. Or was it that he knew he had been caught red-handed? But would a man with all these emotions be carrying on this kind of work?

What kind of work? Suddenly, as though it had been sitting inside my brain all the while, I saw the idea of being kidnapped. It had been happening in Italy—quite recently, in fact, some industrialist had been held for ransom. For all I knew, one of Baldo's journalist buddies may have put in the paper that I was arriving this afternoon. I dug in against dismissing it as ridiculous. The image of Luciano hung in the darkness before me.

The docks of Palermo, just after the war, still lay in pieces in the harbor. The Hôtel des Palmes, a vast Victorian architectural embrace, was nearly empty. The bandit Giuliano was still in the mountains. Vittorio and I were the only tourists in Palermo then, and after unpacking, we walked around the chaotic city, got hungry, and saw a restaurant in a store, a newly rebuilt place that seemed confident of itself. (The two or three others that were open were so evidently apologetic that we had retreated at the doorways.)

Inside, all the tables were empty, but along the right-hand wall a dozen or so had been put together, and about twenty men and women sat in absolute silence, with full plates and wineglasses, staring at us as we sat down. In one sweep of the eye it was possible to see how strange a collection they were. Two men in their forties, dressed in business suits, sat at the center, flanked by a pair of bleached-blond, heavy-breasted girls; then a few men with thick jackets and broad Sicilian country faces and some immense peasant women in shawls and one man who was peaked and thin and wore bent eyeglasses and might have been a journalist or a school-teacher. It was like a cross section of a society assembled for a sociological interview, except that their common silence implied some association, some secret meeting that we had interrupted.

Vittorio and I sat at a table, he facing the banquet, I with my back to it. There was already an awkwardness in the air. I could hear no knife touching a plate, no word spoken behind me, no shuffle of feet. Sunshine poured in through the window. The place was very clean, our tablecloth starched. Presently the owner appeared, a stout man, bald, with a warm look, and a white apron wrapped around his middle. He too was very clean and brought two new menus, nicely typed. He suggested some items, we discussed wines, and he left quite satisfied.

Now Vittorio looked at me with a grin of fear and challenge and whispered, "Don't look now, but there's somebody behind you."

"Who?"

"Lucky Luciano."

"Is that good or bad?"

"Don't laugh."

Then, too, I had to force myself to dig in against the ridiculous but true. Vittorio, who understood gangsters, was clearly wishing we had not come in here, and I tried to share his concern, but all I could feel was the absurdity. Vittorio pretended to go on studying the menu. A fine sweat was glistening on his face, and a fixed smile gave him a masklike look. I put one arm over the back of my chair and turned around.

The banquet table was empty! I had heard no sound of people getting up or leaving. Two men were approaching us from the rear of the restaurant. They came to our table and sat down, one on my right, one on my left. The one on my right was six feet tall or more, and as he sat down I could see the handle of a revolver protruding under the lapel of his well-pressed striped black jacket. The one on my left was undoubtedly Luciano. He had no revolver. His jacket clung beautifully to his chest, his fingers spread out on the tablecloth were manicured and small. He wore a black knitted tie and a steel-gray silk suit. He looked at me and then at Vittorio, who was obviously Italian, and then he looked at the black box containing my movie camera, which I had placed on the table.

He studied the black box quite openly. He was telling us that he wanted to know what was in the black box, which was rectangular and unshaped, unlike most camera boxes. And he kept only a faint smile going, enough to indicate that in principle he had not drawn any conclusions yet. "Where ya from?" he asked.

Then, too, I had found myself in an unwanted relationship in Italy, a pull and tug that had nothing to do with me, and danger inexplicable and absurd. When Vittorio answered, "Brooklyn," I could see Luciano's electricity turn on.

"Where 'bouts?"

Vittorio had an ambivalent attitude toward gangsters. As a lawyer to the underdog he fought against the rackets in unions, made speeches on the waterfront, and was even dabbling with the idea of running for Congress. But at the same time gangsters had a glamour for him, like actors—which is what he would rather have been. They played with power, were an elite, and above all, he thought, they walked in the glory of the courageous. He hated what they stood for but adored what they were; he could not help it. And now he was talking of "Biggie Cassalino," of "Fingers Levine," of "Marty Wholesome," his face close to Luciano's and his skin flushed with pride. He wanted to make good with Lucky, incredibly enough, and in a few minutes of their acquaintance it was clear where Luciano's power came from—himself.

On the right side of his face he looked like a small-town pharmacist. His left eye, however, had died. It blinked and moved normally, but it saw differently, and made judgments unobstructed by the warmth of the other eye. He heard with his right eye but he saw with his left. And it was with his left that he kept glancing at the black box on the table.

It took a long time for me to realize that the black camera box was the issue. Vittorio was now talking about the "boys" as though he hung with them every night. The bodyguard, with the box in front of him, simply stared at it and at me. The owner brought our food, and Luciano made him take back the olives and bring the better ones. He either owned the place or terrorized it. He ordered a glass of milk. They talked of Tom Dewey, who had helped to deport Luciano to Italy a year or two earlier, having convicted him of white-slavery charges. Dewey, then running against Truman, was Luciano's hopeful winner, the heavy implication being that Dewey as president would let him return to the United States because of his services to the Army during the war—he claimed to have fed inside information about the Fascist armies to American intelligence. But his mind was still strung to the black box on the table, and finally he turned to me fully for the first time.

"You lawyer too?"

"No, I'm a writer."

"What paper?"

"No, not papers. I write plays. For the stage."

"Uh huh." He did not believe it, but he did not *not* believe it. He looked at the black box. I reached over and opened it and took out the camera. He nodded. Obviously he wanted the camera opened too. I opened it, and he took it and examined the insides. Then he gave it back to me. I was as relieved as he was.

"So what the hell you doin' in Palermo?" he asked, leaning back now with his hands in his lap.

"Just tourists," Vittorio said.

Luciano had been exiled by the Italian government to Sicily, and it was hard for him to understand why anybody would come here willingly, let alone for pleasure.

"What's there to tour?" he asked, and I could see that the reassurance of the camera was fast wearing thin.

I said, "I have an idea for a play about Sicilians. I wanted to see what it was like here. I know a lot of Sicilians in New York."

He nodded. The left eye, dead as glass, estimated me. I felt I must be blushing. In fact, my whole story suddenly seemed a lie. The bodyguard, a balding man, very strong in the shoulders, said, "You know people here?"

"No," I said, "I don't know anybody here. We were walking around." I thought it might help to add, "And we just happened to see this place." The bodyguard, imitating Luciano, nodded. I thought we might get friendlier. "You come from New York?"

"No, I'm from here. I never been in New York." This obvious lie—obvious because he spoke like every New York Sicilian I had ever known—was said in order to register his conclusion that I had lied. Just as well, probably, because he was either wanted in New York or not wanted. I turned to Luciano, who was again talking to Vittorio, and when I turned back to the bodyguard I found his empty chair. They all moved like cats. And now we had finished eating, and I called for the bill.

Luciano would not hear of it—he took out a round coil of lire and tossed chunks of paper on the table. Vittorio and I both resisted and then gave up and let him pay, but our jab at independence told Luciano our wish to have nothing more to do with him, now that this accidental collision was past, and I felt I had to smooth things over, and I said of the lire— "They're beautiful."

"Funny money," he said. "Gimme one ugly American buck, you can have this crap."

The table was cleared now. There seemed nothing more to say. I made a move of my chair away from the table.

"Lemme drop you, where you going?" Luciano said.

"Just walking around," Vittorio said.

"Where to? I'll drop you. I got my car outside."

"No, we don't want to ride," I said. "We like to walk. We've never seen this place before."

"Well, what do you wanna see?"

Clearly we were not leaving. Not yet. And now I remembered that soon after the bodyguard had vanished I had heard a phone being dialed from the rear of the restaurant. And now the bodyguard returned and stood behind his chair and exchanged a quite open look with Luciano, who then turned to us and said, "Let's go," and we all got up. Some check had been made; another stage had been passed in our clearance.

He would not let us walk. Outside he had a new Lancia, which I openly admired. "Gimme any Chevy," he said in reply. We drove to the Hôtel des Palmes, where, curiously enough, he was also staying. We had had no intention of going to our room, but it seemed the best way to shake Luciano, so when he asked for his key, we asked for ours. The rooms turned out to be adjoining. Luciano looked at the number on the key in my hand, moving my finger open to see it better, then at the number on his. He did not speak at all then. The four of us walked to the elevator. I indicated for him to enter first, but he stood back and silently gestured us in before him. He and the bodyguard stood with their backs against the elevator walls. No one spoke. The fact of our adjoining rooms evidently was disturbing. He walked behind us down the hall and waited until I had unlocked our door. He watched as we went in and barely nodded as we said good-bye.

I closed our door and started to laugh. Vittorio threw himself onto the bed and held his head. Incredibly, he was seriously afraid. "But why?" I asked.

"God, we end up in the next room. He's not going to take this."

"Take what, for Christ's sake?"

"Baby, nobody tours Sicily now. Either we're the FBI or somebody else who doesn't mean him good. Don't laugh. We've got to get out of here."

"Well, let's get out then."

"No, wait. Let's wait half an hour. We don't want him to think we just came up because he wanted us to."

"Well, why the hell else did we come up? I didn't come to Sicily to sit with you in a hotel room."

"Wait a few minutes," Vittorio said.

And we sat there, at least a half an hour—why, neither of us knew exactly, except that it was no more absurd than anything else we might be doing. Suddenly, for no reason, we were in some kind of relationship with a killer. I sat at the long French window, looking down at the sunny street where hardly anything moved.

Now I sat in the Fiat looking out at the darkness with the same sort of feeling, not of being in danger but of not understanding what I should be feeling. Anything, I said to myself, is possible. This is the world now. Unoffending people are found dead every day behind a bush in the park where they went to feed a squirrel. Still, I was bigger than the driver, and he did not frighten me. Unless he had a gun. There my mind slowed to a halt. The choice of optimism or pessimism. Inevitably, the other part of the Luciano episode formed in the air.

To buttress our claim to being tourists, we had told Luciano that we had tried to rent a car and driver to tour the whole island, but we had been informed that it was impossible to buy gas outside Palermo. It had been a passing remark in Luciano's Lancia. Having waited a half hour or so in our hotel room, we opened the door quietly and tiptoed down the hall past Luciano's door. In the lobby a short man in a cape and a wide gray moustache and blue beret came up and hit Vittorio hard on the upper arm. They then embraced. The man was Giuseppe Moro, chief of the communist deputies in the Sicilian parliament. He had known Vittorio in New York, where he had waited a decade for Mussolini to expire. That evening we went to a restaurant with Moro and discovered ourselves two tables away from Luciano, his bodyguard, and the two blond girls. Vittorio had rather boasted—he could not help it—that he had had a long talk with Lucky. Seeing him a few yards away, Vittorio nodded powerfully to him. Moro looked once at Luciano and Luciano at him, and the air froze along their line of vision. Vittorio saw this but went right on telling Moro about our entrapment in the restaurant and later in the hotel. Moro listened sternly. "You were afraid? What were you afraid of?" he said quite loudly, his indignation barely controlled. Vittorio started to back off, explaining that it wasn't really fear but some sort of apprehension, when Moro reached under his arm and slipped out a pistol and laid it on the tablecloth.

"Luciano," he said very loudly—but none of the other guests so much as turned an inch, "is my ——!'"

He said this in English, but the underlying information was clear enough. Luciano went right on eating.

When we returned to our room to sleep that evening, we had hardly gotten our ties off when there was a knock at our door. The end, evidently, had arrived. The knock was repeated. A few minutes earlier we had been laughing near hysteria at this chain of idiotic adventures. Now neither of us could quite make the move to the door, but one of us did, and a handsome man of perhaps twenty-three stood there in a green-plaid Mackinaw, a good tweed cap, peasant's heavy shoes, and a silk shirt open at the collar. He was smiling. His teeth were incredibly white and even, his Sicilian skin nearly black, and he entered the room smiling and chesty, his brown eyes glancing from Vittorio to me to decide which of us could talk to him.

"I understand," he said, "you want to see the country."

"Yes," said Vittorio and shut the door.

"It is possible," the Sicilian said—much amused, it seemed, for he kept on smiling. He could have been a movie star.

"Sit down," Vittorio said.

The Sicilian sat without removing cap or coat. We sat on the bed facing him. "I believe," he said, "that you will be able to find petrol in the country. There is petrol."

Vittorio asked him his name. He said, "Emmanuel," and his smile widened so that we understood it was not his name and that he was beyond the law. Vittorio asked how he knew about us. He said that he knew the people who rented the few cars there were in Palermo. In fact, he knew almost everyone in Palermo. And Vittorio's sense of the Sicilian's power quickened so openly that the young man, seeing it, could not leave his power undescribed. He had been the poor son of a poor peasant in the hills, and when the Germans had come, he had, like all the peasants, sold vegetables to them. Then he had organized the cabbages, later on the beets, still later the entire vegetable production of the area. So that who-ever wanted vegetables called Emmanuel. Finally he had organized the Germans' own gasoline supply by blowing up their trucks in the back country. The Germans at first had retaliated but soon understood the mes-sage and simply ordered their own gasoline from Emmanuel, who issued his own printed forms to be pasted on the trucks' windshields for safe pas-sage. It would therefore be no great problem to organize gasoline for us if we wished to tour the island.

He rose to leave. His smile had never for a moment relaxed. His even white teeth seemed to fill the room. Vittorio asked him how much we should pay him. He held up a lordly palm and gave a brief shake of his head. "I welcome you to Sicily," he said. Vittorio offered him a cigarette from a pack. He took the cigarette, and then he took the pack. Vittorio asked if he wanted more, and he nodded. I took out an unbroken carton from my valise and started to tear the cardboard, and he took the carton and put it under his arm. He stood there waiting. Vittorio took a carton from his bag and handed it to him. Then he held out his hand, shook ours, opened the door, and walked out with a rocking, proud, seaman's gait.

A rattling old green car appeared at eight in the morning, and the driver took us all over Sicily; in tiny hamlets he would pull up at the soli-tary gas pump, a man would come out, fill our tank, hang up the hose, and go into his house with no money passed. Whether this was Luciano's gift or truly Emmanuel's we never knew. And why should Luciano have done this for us? For that matter, why should Emmanuel have done it? The fact, however, was that on mountaintops where there were a dozen slumping peasants' huts, in towns, and along the rivers, wherever our driver stopped before a gas pump a man would appear and without a word fill our tank and hang up the hose and go back to where he had come from.

The outskirts of Rome were surrounding the Fiat now, and the lights of stores bled out the melodrama. I watched the driver carefully. He ex-uded uncertainty, hunching himself down and forward as though to see better where he was going.

I reviewed. He knew my name. He had been happy to see me. The car was not a taxi. But he did not know di Castello or even where I was going. There was guilt on his face. But not the aspect of the operator. In fact, objectively speaking, he seemed a mild man with no secrecy covering his quick emotions. In other words, he did this kind of thing not with a domineering impulse bur rather pitifully. One was supposed to pity him and thus pay double. None of it hung together. With one overnight bag and traveling alone I was obviously not the usual guilty tourist but more likely a man on business. Would men on business be likely to pay double out of pity? Unlikely. My confusion remained absolute.

The streets were beginning to look familiar. The driver had slowed considerably until we were moving at little more than a walking pace, and he was looking around. *"No conosco Hotel d'Inghilterra?"*

"Sì, sì!" he promised, but it was obvious he was lost. How could a gangster, a professional hijacker of foreigners, not know that hotel? We were now passing what I was almost sure was a street leading to the hotel. Emilio's bordello was not far from here. A young man with my name had walked endlessly in this neighborhood, trying to absorb the new age, the age after Fascism was hung up by the feet, the coming-on time of brotherhood and war's educative end, when the whores moved in pairs, hundreds of them everywhere, and if you turned them down they would look you in the eye and say, "When you gonna make us the forty-nine state, Joe?" I saw a policeman on the corner now and quickly leaned forward and shook the driver's shoulder and pointed at the man.

The driver stopped the car, got out, and slammed the door on his thumb. The door bounced open. It had been a direct hit, a real smash. The blood started running over his palm. He took out his handkerchief and hurried to the policeman, wrapping his finger. By the time he returned the handkerchief was soaked. I pointed to his finger. *"Dottore,* hospital," I said. The wound had gone into my stomach.

"No, no," he said and started the car. I repeated "Hospital, *dottore,"* but he waved me away. The sweat was pouring down his cheeks now. He turned a corner and there was the Hotel d'Inghilterra. I got out, taking my bag, but he was upon me at once, and I let him carry it. I reached into my pocket and realized I had no Italian money. We walked into the hotel as I was assuring him not to fear, I had only to change money. He kept nodding and with his good hand assuring me of his trust, it seemed.

It was the same lobby, tiny and confused. In the center a marble table and carved chairs where no one could possibly sit in the flow of guests. A small booth to one side sheltered the concierge, a tall and stout man in a green tail coat and braid. I went to him and said I had a reservation. He knew my face and smiled a welcome. I asked him what the normal rate was from the airport, knowing I could not pay less than double now, now that the driver was trying to hide his wounded hand behind his good one. His face was pale, the eyes spread open wider by the pain, the pain and some tidal wash of guilt that seemed to immobilize him.

The concierge glanced at the driver and then said to me under his lip, "Pay what you like."

"But what's normal?"

The concierge looked at the driver again, sizing him up but without hostility. They were both Italians in a poor country. "Speak to him," I said, giving up.

He came around the small counter and walked up to the driver and said something. The driver shook his head, again with that deeply negative denial, which was the only thing I had seen him do since we had met. It suddenly seemed as though everybody was saying utterly inappropriate things to him and that his whole life was a series of misunderstandings. He was telling the concierge something now, something more lengthy, occasionally pointing at me. For the first time I saw him smile with a little joy, a little release, an unburdening of his heart, it seemed. And as the concierge nodded and returned to me, the driver waited, watching my face.

"He doesn't want anything. He simply recognized you at the airport and wanted to be of help. He admires your plays."

I looked at the driver. A fan. With a bleeding thumb. A suit wrinkled now by his anxiety. Wet hair from the sweat. I strode over to him, started to offer my hand but feared to hurt his thumb and ended by grasping his arm. "I'm terribly sorry," I said.

The concierge translated.

"I thought you might be one of those drivers who overcharge foreign——" I broke off, realizing that all this was of no interest to him at all, a noise down in the valley far below the mountaintop where he lived with books, dramas, poems, God-knows-what loving concourse with beauty and truth. And my embarrassment seemed not to reach him; he merely went on faintly smiling now, a shy man surely, a small private person I had been mortifying for half an hour with talk of fares, *agenzias,* taxis. He said something, something brief, directly to me.

"He is deeply honored to have met you," the concierge said.

"Tell him that I am honored, too."

The concierge translated. The driver shyly nodded. He turned and walked out the doorway, holding his bloody hand a little higher than his heart, to slow the bleeding, I supposed.

1969

The Opera House in Tashkent
(from In Russia)

The opera house in Tashkent looked so inviting, and they were playing *Leila and Mezhdu,* based on the national epic. We must go. Some difficulty in arranging tickets on such short notice. We arrive promptly at seven for a seven-thirty curtain, in order to see what the crowd looks like.

The building is some combination of Moorish, Spanish, City Center–type architecture but nevertheless very white and imposing, with wide-open concrete aprons around it and a nice flat stairway rising up from the street level. A strange quiet, however, as we pass beneath the outer archways, and in fact there is nobody in the lobby. Did we misunderstand the curtain time? It appears not, for the large lady usher takes our ticket and bids us follow her inside. Perhaps Uzbeks do not speak before the curtain goes up?

In the auditorium there is not one soul. Immaculately clean, the seat-arms polished, the carpet soft and well vacuumed—but not a soul. We sit in the third row center. It is a vast house, with perhaps four thousand seats. Endless balconies, galleries, boxes. All empty.

Ten minutes pass like an hour and a half. Another couple comes down the aisle. Action! They are English. One can tell after a few minutes, because they don't speak to one another but sit at polite attention quite as though the seats around them were full. Nothing whatever is odd, remarkable, wrong. If water started rising above their ankles they would not move or take note. One loves them, their truly *interested* attention as they stare at the empty orchestra pit. England will never die.

Movement behind us. Turning around, I spy a customer. An Uzbek worker, he wears a cap sideways, a red bandanna around his neck, no shirt, his black wrinkled jacket and pants and shoes caked with white cement. He is alone, lounging in his seat, staring at the curtain up ahead. Things are moving. Soon we may have the ushers outnumbered and could force a performance.

A disturbance in the orchestra pit. A musician enters from under the stage. A man of sixty, his eyeglasses badly bent, he has no tie, wears a sweater. He sits and opens his violin case. Something wrong with the bridge. He adjusts it for ten minutes.

More action behind us. For some reason about eight people have entered the second balcony. Five or six are now spread out behind us in the orchestra, one man sits alone in a side box. Two more musicians enter the pit. One of them tests his clarinet, the other reads a newspaper. How forlorn. Three or four more come into the pit now. They tune up, but only barely take any notice of one another. Perhaps they have been exiled here? One, for some reason, is wearing a tuxedo. Probably a recent arrival from Moscow, still unaccustomed to frontier mores.

The tuning-up is getting louder and is much better than nothing. Suddenly, as though on cue, they all stop, pack up their instruments, and walk out under the stage! Can it all be over?

Inge is now weeping with laughter, a certain hysteria having entered our relationship. Neither one of us can say anything that is not funny.

A small note of revolt—the audience begins to clap in unison. It is now a quarter past eight. The English couple remains fascinated by the curtain, takes no note of the demonstration. The clapping dies away. Begins all over again.

The house lights go down as the musicians hurry back in. A full orchestra, the members glance out over the gala audience. A kind of utter exhaustion emanates from the conductor, who makes a play at a rapid, sprightly entrance. Somebody up in the gallery claps once.

The curtain rises. An Arab-type chieftain sits before a cardboard tent surrounded by his court. He seems angry as he sings baritone. The others try to placate him. He is stubborn, refusing comfort. Moussorgsky weaves through Tchaikovsky through intermittent Rimsky-Korsakov. Ignorant of the story, one still knows that the chieftain's daughter must soon appear. She sure as hell does. Beautiful girl but can't sing. Which is the hero? Two or three young bravos appear, and one knows which is the hero because he is the shortest and stands at the center, and whenever he points at something he also takes a gliding step in the same direction, while the others only point without taking a step. Very gradually one's sympathy begins to go out to all of them knocking themselves out for the empty house. What dreams of glory they must have had once! It is terribly hard work, this opera. Queen Victoria would have adored the purity of its emotions, the sweep of the music. It is all Cultural. Somewhere in this city must be some guys and girls hiding in a cellar playing some stringed instrument and singing to each other without a committee. The public has vetoed this opera, is all one can say. It has definitely decided to risk everything and not come. There is something heartening and universal, finally. As the box-office man on Broadway once said to me, "There is no power on earth that can keep the public from staying home."

Intermission. The audience rises. The combined sound is like eleven chickens scratching in Madison Square Garden. We stroll idly, politely, toward the lobby. The English couple, still *interested,* appears a few yards away. I confide to Inge that we are not remaining for the second act, although there is no doubt the English couple will do their national duty. We stroll out the front door rather as though wanting a breath of the night air. We keep on strolling at a sort of trot. Glancing behind, we see the English couple also strolling, looking about at the nonexistent native audience but disappearing nevertheless into the bowels of Tashkent. And yet—what's the opera situation on a weekday night in Duluth, Minnesota?

Making Crowds

As in Chicago so in Miami—this had to be the Last Convention. So said half-a-dozen newsmen of my acquaintance, and I felt the same myself a good part of the time. There is the shock and charm of the American crowd in all its variety and sheer animal power, but in any real sense the thing simply cannot work. How can the same man "represent" Richard Daley and Bella Abzug? For that matter how could Franklin Roosevelt stand for the principles of Georgia's Governor Talmadge and his red suspenders and simultaneously for the young trade-union movement whose organizers were being crucified in the South?

But this is too rational. Democracy is first of all a state of feeling. A nominee, and later a president, is not a sort of methodical lawyer hired to win a client's claim but an ambiguously symbolic figure upon whom is projected the conflicting desires of an audience. Like the protagonist in a drama he rises to a level of the fictional. As he comes closer to being the nominee he becomes less an ordinary man than a performer who is merely like a man. One proof of this is that we demand a perfection of character of him which would be absurd and childish were he not a nominee but which is somehow reasonable as he approaches that status. For he is now a hero who must act out what we would believe is the best in our own faulted personalities.

So it is inevitable that the Issues dim in a convention quite as they do in a good play whose moral conclusions and thematic point, while necessary to give it form, recede in importance for the mind which is swayed by personalities, color, the surprises and sudden switches of the action itself.

As a Connecticut delegate in '68 I was at first surprised by the relative impotence of the Issues for the Humphrey men who made up the bulk of our delegation. I had assumed that as machine politicians whose very livelihoods depended on winning the election they would be ruled by this consideration, but I could not find one who believed Humphrey had a chance against Nixon. One would assume they would therefore be casting about for an alternative. This would be rational. Nor were they under the illusion that continuing the war would do anything but hurt their cause. Yet they would not hear of any idea to set themselves against Johnson's policy, which had no hope of bringing peace reasonably soon.

It was clear then that it came down to their *belonging* somewhere, the way people belong in a certain neighborhood and are strangers in another in no objective way different than their own. Win or no win, issues or no issues, they belonged with Humphrey and the binding tie was visceral. And when I thought about it later in the calm of total disaster for our side, I found my own case too similar. Had Humphrey by some miracle turned against the war and come out for immediate withdrawal I knew it would be hard for me to go with him. I did not belong with him. Objectively, his record on other issues was as good or better than McCarthy's, yet in his camp I'd have been a stranger and at odds with myself. It is a bit like asking an audience in the last act of *Hamlet* to side with the king. Assume we suddenly learn that the king might well be literally innocent of the murder of Hamlet's father, could it change our nonidentification with him? Hamlet has already said too many things which moved us and carried us with him, and mere facts could never prevail over expended feelings.

It could have been a feeling of déjà vu which made the Miami thing seem so manifestly theatrical an occasion, but there were also striking signs that whatever principles they had come to fight for the delegates were *on;* they had come to symbolize, not merely to transact public business. It was another element in the transformation of the party which had now become contemporary. Nobody vomiting rye or smoking Admirations, no rebel yells from blue-eyed yahoos, and surely the highest IQ level in any convention in history—they actually kept up with most of the parliamentary maneuvering which was lost on the crowd in Chicago. To be sure there was the same air of total disorientation in the first days, like a freshman class at a large university asking where the gym is, but these people bore a double perspective; like actors they related to the reality around them, but at the same time they played it for the home screen.

One could remember when people went shy and reticent before the

TV lights and camera, and the old-time delegate caught by a TV interviewer would either puff himself up and try to look like a statesman, or wave to his mother through the lens. These young, suckled on TV, knew that you never look into the lens and that you have to condense the statement of your position or be cut off, and they did both with ease and naturalness. The old guard had been more cagey than this before the camera, suspicious of the interloper, for a convention was an authentic rather than an artistic occasion. The new understood that the camera is the main thing and that nothing could be said to *happen* until it had been filmed.

These shadings are politically instructive. The men of Chicago knew it was all as staged a performance as *The Follies* and that their part in it was to obey instructions while evincing the requisite enthusiasms on cue. They too were acting, but the difference was that they believed in the form itself while the new delegates were ironical toward the very idea of a convention and even the party. After all, McGovern had let slip that if he lost the nomination he would bolt. They were here to win their demands upon society, would use the form as long as it was usable and if the form failed them they were capable of walking off the stage and out of the theater. For the old, the stakes used to be the party and the convention. For the young it was to dominate the age itself, and when the young were tapped by the TV men they played it fully, not strategically and strained as the old men used to. In theater terms, the classic fourth wall of the stage was no more—they were trying to mingle with the audience, but they were playing nonetheless.

It has been said that this convention had much more content than previous ones, but it was not merely that there were so many blacks, and actual girls in jeans rather than the fat ladies led in from hard precinct chairs. It was that—had McGovern not been nominated—they would have burst the form itself, abandoned the convention, and burst through into the streets and real life. No such implicit threat hung over Chicago against the possibility of a Humphrey defeat. So in Chicago and Miami were two levels of art, one more naïve than the other perhaps, but both were performances. And in the mind vague prospects rose of some more authentic means of choosing the most powerful officeholder on the planet.

This performance-orientation, I thought, suppurated the city itself, the people's tone of voice became unreal and emblematic. Unable to park the car I had foolishly rented I reverted to cabs, and I had no sooner sat down in one than the driver in his New York accent announced, "I'm a Republican, been one thirty-five years. Who likes Nixon? You can't like Nixon. But I'm a Republican. Because my father-in-law's a Democrat." He laughed. "I like to get the knife in. It's all shit." I hadn't mentioned I was a writer, but it wasn't necessary—we are a nation of the interviewed.

This outer-directedness took stranger forms than usual in Miami. Flamingo Park, normally a preserve for the arthritic aged, the pensioner, and the babysitter, had by mutual agreement become a corral for the Outraged, the much-feared hippies who now lay about in the shade of dusty palms like the cast of an abandoned show. Some, veterans of the Chicago battles, others new recruits, they sent up dutiful wisps of grass smoke, demonstrating, as it were, their fundamental intelligence rather than the advertised rage. In fact, by the middle of our Passion Week the TV people had already sucked the marrow of their news and had abandoned them to life's ironies, which can be crueler than the clubs of the police. Even the lawn looked tired. I heard through the terrible moist heat the voice of a girl and The Gospel According to Saint Matthew.

At an impromptu pulpit made of a crate over which a faded purple cloth was draped, she stood alone, reading the Bible to Miami, a pretty seventeen-year-old totally ignored by the few strollers from the straight world who had come to see the animals and unheard by her contemporaries who blinked cruddy eyes at the morning sun or stared dead-brained at the old, half-crippled Jews sliding the shuffleboard disks along the baking concrete slabs. The dust, it seemed, had settled again, and America had once more transformed her revolutionaries into screwballs, as in my youth she had hung the hobo's mask on the Depression unemployed who, in their hour, had made a bid to characterize the country and had failed. Then I heard actual Hebrew.

A small drooping pup tent, one of several propped up on these deserted fairgrounds, and before it stood a young Jew with a yarmulke on his head, doing something with a man of sixty-five or so who wore a brown felt hat, a blue vest without a shirt, and had a two-day gray stubble on his cheeks. Amazed and unbelieving, I approached—the young Jew was teaching the old man how to wind phylacteries around his arm! I saw now that under the old guy's hat brim was the single strand of leather attached to which was the leather box containing the Holy Word pressed to his forehead. He was having trouble learning how to wind the leather reins around his fingers, but the young teacher was patiently redoing the procedure. And all the while a few yards away stood another Orthodox, a confederate of nineteen who, as I came near, asked if I wanted to be next.

"Are you proselytizing?" I asked.

"No, we don't proselytize. We're only interested in Jews. Come on, try it."

"I gave that up when I was fourteen."

"Try it. You might like it again."

The confederate's sublime arrogance, irritating as it was, nevertheless contrasted with the surrounding air of cultivated purposelessness and was strangely fitting in this highly political, outer-directed city. But the worst was yet to come—I heard the old pupil *counting*. I went closer to hear what to my atavistic heart seemed an abomination, for when you wind the phylacteries you are talking to God. But he was, he was counting even as he at last had managed to correctly wind the narrow leather rein around his fingers and up his arm.

"One thousand, two thousand, three thousand," he muttered, hardly moving his lips. Why was he counting? And why did not the young Orthodox soul-fisher seem to notice? Was this all a mockery, and the two young Jews acting out some kind of travesty of holy instruction, hoping to kill their parents with heart attacks? But now the old pupil glanced past me and I followed his gaze to another man, a companion his own age, who was standing there photographing his friend's conversion with a home movie camera.

The old pupil, who to the naked eye, or rather to the silent film, was the very picture of the hatted old pious Jew performing one of the most ancient of rituals, now lowered his arm and having rehearsed sufficiently ordered his cameraman to begin shooting; "Count to ten, one thousand, two thousand, up to ten," he instructed him, and then turned back to perform the winding of the phylactery. Meanwhile, the shill never ceased inviting me to join the fun, but the thing that brought me back to my twentieth-century senses was the fact that the two Orthodox, who I have no reason to think were anything less than sincere fishers of men, were also cooperating and knew how to place themselves on each side of the new convert so that their ministrations would show to good effect on film. Meanwhile— and this is the final note on this edifying scene—the convert put on a look of such powerful piety as he performed his newly rediscovered Godly duty that I had to wonder whether this was as faked as it appeared to be. For all

I know he would from that day return to the synagogue and the Jewish life, the more so when it has all been filmed, registered, you might say, in God's very eye. Flamingo Park, this whole city in fact, had taken on the air of scenery, the MGM back lot in whose perfect imitations of streets the extras and featured players filled up waiting time with games, naps, and horse-play while the stars and the producers worried out the continuity in closed rooms somewhere up high.

Which reminds me of my shock on first learning that Eisenhower had his makeup man. But what did I expect—a presidential candidate sweating on television and his wrinkles showing? What is this nostalgia for the authentic? Must not Lincoln have had some crowd-related object in mind when he trimmed his beard just so? Still, the idea of Lincoln pausing for his pancake and going over in his mind, "Fourscore and seven years ago . . ."

And were we not set up for this by the Renaissance painters who made the miserable Magdalen so beautiful, Jesus so unearthly? Was it at least part of his motivation in a Roman colony where every official action was surrounded with show business that Jesus knew he must really die to break through with the message? Did the wild men of the '68 Chicago streets understand that they'd be clowns until they bled real blood on a medium where blood was as ketchup theretofore?

It seems that even George Meany was carried away by the pull of the symbolic. One assumed an ideological cleavage behind his and I. W. Abel's refusal to go with the convention's choice, and the cynical would make the stakes even more material—McGovern was not in debt to labor and so would be independent of its claims on the presidency. But surely Meany knew what later was revealed, that the pro-McGovern unions controlled more campaign money than the unions he and Abel held in their grip, so we are face-to-face again with symbolic gestures. To Meany and such standard types this convention might as well have been a Mayan ritual whose application to himself or anyone he knew was simply not possible. The whole thing just wasn't real, a lot of kids acting out a drama of power politics when they had never even *worked,* owned businesses, met a payroll, or paid homage to the industrial machine in any form. They watched it all like legionnaires at a convention in Sandusky, Ohio, before a performance of *Waiting for Godot* or *The Bald Soprano.* What the hell is this?

You can call it a culture gap, but you'd think that faced with another four Nixon years they would have been able to temper outrage, if only for the sake of the lesser evil. Men acting rationally surely could have done so. But they had been reached where art reaches men—in the hollows of disgust and primordial rage, until they left their famous hardheaded objectivity behind and retreated to a gesture of revolt, which had to be mostly empty since the forces to inflict damage were not theirs to command. And so George Meany for a moment joined the cast, long enough to curse a world he never made and departing a play too spurious for any belief. It was a revulsion of taste, but taste is always a matter of identification, as the history of art makes clear enough.

When I went to Miami Beach it was with the near certainty that the pros would rob George McGovern of the nomination; after a day in the lobbies looking in vain for the Old Boys I was afraid he would win everything but the power that goes with the nomination. It seemed to me then that underneath the conflict of issues and lifestyles and the rest, what we were witnessing, and still are as the election battles shape up, is the most complicated and ambiguous construction man makes—the Crowd.

To put it briefly, a Crowd is not merely a large collection of people but an organism in itself, having its own energies which are aimed at a discharge. The McGovern phenomenon can be seen as the creation of a new Crowd whose existence, in terms of its individual members, was previously known but as a Crowd was unforeseen. The common assumption was that the two parties—that is, the two Crowds—had preempted the field and the most that could happen was perhaps a lowering of the age of the Democratic crowd, which would demand a quicker peace in Vietnam and some changes in the tax and welfare systems. What McGovern demonstrated, surprisingly, was that a new Crowd has in fact secretly been forming itself not only among the previously ignored and dispossessed but also in some undetermined degree among that eight to ten percent of the straight people as well, that mercurial group of the unaligned which may shift to or away from either party and decide an election. By pulling out, the Meanys are signaling their hope and belief that this new construction is merely that—a rather adventitious seizure of party power by a fragment which is not, in fact, a crowd at all but a self-announced facsimile.

A merely random collection of people becomes an operative Crowd at the point when each of its members begins to feel a strong sense of equality with all the others. This must not be mistaken for a virtue or an evil; a Nazi crowd and a Democratic one are subject to the same generic sensations regardless of their opposing ideologies. William L. Shirer once told me that when he attended Hitler's mass meetings as a hostile reporter he often felt the skin crawling on his neck as he realized that something within him was being sucked into the general sweep of the crowd's fused identity. Whatever the crowd's larger social purposes its first purpose is to exist as a crowd, and it achieves its existence when differences have been eradicated among its members. At this moment, like any organism, a crowd tends to expel what is alien to itself, and that is when its Crowd-life begins. The phenomenon is common in the theater where a lot of unrelated people gather and fuse only if and when a common, equal response is ignited in them by what they are seeing. The play which fails, in effect, to make a crowd out of a disparate collection of people has simply left their differences intact. So it is that the politician, like the writer or actor, must make a crowd for himself by providing that locus around which a great many people may transcend their ordinary bounds of feeling and join in the crowd's equality.

What has misled observers of the McGovern phenomenon is that its adherents' viewpoints and class memberships are so various and even conflicting. A great many well-to-do people, for example, have contributed a lot of money even in the face of McGovern's announced intention to raise their taxes; the professional women continue working for him despite a nearly total refusal on his part to adopt their positions; blacks who until very recently swore to support only candidates vowing fealty to their cause have gone for McGovern, who has not. And so on. Contrariwise, the Jews, or a lot of them, have conceived McGovern as lukewarm at best about Israel despite his avowals of continuation of past U.S. policy.

Something more than the sheer consideration of issues is working here, and it is obviously so when Wallaceites can regard McGovern without falling to pieces.

To put it this way is not to make Issues disappear but to set them in their place below the question of symbolic identification. At the least, it is certain that McGovern's Crowd is a real one and not a facsimile and that it has important possibilities for growth. But this is due as much to the openness—you might call it vagueness—of his positions as their sharpness. With some surprise I found, for whatever one man's experience may be worth, that to his own followers McGovern stands for more than his orientation toward Issues, and this may be the basic reason why the Republicans—at least around convention time—had stopped laughing.

Driving to my lodgings in the small hours, I picked up hitchhikers, all of them the McGovern Young. At half-past four one morning my headlights flashed on a girl walking alone along Collins Avenue. She was twenty-one, short-bobbed, wore white slacks with fake stiff lace around the bells, a black jersey, and came all the way from Alaska to this hot place. But she was not even a delegate, just a "worker" for George; she had scraped the fare together and was now stone broke, trying to walk the seven miles way out to her motel in the next town, Hollywood. In fact, she was eating once a day at the canteen in the Convention Hall where the Democratic Party provided fried chicken to just such faithful. I offered to give or loan her money, but she refused, either on some arcane principle or for fear of a sexual approach. In any case, she was placidly resentful that McGovern workers were not being paid as evidently they had been promised. This did not amount to a betrayal in her mind but simply a fact. Like the other Georgeans I came to meet, she was remarkably factual. For example, she had accompanied an Eskimo delegate (there exploded in my mind a furred man in this frightful heat) who also had to surmount barriers in order to get here. "He had to borrow his brother's plane to fly to Nome."

She said this with a certain hurt. I doubt that in all the history of revolutionary gatherings a delegate has been reduced to borrowing his brother's plane, but in surreal Miami I must admit that this piece of information seemed perfectly ordinary. And what, I asked, had moved her toward McGovern? The war? Ecology? The Alaskan pipeline?

"I wouldn't say it was those things," she said, and her tone made "those things" seem distant indeed. "I just wanted to participate."

It was a longer drive to Hollywood than I had booked in my mind when I picked her up, and in the surrounding blackness between the towns our interview gave way to conversation. She was studying biology and lived alone in a cabin heated by a kerosene stove on the outskirts of whatever Alaskan town, eating out of cans. Her parents were divorced. I looked at her more carefully now—she was rather plain, a turned-up nose, round face, straight black hair, pudgy. A lonely girl. One understood the issue. It is not to denigrate it or its political force to make note of it this way. She had felt the pull of her Crowd and had answered it as she never could have by watching it all on the tube.

I had told her I also was for McGovern, and before her motel door she smiled for the first time and offered her hand. In the morning she would awaken hungry and suffer through the day until the Democratic fried chicken in the evening. But, as she said, it was helping her to lose weight. This whole experience had innumerable benefits, and should Nixon solve the war before election time or even make the air pure, she would remain a McGovern worker. And this is strength, not weakness, in a political movement.

In full sunlight another partisan, a boy from Vermont, sat beside me on the way to the Doral Hotel, McGovern's headquarters, but he was not only a delegate; he had been on TV as the youngest delegate in history, eighteen. He seemed extremely tired, with an inner exhaustion known especially to performers who must go on despite everything. Yet he was already a little sick of his notoriety, he said. "I'm not sure I'll go on in politics. I don't feel like it right now."

Had something disillusioned him?

"Not exactly. But I don't think he should have said that to Wall Street."

Said what?

"How they hadn't to worry none about his tax reforms. He had no call saying a thing like that to Wall Street. I mean is he serious?"

Then you've gone sour on him?

"No—no, I'm for him. But I wish he hadn't said those things."

And what had brought him in? The war? Ecology? Unemployment?

He glanced at me. I could, I thought, hear his mind saying, "What war?"—he gave me that kind of blank. But what had brought him out to do political work?

"It was interesting. I met a lot of people, and I enjoy that. I don't know, I just felt I wanted to get into it. But I don't think I'd make it a life's work."

A third was Boston Irish and feverish with all his appointments and the caucuses; red-haired, twenty-three, he was having the time of his life. But he was serious. "I think we can take Massachusetts."

And why was he in it? The war? Ecology? What?

Again that surprised look.

Or maybe, I said, you're Irish and just like the game.

He laughed. "It's not the Irish, but I do, I like the game. I want to do it all my life."

Why? What's there about it?

"I just like it. I like doing it. I think we can take Massachusetts."

There would be an opportunity later to learn about those issues (or the lack of them) and the young, but a conversation over breakfast reminded me of the complications in the hearts of the other Crowd, the one that had stopped growing. Two or three times I had passed these two immense men in the Americana lobby—I would go there to sleep in my room or simply because, as Muskie's headquarters, it was the only place you could park. As in Shakespeare, it was separated from the chief contenders' camps, housing Meany's entourage as well as John Bailey's Connecticut troops. Thus it was the quietest lobby of all, and you could find middle-aged and elderly John of Gaunts bemoaning the partition of this England, this blessed Isle and so forth. I had exchanged waves with these two giants, who, I figured, must know my face, so polite and friendly were they every time our paths crossed. On this morning I found myself at the next table, and since they looked kind of lonely and in need, for some reason, of my company I moved over and joined them over eggs. I discovered they had merely waved to be friendly. Also, to talk with someone who might, hopefully, help them understand what had happened to their kind in Miami.

This was Wednesday, when McGovern had already turned back the California challenge and had the nomination in the bag.

I asked, "You fellas for Humphrey?"

"I am. He's for Muskie," said the black-haired man, relieving his thick wrist by stretching his watch band which was extended near to bursting.

"You delegates?"

"No. Just here. You?"

"No, I'm trying to write about it."

"The papers."

"Magazine. But I'm for McGovern."

"I seen you somewhere."

I knew he wouldn't like what he dimly saw, and I waited, and he finally pointed a finger. "You were with the McCarthy side at the '68 Convention."

"That's it. I'm Miller."

"Oooh ya." Then he turned to his friend. "He's that writer."

"O-o-h ya," the brown-haired man said. Their curiosity overtook their distaste. The black-haired man's eyes flickered at notoriety so close. "Well, he'll never win Connecticut."

"Still, he certainly came up fast for the nomination."

"He got that for one statement. When he said he'd end the war on Inauguration Day."

"That's how Eisenhower beat Stevenson, wasn't it? When he said he'd go to Korea? Stevenson said we'd have to fight on forever."

"That's true." He opened a little, his uncertainty peeked out. "You think he's got a chance?"

"What've you got against him?"

"He's not honest." And the brown-haired friend nodded.

"By the way, where you from?"

"Hartford."

"What do you do?"

"I'm a Sheriff. We both are." The brown-haired man nodded again, and said, "Sheriffs." I could see them both emerging from the squad car, chests immense, holsters shining, Americans in charge.

"How do you mean, not honest?"

"Well, Humphrey . . . a man goes out and works for him, he takes care of you. McGovern, I'm afraid, is gonna tell you if you don't qualify, get out."

Unhorsed by his unblinking honesty, the whole convention came alive for the first time. "But you could work with him, couldn't you? With his people?"

The brown-haired man spoke; "They've got no use for ethnics. I'm a Ukrainian. You don't see any Ukrainians up there" (on the convention platform).

"Or Poles either. I'm a Pole. Fifteen percent of the delegates are black. Which is all right, but where's the others?"

They looked hurt. Beetle-browed, appealing for justice. "You're right about that. He's going to have to come to you people."

"I don't know what you are, but . . ."

"I'm Jewish."

"Okay. If Ribicoff was made vice president . . ."

"He won't take it. I just talked to him."

"Sure he won't take it," the Pole said; "he's not going to sink with a loser."

"I don't think that's it. He's been sponsoring McGovern for years. He just doesn't want any more than he's got. He's a senator and that's what he likes."

"And he's got the scratch," the Pole said.

"Plenty," the Ukrainian added, rubbing two fingers.

"But say he was vice presidential nominee," the Pole said; "that'd be a terrific feather in your cap, now wouldn't it."

"Sure."

"Well that's it."

The point driven home, they both leaned back heavily in their chairs. But they wanted another move; mine. It surprised me.

"Under Roosevelt they had all kinds of Democratic clubs where I come from. Ukrainian, Polish, Irish, Lith . . ."

"Sure!" the Pole agreed. "Roosevelt *came* to the ethnic people."

"Supposing McGovern came to you people. Is it too late? Could he make a difference now?"

"He won't do it. He comes from that place out there. They got no ethnics out there."

"But if he did, would you accept him?"

"You can't live on 'ifs.' What he likes is these hippies. If it wasn't for them in Chicago, where they made such a bad impression, Humphrey'd have been elected. Those riots destroyed the Democratic Party."

"The war did that."

"Well, naturally the war. Without the war it'd been heaven. Even now, people don't realize there's a lot of boys out there."

"McGovern's trying to bring them home."

"That's right." They both nodded agreement. They believed or disbelieved each separate thing separately. There was no ideology to wrack falsehoods into a straight line. I didn't think they were lost to McGovern at all. If he cared enough, and if he, as native as an Indian, could project himself into the immigrant heart which is torn between shame of the old-country beginnings and resentment of that shame. Their most heartfelt emotion is a piece of the dignity pie which Nixon even more than McGovern cannot ever give them. I have heard deeply anticommunist, Catholic Poles evince pride that Poland is advancing, has stood up to Moscow, and can boast of artists and writers, even if they are Reds. Similarly Italians. McGovern, strange as it sounds, is in the best position to fire these people up. Nobody is more American than he, none could more legitimately show them the recognition that would bring them home. Looking at these men I was mystified that they had been left so far out on a limb. Is it possible McGovern thinks they are lost to him? Or can he really lack the requisite sympathy as they suppose? Or is it that they represent the outer limits of the new Crowd? Surely a Kennedy would have long since visited Hamtramck and Hartford by this time. But the Kennedys are immigrants.

A politician, like a playwright, has to work with his viscera as well as his head or he's no good. Humphrey, Daley, Meany, Muskie cannot feel the changes in the country. Senator Abe Ribicoff at eight-thirty in the morning in the lobby of the Americana. His car was waiting outside the revolving door to take him over to McGovern at the Doral, but he sat down to talk; he has evidently learned how to relax into the moment and not be rushed by time. In Chicago on the worst night of the carnage in the streets, he had stood at the podium of the convention over the heads of the Illinois delegation and, looking directly down at Richard Daley, had been the first official Democrat to flash the facts of life to the grand and doomed machine, declaring his horror that the Chicago police department was using "Gestapo tactics." At which the crevasse opened and the waters of Miami rushed through the dikes, for that was when Daley had drawn a finger over his throat as he glared up at Ribicoff and told him to drop dead. Connecticut had been placed on Illinois' flank so that I was close to Daley's troops, whose size-eighteen necks swelled, it seeming, for a moment, that if Daley gave the signal they would have gladly rushed the platform and torn Abe's head from his shoulders. The parliamentary system is a paraphrase for murder, and Abe could feel the killing waves. I thought I saw his head shake, but he stood and nodded back to Daley's gesture and curse, affirming again what he had declared. If there was a single instant when the new Crowd split from the old and began to form a separate entity it was then, when Ribicoff's heel drew the borders of the old Crowd's growth.

Apart from his courage, and it took a great deal of it in that moment of ignition, I suppose he could be the one to tell the party the time of day, because there is something in him that has had enough of politics. I wanted to know if he would accept the vice presidential nomination, about which there was much talk. "I'm going to tell them that after thirty-nine years in politics I'd prefer to run for local office with McGovern. It's the only enthusiasm I have left for politics. There are other things I want to do with my life." A recent widower, he seemed to see the turmoil through the quietus of mortality. For over two years he has been McGovern's sponsor in the Senate and, from all accounts, foresaw every step of his rise from what at first seemed an impossibly obscure beginning. In fact, he sensed early on the real extent of the new third Crowd—McGovern's—and now showed no surprise that it turned out to be there. But at least until very recently the general opinion of McGovern was that he was too colorless, even mildly professorial, and no leader. "McGovern is a very ambitious man. I asked him two years ago, 'But are you ready to give up everything for this?

Your family life, your own peace, every minute of your existence?' He said, 'I want to be president.' He's a very great organizer, and he's tough. I believe he's going to make it."

I thought again of our mythmaking apparatus. For no solid reason I can name I also had had the idea of a professorial McGovern, the first Ph.D. since Wilson to run for high office, but two years ago he had shown up at my neighbor's house at a party for Joe Duffey's campaign for the Senate, and he looked to me then like a beautifully tailored, middle-aged cowboy with that long blue gaze and thick thumbs. Maybe it was his dovish antiwar stance that had characterized him so softly or maybe just the journalistic shorthand which bedevils us all. I could not help thinking of our other great figures of myth, movie stars when there still were stars, and the hilarious misapprehensions of their characters which the public, especially intellectuals, devour. It is a rule never to be broken that the most lasting picture of a star is always created by his or her earliest interviews. The reason is simply that lazy journalists forever after unearth the file and basically rewrite what was written before. The same is true of politicians who are tagged early on. Someone somewhere must have portrayed McGovern as an overcivilized professor, when in fact he is the most direct political descendant of the Kennedy operational technique.

That technique was most spontaneously demonstrated not so much on the podium in Miami but in the lobby of the Doral Hotel when about three hundred hippies, SDS, Progressive Labor Party, and assorted Outraged suddenly filed in and sat down on the floor, demanding to see McGovern, who had to explain himself then and there as to why, the previous evening, he had stated that he would retain the U.S. armed presence in Thailand. The entire hotel was promptly shut down tight, the management cutting off the elevators for fear the invasion would spread through the upper floors. A squad of police soon arrived and were quickly ordered out, for violence in that narrow lobby would have left a lot of red meat lying about. Besides, it is a part of our awareness in post-Chicago times that the young savages are daughters and sons of the middle class and bear a political legitimacy which, as always in every era, is the reward given the violent and the brave. In the bargain, you can see long-haired cops everywhere now, four years after Chicago.

But arriving quite by chance an hour or more after the sit-down had begun it was hard to gauge the beat. Beneath the uproar the kids were clearly disciplined, and when a thin girl of nineteen or so ordered them through a bullhorn to sit, they formed in ranks and sat facing her as in class. Many were shirtless, and all were styled in the latest Army–Navy store bargains. I could not help my mind's resurrection of the continuity here—the last sit-down I had seen was in Flint, Michigan, in 1936, when the auto workers shut down Fisher Body Plant Number 2, and this was a reassurance, for the act of sitting together on signal is political, not temperamental, a call for parley rather than riot. Nevertheless, even to the untutored eye the taunting factions stood out, primarily the Zippies, who clustered—all fifteen of them—in one corner with their own portable p.a. system, holding up a six-by-ten-foot photo of Johnson which they had stolen out of the Convention Hall where it had hung in a line of the Great Democratic Leaders of the past. Over LBJ's forehead they had stuck a McGovern bumper sticker. The echo of their yells and latter-day Dadaist ebullience, rapping against the marble lobby walls combined with the rhythmic chants of the sitters led by the young girl, left all options open. Three TV cameras with their crews were ranged on a platform to one side, but no photo lights were on yet, the opening curtain evidently being delayed, for what cause no one seemed to know. It needs be mentioned that in a more open area nearer the entrance doors a dozen or so straights in conventional clothes were standing around, people with Midwestern eyeglasses and flowered dresses, who looked on with more curiosity than the apprehension which the occasion seemed to deserve; their estimate of the mood turned out to be quite correct, probably because the riots they had seen on TV numerous times had never harmed them.

The sitters, split though they were among their factions, were nevertheless united in one object, to force McGovern down from his suite; understanding the program, the TV men were not wasting light and tape on the preliminaries. "We want McGovern! We want McGovern!" For half an hour the demand repeated itself under the orchestrating arms of the young girl at their head, and now, having achieved the inner organization of a true Crowd, which was their mutual equality and unanimity, a victory or discharge beyond mere chanting had to be found. But nothing of that kind seemed about to happen, so hands were raised quite as in the classroom, their sole previous experience of purposeful action, and from the floor came proposals to climb the stairs to McGovern or to physically force the management to turn an elevator on. Now the TV men stirred but continued smoking and drinking their Cokes. Meanwhile the Zippies, mocking McGovern as well as the political purposefulness implied in the surrounding orderliness, had raised the volume of their p.a. to drown it all. Long since used to the blasts of rock music, the seated majority was immune to interruption. That pall of stalemate descended when anything can happen; they had committed themselves symbolically, and there could be no retreat this side of confrontation or violence. And the sense of timing in headquarters upstairs caught the danger by some telepathic means, for an elevator door opened and Mankiewicz appeared. A roar of curses, applause and yells greeted him. He seemed an even smaller and more fragile man than he is, possibly because by this time the girl leader was sitting on the shoulders of a boy and was bent over looking down at him, while she carefully held her microphone close to her mouth so that her rage would carry throughout the lobby's chaotic acoustics.

Now one camera was trucking into the center of the lobby from the common roost at one side, and the Outraged carefully made way for it. From the ranked PL group came the rhythmic chant, "Fuck McGovern!" but the camera's lights were not yet on, and this soon died away. Now the Zippies, who had been left behind by the moving camera, pressed ahead into the crowd with their immense Johnson photograph, screaming at lung-bursting levels through their p.a. but suddenly going silent to hear the camera crew's advice not to block the entire view. They moved accordingly and, once properly positioned, resumed their particular version of passion, grouped at the right-hand bank of elevators opposite the Progressive Laborites who were standing on the other flank of the sitting majority. So we had the full panoply—against the left wall the PL's program summed up in Fuck McGovern, in the center the bulk of the sitters waiting for orders from the sharp-faced girl perched next to a very serious if not humiliated Mankiewicz, and on the right flank the Zippies carrying on where Tristan Tzara had left off in Zurich, 1924.

I can't vouch for the accuracy of Mankiewicz' dialogue with the girl leader, because his appearance caught me so by surprise. A moment before his arrival I had seen three boxes of a dozen eggs each handed up from the crowd on the floor to the leadership around the girl—food had been brought in for a long sit, if necessary—and even she had involuntarily to register a disclaimer, however humorously, of the purpose these potential missiles would serve. Laughing, she said they were hard-boiled, but there was room for doubt. The vision of McGovern being pelted by three dozen eggs from a crowd of young, usually identified as his most fervent supporters, would on TV have changed even bad odds to none at all.

In addition, as these boxes of eggs were moving from hand to hand up to the front, a haggard, bearded fellow in torn cut-off-at-the-knee dungarees came up to me and said he had played in *The Crucible* in college and thought now that he should straighten me out as to what was happening here. Indicating the Progressive Laborites and their Fuck McGovernism, he said, "They're trying to puddle him right here and now. They think the Vietcong are bourgeois and Mao is ready for his Cadillac. You're looking at the stormbirds of American fascism—the worse it gets the quicker the workers will turn against capitalism, you see?" I saw. He looked sickened, in which case what was he doing here at all? "I thought we had to call McGovern on that statement he gave out about keeping forces in Thailand. But this is therapy time, and it's going through the roof. He's out of his head if he comes down now. They'll ruin him right in the living room. It's awful. We're in prime time now."

I caught the end of the Mankiewicz confrontation. The girl, beet red in the face, arching over from her perch on the boy's shoulders, was screaming, "Okay, in fifteen minutes we're either getting an answer or McGovern is coming down. Within fifteen minutes, is that right?"

Mankiewicz kept his eyes down. He had evidently agreed to this already, but she wanted it loud and clear. I thought I could hear his teeth gritting. "That's right."

"Okay, get going!" she dismissed him. He disappeared to the triumphant screams of the mob, and she turned with electric eyes to the whooping audience, a thin-lipped grin gashing her face. A stout girl in a once-white blouse and a skirt stepped up beside her with a pad and pencil and called out, "Okay, cool it. Now let's get the issues!"

As slices of white bread and pieces of cheese were being handed around and the Dadas were going wild with satire of this participatory democracy, the white-bloused girl was having trouble dredging issues from the orderly majority. "Abortion!" finally sounded loud and clear, and she dutifully wrote it down and turning her eyes over the whole assembly for its agreement, said, "Abortion—right?" "Right on!" Then after some more soul searching in which hiatus it was clearer than ever that the issues were being dragged behind them rather than leading them forward, they resurrected the litany of the vanguard. A PL boy cried out, "Socialism now!" but was cut off by his fellows who knew better. They were still seated on the floor but pressing on into history and scrambling for their declarations, their flags, as it were, and the only sure thing in them was their existence now that the perhaps future president of the United States was descending from his sequestered throne room to pay homage to their power. For myself, a mixture of resentment and a hard-to-win confession; they were right in insisting McGovern face the contradiction of his peace position which his previous night's statement clearly implied, perhaps even at the cost of his national humiliation on the tube, for betrayal by politicians has been the brand upon the forehead of this system. But I was flummoxed by their contempt for human dignity, let alone the dignity of their own demand for honesty. Mankiewicz, after all, was still a human being, and the girl had all but urinated on his head to the crowd's apparent appreciation. No country could be led by such contempt, excepting to a very dark place.

Like heavy cannon the two remaining TV cameras lumbered into place amid the crowd, which now got to its feet as the TV lights burst on, illuminating the bottom of a curving stairway to one side of the lobby. My mind was on three dozen eggs secreted somewhere, cradled in pairs of children's hands. McGovern arrived at the bottom of the stairs to find the girl leader swaying over his head with her microphone pressed to her mouth. I cannot recall her lines, but the command in them was filled to bursting with the audience's fantasy of power which had been sucked up from so many sources—the snarling orders of the tough cops on TV, the Chinese students' interrogations of erring professors and landlords, Perry Mason, and their dreams dreamed not long ago in Larchmont bedrooms surrounded by the hated chintz. Surely, an authentic rather than a role-playing voice here could not have sought to demean the one senator who has stood alone for so many years against their hated war. But despite myself I realized now that McGovern had correctly chosen to recognize his duty to answer for his press statement which had trimmed his peace position.

McGovern appeared in the white light at the foot of the stairway, and if an observer had arrived at that very moment he could not have known whether the roar of the crowd was hostile or friendly. For the crowd had already won by this giving-birth, and the sound was the sound of relief after labor, from enemy and friend alike. He spoke right through the din of the Zippies' mockery and the counterincoherence of his supporters, in a voice amazingly the same as it had been in my neighbor's house, without a trace of apology or trepidation and yet not with that false charm designed to kid away the conflict. His references are from within. There was about him not the slightest air of being put upon, no sign of anger, but an even estimation of the trouble he was in, neither more nor less. All three cameras were on now, and he was speaking on prime time to America, but the inevitable tension of performing fused with his being here before this particular group of young. It was the first authentic feeling any of them had heard since the demonstration began.

He came directly to the issue of his previous press statement and overrode it; he would say now precisely what he had been saying all along, that on Inauguration Day the war would end and all American forces would be out of Indochina within ninety days. The inevitable cheer went up and the inevitable digging in of heels—what about abortion, a guaranteed annual wage, legalization of pot, amnesty? He lobbed the ball back— surely they accepted that human beings could not agree on absolutely everything. This summoning up of their own creed derailed them, for it did not sound strategic or cynical but a genuine aspect of his character. He had still left unexplained his paradoxical statement, but it had fallen away, lost in the discharge of their feelings of common identity which had succeeded in materializing him before them as though they had created him. The sharp-faced girl yelled on in vain, and when he said that they would surely understand he had a lot of things he must do and waved farewell, the applause swept up to the ranks of the PL's who were now mounted on each other's shoulders, middle fingers raised, hands jerking upward in the air, shouting, "Fuck McGovern!" But they had fallen into place, they too were enjoying now, and the fabled Issues had gone by, were merged in the climactic fact that he had come down because they had demanded him, had grown him. Moses smashed the tablets in a fury with the Jews for their failure to rise to the sublime commandments, but despite everything he had forged a tribe of many disparate peoples, for what mattered was not the words but the mime, the fact that they had been present when he went up and when he came down from the Lord, and if few would remember exactly what was said or settled, none would forget the essential—that they had been there when for their sake he had climbed Sinai, they had seen it and had been the cause and were the sinews of a leader and thus transcended.

As they dispersed and the white lights of the cameras flowed out, I walked out into the heat of night and was stopped by another bearded one naked to a pair of murky shorts. "I played in *The Crucible* at Louisiana State. Terrific, wasn't it?" I wasn't so sure, although I was surer than I had been ten minutes earlier. He was an associate professor somewhere. I was curious whether he dressed like this for class. No, of course not—"This is theater," he said with a pleased smile, "you don't go onstage in your ordinary clothes." We both laughed. "Come over to Flamingo Park in the morning. I'll show you our plans to trash the Republicans in August." It was precisely the same tone a director might use toward his next production, that suppressed brag about a coming masterpiece, that basic joyfulness in being an artist at all.

I find I have left the convention itself for last, and it isn't by accident since it was so anticlimactic after the second day. Certainly it signified a renovation of politics, a major party opened at last to the streets, the teacher, the student, the amateur. It showed that a new machine has been born, but the question remains the depth of its reach into the country. The truth is that the legitimitizing weight of the working class was not there to make it the real reflection of America it wanted to be. If only for this absence it can be but a stage along the way. But it is equally true that there never has been a new movement, be it Abolition, the New Deal, or Wilson's New Democracy, which did not first arrive in the heads of intellectuals. Still, there was not yet Power, only an aversion for what is, and these are not the same. So there was a certain surreality, as though a new king had just been crowned but the old one had neither died nor could he be located, he had simply wandered off.

Which probably symbolizes the pervading sense of an inner unrelatedness in the country itself. Ours is a president whose paternality has never settled on him. Patricides, we live now in the shadow of something homogenized, whose leadership consists at best of a benign distrust between the people and itself and at worst of its implicit violence. This vagueness of a ruling personality had to enter the convention where, quite strangely, the enemy Nixon's name was barely mentioned at all. The one moment when an authentic emotion was felt was Teddy Kennedy's evocation of the nostalgia of the past when indeed there had been kings even if you didn't altogether admire them. But otherwise there was nothing handed down, no grail, no flag, no helmet emptied of its immortal knight, and so nothing was quite won, not yet. But something may have created itself if history is kind.

It was literally as though we had no past at all. A man from Mars must surely have wondered if this race was new. Yet we live under the oldest continuous government on earth, and, strangely, the convention could not find one old man loved enough to bless the new leader and send him forth with something memorable and good. Within the bounds of convention-eering there was less a classic conflict with the dying than a sheer asser-tion of new birth, a dangerously immaculate conception.

But it could turn out yet to have been realer than it seemed. Within America a certain Crowd has certainly lost its old cohesion, and the lines of force no longer hold. The vote is floating. As late as Jack Kennedy's campaign one could still speak of Left and Right, but this time only of a mood. What else than a mood could have found a leader for so city-bred a revolution in a man from the sparsest population in the country? If histor-ical formulations had their classic impress, how could so ministerial a man be leader of an avant-garde whose advertised faith is in smoke, a movement of women clamoring for the right to abort, students for whom the conventional disciplines are laughable?

It may be that in some primordial way there is a reaching back to roots in the raising-up of George McGovern. Even for his enemies his menace is not radicalism but righteousness, that quality which always hovers on the ridiculous but when it stands and holds can smash through all confusion. It could well be that righteousness is all we have left. If Kennedy was of the Left, if only symbolically, he was also as much the author of the Green Berets and the war as any man was, and if Nixon is the Right he has thrown the line to China. Yet few know how to call Kennedy bad, and this country has enormous trouble trying to think of Nixon as good. But it is in-deed a word McGovern suggests to the mind despite everything, not that one really knows his character but that he seems to be seriously obsessed with the creativity of the people rather than the manipulability of institu-tions. If he truly is so, and can make it palpable, anything can happen.

As for conventions themselves, they will surely have to go. Perhaps a national primary is the answer, something at least more straightforward than this travesty which all of us know is but a time-honored means of ma-nipulating symbols. The much-touted finesse of the new machine is a doubtful achievement, finally; it has only proved that amateurs can learn cynicism fast. The nominees will have to make the fight at the supermar-ket and on film, which brings us back to where we started—to the man on the stump attempting with directness to make his Crowd.

1972

Miracles

Sometime back in the Fifties, *Life* sent out a questionnaire asking opinions on the new revolution then taking place, allegedly. I sent mine back unanswered, with the note that there was no revolution. It seems to me now that I was right and wrong.

The only moment of near revolution I know about, at least in my lifetime, was in the winter of 1932 when the leading bankers went to Washington and seriously discussed with the Treasury Department the idea of the Government taking over all the banks. That, and a few days in Flint, Michigan, during the sit-down strikes. These events—along with the widespread talk in business circles and among the people, that the system was actually at an end and some form of socialist ownership had to be the next step lest total chaos overwhelm the United States—had the look of the real thing. In the ensuing one hundred days, the Roosevelt Administration devised a flood of legislation that saved capitalism by laying down what essentially were limits to how crooked you were allowed to be, or how rapacious, without going to jail. And direct money payments to desperate people was made public policy. It was a revolutionary moment, and it lasted for perhaps four or five years, primarily, I think, because the Establishment had lost its nerve, did not really have a clue to solving mass unemployment. Inevitably, to stand in the avant-garde meant espousing socialism; it meant being political.

The turmoil of the Fifties and Sixties came to a head in a booming economy, just after the Establishment had retrieved its poise to the point where it had cleaned out—through McCarthyism—the universities, the arts, of the last of the people who had a social, let alone a socialist, vision.

If there were one concept that might stand for the Thirties avant-garde, it was the solidarity of humanity, and if the Fifties had an emblem, it was loneliness. The Thirties radical, of whatever stripe, saw a pattern of deliquescence in the American system; the Fifties youth was bereft of any such comfort. When the new struggle came, it was inevitably a personal and not a political one—because American politics had its strength back and was at least working again.

But if the Sixties was not a revolution in any classic sense—a transfer of power between classes—it did partake of the revolutionary process by overturning certain attitudes toward what a human being is and what he might be. More, the latter-day revolt has offered a new pattern, just as the one in the Thirties attempted to do, to account for the human condition, a hidden matrix which guided us all. So, in the psychological sense, there is a continuity between both generations, and there are others too.

It is commonplace to say that the Thirties revolt was one of the mind while the latest is one of the gut, a contrast between rationalism and mysticism. This distinction is too neat to be true. Of course a lot of people, probably the majority who became radical in the Thirties, were inspired by unfilled bellies and narrowed-down chances to make a buck. Which is natural and legitimate. As natural and legitimate as the number of Fifties and Sixties revolutionaries whose new vision was limited to the idea of getting laid without the etiquette of courting and bullshit.

I was about fourteen when the Depression hit, and like a lot of others who were more or less my age, the first sign of a new age was borne into the house by my father. It was a bad time for fathers who were suddenly no longer leaders, confident family heads, but instead men at a loss as to what to do with themselves tomorrow. The money had stopped, and these men were trained by American individualism to take the guilt on themselves for their failures, just as they had taken the credit for their successes. Under the streetlamp at the corner drugstore the talk was suddenly shifting from whether you were going to be a doctor, lawyer, businessman, or scientist, to what the hell you were going to do after the dreaded day you were graduated from high school. There were suicides in the neighborhood. We had all been sailing this proud and powerful ship, and right there in the middle of the ocean it was beached, stuck on some invisible reef.

It seems easy to tell how it was to live in those years, but I have made several attempts to tell it, and when I do try I know I cannot quite touch that mysterious underwater thing. A catastrophe of such magnitude cannot be delivered up by facts, for it was not merely facts whose impact one felt, not merely the changes in family and friends but a sense that we were in the grip of a mystery deeper and broader and more interior than an economic disaster. The image I have of the Depression is of a blazing sun that never sets, burning down on a dazed, parched people, dust hanging over the streets, the furniture, the kitchen table. It wasn't only that so many high-class men, leaders, august personages, were turning out to be empty barrels—or common crooks, like the head of the stock exchange. It was that absolutely nothing one had believed was true, and the entire older generation was a horse's ass.

So I went back to the synagogue—an Orthodox synagogue. And there I found three old men playing pinochle in the entrance corridor of that ugly building. I drew up a chair and sat with them. I had no idea what I wanted there. I could read Hebrew but understand little of what I had been saying. I walked inside and looked at the altar. I thought something would speak to me, but nothing did. I went home and came back a few more times. But the sun stood as still in the heavens as it ever had, and nothing spoke. I even joined the little choir, but still nothing happened to me, nothing moved within me.

The mute threat underlying unemployment is that you will never cease being a child. I was favored—I had gotten a job delivering rolls and bread from four to seven every morning, for four dollars a week. Freezing cats followed my bike from house to house, crying in pain. The summer dawns were lovely over the sleeping one-family houses, but they were spoiled by my fear of time bringing me closer to graduation. A man was not wanted anywhere, and the job ads in the *New York Times* specified "White," or "Christian," although there were never more than a dozen openings, anyway. A man, let alone a boy, wasn't worth anything. There was no way at all to touch the world.

One afternoon on a windy street corner, while I was waiting my turn to play handball against the pharmacist's brick wall, a guy who was already in college started talking about capitalism. I had never heard of capitalism. I didn't know we lived under a system. I thought it had always been this way. He said that the history of the world (what history?) was the history of the class struggle (what is a class?). He was incomprehensible but a hell of a handball player, so I respected him. He was unique, the only one I knew who stayed on the same subject every time I met him. He kept pouring this stuff over my head, but none of it was sticking; what he was saying didn't seem to have anything to do with me. I was listening only for what I wanted to know—how to restore my family. How to be their benefactor. How to bring the good times back. How to fix it so my father would again stand there as the leader, instead of coming home at night exhausted, guilty.

This guy kicked the trip wire one afternoon. We were on the beach at Coney Island. In those days families were living under the boardwalk in scrap-metal or wood-slat shacks. We could smell feces and cooking there in the sun. And this guy said, "You are part of the declassed bourgeoisie."

Life quickened, insane as it sounds, because . . .

My father was no longer to blame. It wasn't he who had failed; it was that we were all in a drama, determined by history, whose plot was the gradual impoverishment of the middle class, the enrichment of the upper, and the joining of the middle with the workers to set up a socialist economy. I had gotten what the synagogue had not given me—the ennobling overview. It was possible again to think that people were important, that a pattern lay hidden beneath the despair and the hysteria of the mothers, that the fathers would again be in their places. Life suddenly had a transcendent purpose, to spread this news, to lift consciousness. For the day would arrive when conflict would end. Things would no longer have value, the machines would provide. We would all live, like people in a park on Sunday, quietly, smiling, dignified. The age of Things was over. All that remained was for people to know it.

They usually call this the experience of materialist religion, but it had little materialism for me. I wasn't looking to it for anything like money or a better job but for a place, literally, in the universe. Through Marxism you extended your affection to the human race. The emptiness of days filled with a maturing purpose—the deepening crisis of capitalism, bursting into the new age, the inexorable approach of nirvana.

It was the last of the forgoing philosophies. The deeds of the present, the moment, had no intrinsic importance, but only counted insofar as they brought closer or held back the coming of the new. Man-as-sacrifice was its essence; heroism was what mattered. We were in the Last Days, all signs pointed to Apocalypse. Self was anathema, a throwback; individual people were dematerialized. A Russian, Ostrovsky, wrote *An Optimistic Tragedy,* and the title signified the mood, I think, wherever Marx's vision had taken root. Joy was coming—no matter what.

The Thirties has never been rendered in literature, because the emotions reported are all coiled around political and economic events, when in truth a religious sweep was central to everything one felt, an utter renewal of mankind, nothing less. The mystic element was usually elided, I imagine, because to share Marx was to feel contempt for all irrationality. It was capitalism that was irrational, religious, obscure in the head, and Hitler was its screaming archangel. Pride lay not in what one felt but what one was capable of analyzing into its class components. The story went around that Wall Street stockbrokers were calling Earl Browder, head of the Communist Party, for his analysis of the economy. A communist *knew*, had glimpsed the inevitable.

Similarly, the movement in the Sixties was hermetic and, like its ancestor, was unable to penetrate the national mind with anything more than its crude, materialist side. To the man on the street, it was merely a generation lying across the road of Progress, crying out F—— Work. And its worst proponents so defined it, too. In the case of both "revolutions," a redemptive thrust, without which such movements are never propelled, could not be transmitted beyond the ranks, and both revolutions appeared to the outsider as contemptuous of man's higher ideals, spirituality, and innate goodness. To most supporters of the Spanish loyalists, their struggle was far more profound than any politics could embrace; the Spanish civil war was a battle of angels as well as the lowly poor against the murderous rich. When the dark spirit won, it was not only a factional victory but the shaking of Inevitability, human future itself had been overwhelmed. While Picasso painted *Guernica,* the State Department, business and religious leaders, and most of the press were oddly hesitant about saying unkind words about Hitler and Mussolini, the law-and-order boys behind Franco. Of the minority of Americans who even knew a war was going on in Spain, probably half were on the side of the Church and fascism. To these people, the republic stood for license, atheism, radicalism, and—yes, even the socialization of women, whatever that meant. So for me the commonly held attitude toward Sixties youth had echoes. The country was fixated on the body of the new revolt while its spirit went either unnoticed or was mangled by the media or the movement's own confused reporters.

The Thirties and Sixties "revolutions," for want of a better word, show certain stylistic similarities and differences. The earlier radical took on a new—for the middle class—proletarian speech, often stopped shaving and wore the worker's brogans and the lumberjack's mackinaw: his tailor, too, was the Army-Navy surplus store. He found black jazz more real than the big band's arranged sentimentality, found Woody Guthrie and Ledbetter and folk music authentic because they were not creations of the merchandiser but a cry of pain. He turned his back, or tried to, on the bounds of family, to embrace instead all humankind, and was compromised—when he found himself lifted up the economic ladder—in his effort to keep his alienation intact. When he married he vowed never to reconstruct the burdensome household he had left behind, the pots and pans, the life of things. The goal was the unillusioned life, the opposite of the American Way in nearly all respects. The people were under a pall of materialism, whipped on unto death in a pursuit of rust. The list of similarities is longer than this, but the differences are the point.

Once nipped by Marx, the Thirties radical felt he was leading a conditional life. He might contribute money, or himself, to help organize a new union, but important as the union was, it paled before its real, its secret, meaning—which was that it taught the worker his strength and was a step toward taking state power away from the capitalist class. If the Thirties radical viewed a work of art or a friend, the measure of value came to be whether socialism was being brought closer or pushed farther away by that art or that friend. And so his life moved into a path of symbols, initially ways to locate himself in history and in society, but ultimately that which ruled his mind while reality escaped.

The Thirties radical soon settled into living for the future, and in this he shared the room of his mind with the bourgeoisie. It could not have been otherwise. Capitalism and socialism are forgoing systems; and you cannot tend the machine, on which both systems are based, whenever the spirit moves you, but *on time,* even when you would rather be making love or getting drunk. Remember the radical of the Thirties came out of a system that had stopped, and the prime job was to organize new production relations that would start it up again. The Sixties radical opened his eyes to a system pouring its junk over everybody, or nearly everybody, and the problem was to stop just that, to escape being overwhelmed by the mindless, goalless flood that marooned each person on his island of commodities.

The Sixties people would stop time, money time, production time, and its concomitant futurism. Their Marxist ancestors had also wanted man as the measure of all things but sought to center man again by empowering the then-powerless. What came of it was Russia and, at home, the porkchop trade-union leaders and their cigars. So power itself was now the spook, and the only alternative, if humankind was to show a human face again, was to break the engagement with the future, with even sublimation itself. You lived now, lied now, loved now, died now. And the Thirties people, radical or bourgeois, were horrified and threatened by this reversal because they possessed the same inner relation to the future, the self-abnegating masochism that living for any future entails.

Dope stops time. More accurately, money time and production time and social time. In the head is created a more or less amiable society, with one member—and a religion, with a single believer. The pulsing of your heart is the clock, and the future is measured by prospective trips or interior discoveries yet to come. Kesey, who found his voice in the Sixties, once saw America saved by LSD, the chemical exploding the future forever and opening the mind and heart to the now, to the precious life being traded away for a handful of dust. Which leads to another big difference between the two generations and something that I think informs the antic jokiness in the Sixties radical style.

The Thirties radical never dreamed the world could really explode. In fact, as Clausewitz had said and Marx would have agreed, war was merely politics by other means. If we hated fascism, it too was merely politics, even the clubbing of radicals and Jews. That even fascists could burn up people in ovens was unthinkable. What the Holocaust did was posit a new enemy who indeed was beyond the dialectic, beyond political definition. It was man.

So that Apocalypse, as inherited by the Sixties generation, was not what it used to be, the orderly consequence of a dying system, but an already-visual scene in Hiroshima and Auschwitz whose authors were, in one case, parliamentary politicians. Oppenheimer-like humanists quoting the Upanishads, decent fellows all and, in the other, their tyrant enemies. Political differences and principles guaranteed nothing at all. What had to be projected instead was a human nowness, Leary's turning on and dropping out, lest the whole dark quackery of political side-taking burn us all in our noble motives. The very notion of thinking, conceptualizing, theorizing—the mind itself—went up the flue; and many bourgeois governments, for a little while, backed up in fear not of an ideology but of a lifestyle—a mass refusal to forgo.

For myself, I knew this had no hope and not because it eschewed a political vision but because its idea of man was wrong. Because a man cries "Brother!" doesn't make him one, any more than when his father muttered

"Comrade." The struggle with evil doesn't cancel out that easily, as the fate of Marxists had shown. More, from where I sat, the religious accents of Sixties radicalism were not entirely apart from those of Thirties radicalism. Like the Christians, Marx had projected a Judgment Day on the barricades, an Armageddon out of which the last would rise to be first, then to direct the withering away of the state itself once socialism came to pass, the veritable kingdom where conflict is no more and money itself vanished in an abounding surplus of goods. You wanted a car, you just picked one up and left it when you didn't need it anymore—a sort of celestial Hertz. If the last thing Jesus or Marx had in mind was a new fatalism, that was nevertheless what most human beings made of the stringent and muscular admonitions these prophets pronounced, and what most of the voyagers into the Age of Aquarius were making, I thought, of the punishing, disciplined yoga that had evolved this new vision. Once you have thought yourself into an alignment with Fate, you are a sort of Saving Remnant for whom mere reality is but an evolution of symbolic events, until finally you are no longer really anything at all except a knower—and thus your deeds cannot be judged by mortal judgment, so anything goes. Differences there are, of course, but Manson, Stalin and that long line of Christian crusaders join hands in this particular dance. How often have I heard survivors of the Thirties astonished that they could have said the things they said, believed what they had believed. A faith had been running underneath that newfound pride in objective social analysis, that sense of merging with the long line into the Inevitable, and a faith exploded is as unrecoverable to the heart in its original intensity as a lost love.

The latter-day Edenism of the Sixties had a sour flavor, for me at least: it was repeating another first act of another disillusioned play. I saw the love-girls, free at last, but what would happen when the babies came?

Most girls with babies are funny. They like to know exactly *where they are.* If only because babies reintroduce linear time and long-term obligation, high-flying anarchy must come to earth.

Kesey's new book *Garage Sale,* a mélange of his own and his friends' writing, is a sort of geologic section of some thirteen years in the wilderness. But his screenplay, which appears in this book, is the real surprise, a hail and farewell to the era. From the height of its final pages you can look down and begin to sense a form at last in the whole insane pageant. For Kesey had not merely taken a dive into his bloodstream and glimpsed, as it were, the interior of his eyes, but emerged into the ring where the

Others are, the brothers and sisters toward whom a newfound responsibility flows, and toward the world itself. The time-honored way to make that discovery was the Hebrew-Christian self-torture—the near-dissolution of the body inviting God. Here it is otherwise, the enhancing of the senses and pleasure, the blending of the physicality of Eastern mysticism with the Mosaic injunction to serve the People, whose well-being is the measure of all truth. If responsibility can be reached through pleasure, then something new is on the earth.

Skeptic that I am, I could believe in this. My zodiacal friends tell me that in terms of an individual, the Great Wheel says the human race is now thirty-five years of age, and that's when human beings are most creative, when Jesus gathered together all that he was and died. So Love is coming toward us, the Age of Aquarius. Scorched by an earlier Inevitable, I shy from this one, and I warn whoever will listen that the tension with evil has no end, or, when it does, the man within has died. Nevertheless, when I think back to what life was like in the Thirties and see from that long-ago vantage what is happening now, I stand in the glistening presence of miracles.

Radical or conservative, we worshipped the big and the smoke from the chimney, and the earth was only there to chew up and drill holes in, the air a bottomless garbage pail. Now my ten-year-old daughter turns the key off when I am parked and waiting for someone. How miraculous. We got out of Vietnam because the Army wouldn't fight it anymore. That's the simple truth and how miraculous. Nixon—Billy Graham and prayer breakfasts notwithstanding—has revealed himself—and, really, by himself. As though the earth had squeezed up his roots and he rotted where he stood, this lawless man of disorder. How miraculous. The seed of the visionless has spent itself in him. How miraculous. In the early Fifties a Catholic university survey asked me why I thought there were so few of the faith in the arts or in the contentions of social debate. I wrote back that Irish Catholicism and Yankee Puritanism had combined in this country to sink the inquiring mind without a trace. Now? The spectacle of a Catholic priest demonstrating, leading the poor, is miraculous. Reporters stand up and yell at a presidential press officer, accusing him of having told them lies, and this in the White House, with the flag on the platform. How miraculous. The power company wants to run a high-tension line across my countryside and my neighbors, many of them having voted for Nixon, descend on what used to be routine, company-dominated "hearings," and invoke beauty and demand their aesthetic rights as though they were poets. How miraculous. Notre Dame University invites me to read. How miraculous. The stock market drops at rumors of war and soars with signs of peace. Incredible. I speak at West Point. Not believable. And tell them, a week after Nixon's invasion of Cambodia, from where I had just returned, that it is a disaster, a disgrace, and will surely bomb the Cambodians into the communist camp. A sixty-year-old colonel, with a horizontal Guards moustache, ramrod fellow beribboned up to his chin, stands and says he was U.S. Military Attaché in Phnom Penh for nine years and that Mr. Miller has spoken the truth. How miraculous. Only one cadet stands to ask why I choose to undermine their morale, and he is the son of the union chief in Chicago. How miraculous. And afterward, on the porch of an officer's house with a dozen colonels, all Vietnam vets, close-cropped and loose on scotch, they confide their mourning—for the Corps, the country, and a dwindling sense of honor. They talk of resigning, of being ashamed to wear the uniform into New York and, longingly, of Eisenhower's Order of the Day to the legions about to storm the Normandy beaches because that order spoke of mankind, of lifting the yoke of tyranny, and one man exclaims: "Imagine those words in an order anymore!" Would they ever know a rightful cause again, in or out of war? They were acolytes in a sullied church, and if these men blamed the politicians for defeat, they were also no longer sure we had deserved to win. That ancient scorn for human circumstances was faltering, even here, in the cannon's heart. Something is changing.

I suppose that in part I have been looking at Sixties radicalism from the Left Bank, from Prague and Red Square, as well as from my own home. It is always disappointing to American radicals to hear that things are worse abroad. Sounds like liberal smuggery. But I don't mean conditions, only the spirit. Especially is this difficult to swallow right now when the tide has played out here, the revolution eddying, and indifference again prevails. Who has gained from it all except MGM Records and the department stores with their new lines of eighty-dollar jeans? What came of the love-ins but fatherless children? And heavier contracts for the stars? And the sharp-eyed managers of perfidious guitars? What comfort that the cop looking for hash under the mattress has curls sticking out behind his helmet? The truth is that the fundamental demand of the French students in the 1968 revolution was that their universities be changed into the utilitarian American kind.

In 1968 I met with some thirty writers and editors and other hairy types in the office of *Listy,* the Prague literary magazine. They wanted someone from outside to know they were about to be jailed by the Russian toadies running the government. They asked me to come because I am an American, and only the Americans *might* respond to their disaster. These fellows had little hope, but it was all they did have. The Vietnam war was raging then, and they could read the *New York Times* and know we were imperialists and racists and lacked anything you could call culture, and yet the hope, what there was of it, pointed toward us. A few of them had been here and knew the score, had seen Harlem and Bedford-Stuyvesant and our wrecked cities—compared to their Prague, barbaric, corrupt, incredibly hard places, and merciless to the unsuccessful. Yet it was as though from this insane country were the impossible help possible—from this armed place that was at the moment killing another struggling people.

Under the Kremlin wall one day I remarked to my Soviet interpreter, a bright chap, that there must have been some fast footwork in that palace. . . . To my surprise the fellow was offended and said, "It is not our business." And the few who try to make it their business keep a bag packed with clean underwear, for jail. Those few, to my amazement, look to Americans as the free-swinging opposites of what their countrymen are. Not really to the American radical but to what they see as a man-centered idea still alive among us.

One of the owners of a German automobile company, this man naturalized now and based in New York, tells me he had to bring over the company's engineers and make them attend Senate hearings on auto emissions to convince them that they must take seriously the problem of auto pollution—because the Americans meant business, something these engineers had refused to believe because nobody in Europe meant business. A swim in the Mediterranean off Nice, a sail in the Sea of Japan, or a water-ski off the Italian west coast makes Coney Island look as pristine as Thoreau's pond.

But no listing of hopeful improvements can really alter the despair with modern life which is shared everywhere; the difference, if there is one, is a residual eagerness in Americans to believe despair is not life's fixed condition but only another frontier to be crossed. Perhaps only the black man can know the more universal despair—which changes only to remain forever the same—yet he has certainly evolved out of his passivity toward it.

In the central square of Wilmington, North Carolina, in the twilight of a fall 1940 evening, about a thousand blacks spread out along the storefronts and sat down or lounged among their jalopies and busted trucks. I happened to be there, temporarily employed by the Library of Congress to record speech patterns, no less, in that state. Quite accidentally I came upon this strange display. Eerie—for I knew instantly that they were not there to no purpose, and in 1940 you simply did not connect black people with assertion, let alone protest. (Blacks had stood apart from the whole radical Thirties, except for a handful who had never succeeded in rousing their own people.) I used the excuse of my microphone to find out what was going on, and I collected a crowd of men who were somewhat reassured by the Great Seal of the U.S. painted in gold on my truck—in those days the Federal Government was Roosevelt, whom white racists hated.

They were diffident country people, shy and suspicious, but pieced out for me the fact that they had been recruited from backwoods farms and hamlets to build the new Wilmington shipyard in the swamps nearby, a mucky, mosquito-tormented job. Now that the yard was finished, they had all been summarily fired to make way for white workers to come in and take the clean shipbuilding jobs. Only one of the men so much as raised his voice, a large fellow with powerful arms and a heavy bass voice. He stepped out of the polite shyness and roared, "Captain, we just about tripped! We got *no place to go!*" Then they dispersed. No police came to ride them down. By nine that night these people had all vanished, presumably into the woods from which they came. White Wilmington had barely taken notice of the occupation of the square, and in fact these black people had hardly raised their voices. Next day I interviewed the chief of Bethlehem's operation there and he was bewildered that there could even be an issue. Blacks hired in a shipyard to work alongside *whites?* That level of awareness is not possible anymore, even if so many blacks still live as though in an occupied country, a territory the Depression never left.

If only because the good news of Aquarius never touched our racism, it left an uneasiness; but there is another disquiet as well. Like the Thirties, the Sixties did not know quite what to do with evil. In the fever of the newfound Marxism, evil was seen evaporating with the disappearance of the private owner and his exploitation of people, but the snob T. S. Eliot said it better—"They are trying to make a world where no one will have to be good." Now again, by means of drugs or prayer or sex, we'll merge all impulses into a morally undifferentiated receptivity to life, and evil will shrivel once exposed to the sun. It is as though evil were merely fear, fear of what we conceal within, and by letting it all hang out we leap across the categories of good and bad. To both "revolutions," good and bad were inventions of the Establishment, mere social norms, and so it seemed that Stalin was liquidating not people but the dying past. Just as Manson, to many, is an ambiguous villain—the faces of his victims fade beside his victory over self-repression. There was something strangely pure in his massacre, since he did not even know his victims. André Gide wrote this story long ago—of a man who fires his gun in a railroad car and kills a man he never saw before—this in order to spring free of the ultimate repression through a totally gratuitous act, to find the irreducible self. Nihilism may save pride but it leaves its casualties and no fewer than does the moral code it sought to squash. Embittered now and defeated, the Sixties people find themselves no longer trained for nirvana but, yet again, in the United States. Still, they changed it forever, if this is a comfort.

By 1949, a Thirties man would never know there had ever existed, only a few years before, a movement for social justice, loud and pervasive. By 1949 the word "society" had become suspect again. But ten years later, justice was once more the issue. It was simply that the inventions of the Thirties had been absorbed, just as now the nation has both rejected and digested the Sixties idea. And this may be why, in my case anyway, a return from abroad always yields a faintly surprising experience of hope. It does keep changing here, it does go on: the blind, blundering search— which is not the case in more completed places. Evidently we are not fated to be wise, to be still in a contemplation of our cyclical repetitiousness, but must spawn new generations that refuse the past absolutely and set out yet again for that space where evil and conflict are no more.

It will not come—and it is coming.

1973

What's Wrong with This Picture?
Speculations on a homemade greeting card

Here is a New Year's card I recently received many months late. Like couples everywhere, this one decided to celebrate the occasion with a humorous photograph. It could have been taken in any one of a number of countries. It happens to have been made in Czechoslovakia.

The wife is wearing just the right smile for a woman standing hip-deep in water with her clothes on. It is a warm and relaxed smile. The husband, likewise, expresses the occasion with his look of grave responsibility, his walking stick and dark suit, his reassuring hand on Eda, their beloved dog.

The wife's floppy hat and gaily printed dress and the husband's polka-dot tie and pocket handkerchief suggest that the couple might have started off for a stroll down a Prague boulevard when, for some reason unstated, they found themselves standing in the water. One sees, in any case, that they are fundamentally law-abiding people who do not make a fuss about temporary inconvenience. Instead, the couple displays almost exhilarating confidence in the way things are.

Actually—although of course it does not show in the picture—the man and woman are within a short drive from the encampments of the Red Army, which entered their country some six years ago to protect it from its enemies, and has never left. This contributes to the calm atmosphere of the photograph, for with the Red Army so close by there is no reason to fear anything beyond the Czech borders, or, for that matter, within them.

One can see, in short, that these people live in a country blessed by peace. True, a certain tension arises from one's not being certain whether the water they are standing in is rising or falling. But, either way, it seems certain these people will know how to behave. Should the water rise to their chins, the man and woman will swim away, without in the least altering the amused resignation that animates them now. They will be accompanied, of course, by their dog, whose life preserver they will continue to grasp.

So we may conclude that here is a couple that has learned how to live without illusions and thus without severe disappointment. He happens to be on a list of 152 Czech writers who are forbidden to publish anything within the borders of the Czechoslovak Socialist Republic or to have their plays produced on a Czech stage. But one does not see the man and his wife thrashing about angrily in the water, as might be expected.

Instead, they stand in the water for their New Year's photograph, not in the least resentful or angry but with the optimistic obedience the present leadership of Czechoslovakia expects of all its citizens. Since it has been decreed that the couple stand in the water, so to speak, then that is where they will stand, and nothing could be simpler. Their dog, of course, is not blacklisted, but she always follows them so closely that they allow her to share their fate.

Considering all this, one might conclude the husband and wife are expressing utter hopelessness, and there is indeed some truth in this interpretation. In its desire for peace, the United States, much as it might wish to, cannot officially raise the issue with the Soviet Union, and this leaves the writer and his wife standing in the water.

On the other hand, the Soviet Union, much as it might wish to, cannot withdraw its military support of the regime it placed in power in 1968. At the same time, however, many Czechs believe the cultural cemetery their country has become is even too extreme for the Russian taste. The problem is that only mediocrities have been willing to take positions in the regime, and of course mediocrities lack the finesse to deal with the country's intellectuals, except to sentence them to an internal exile or force them to emigrate.

When some people, like the writer in this photograph, refuse to emigrate, they are nevertheless described in the controlled press as having left the country. A more bloodless and efficient solution is hard to imagine, but it is another reason why the writer is standing in the water fully dressed. When he and his wife are on dry land, walking down the streets of their neighborhood, they know that the official version is that they are living in another country; therefore, the couple's hold on reality—all that is really left for them—requires some expression, and so they occasionally stand hip deep in a lake or a river.

Yet another reason is that fellow intellectuals abroad, specifically those who espouse socialism or radical reforms in their own capitalist states, often march with placards denouncing tyranny in countries like Greece, Spain, Brazil or Chile, but none of these people seems to have noticed what is happening in Czechoslovakia. This is because Czechoslovakia is already a socialist country. And for this reason too the writer's wife smiles as cutely as she does and the writer himself shows no sign of surprise as the couple stands together in the water. Indeed, there is yet another reason for their expressions—namely, that the writer has for many years been advocating communism.

If the photograph could have been much wider, it would have revealed a veritable crowd of writers, professors, and intellectuals and their families, standing in the water. Not a few of these would be authors whose works come out in France, England, America—other places and other languages. For this these artists are not punished, although the government tries to discourage foreign publishers. Also, royalties are specially taxed so as to leave the artists with next to nothing. Thus they are quite successful in other countries but are forbidden to publish in their own language. And this also helps explain why the writer and his wife do not feel it so extraordinary to be standing hip-deep in water with their clothes on.

In Russia, quite otherwise, writers do not have themselves photographed in this curious way, because the Soviet government simply forbids their publishing abroad without official permission to do so. So Russian writers are photographed on perfectly dry land. The unique situation has therefore arisen whereby Czech writers would be delighted if foreign publishers or foundations would put out their work not only in foreign languages but in *Czech*. So persecuted a national pride is unequaled in any of the other socialist countries!

As matters stand, Czech writers can never read their work in other than strange languages, and this makes some of these writers feel they are instead the authors of translations. This is also why the couple is photographed standing hip deep in water with their clothes on.

The man in the picture has had half a dozen plays produced abroad and receives press notices now and then from Paris, London, Frankfurt or New York, but he does not feel he has ever finished a play, since a play is usually finished inside a theater and he is not allowed inside a theater in Czechoslovakia to work with actors and a production. This is also why he is standing in the water with his clothes on.

At the risk of overelaborating on so simple a picture, it is nevertheless necessary to add that a path, so to speak, lies open before this couple, if they would only take it. It would be the work of half an hour for this playwright to secure for himself a place on dry land. He need only appear before the proper authorities and deliver a confession that he was wrong in 1968 to oppose the Russian invasion, the elimination of human rights, et cetera, ending with praise for the present regime and a confirmation of its correct and humane position. His confession would then be widely published—in Czech, of course—and with it his condemnation of friends who still insist on standing in water, calling upon them to come out against alien, imperialist ideas and to take up their part in the building of a new Czechoslovakia instead of pretending, as they do now, that their consciences are more valuable and right than the wisdom of the present rulers. With a few well-chosen words, the couple and the dog could dry off and become real Czechs.

That the playwright finds himself unable either to accommodate the government in this or to emigrate and write freely in a foreign country indicates a certain stubborn affection for his own land. This is also why his wife smiles as she does and why he seems on the verge of either laughing or crying, it is not clear which.

It is not to be assumed, however, that his seeming imperturbability extends into the depths of his heart, let alone that the scores of other writers who would be visible in a wider picture have left to them the humor which this playwright is still capable of showing. Some, for example, will say that they are writing more purely, more personally, now that they can only write for their circle of friends. But others feel reality is closing down around them, that in their enforced isolation they are losing their grasp on life itself. These last, if photographed, would be shown farther out, in deeper water, with only their noses visible.

If the whole crowd of intellectuals could be shown where they are—in the water, that is, and fully clothed—and if they could be heard announcing their preference as to what sort of system they would want for their country, hardly one would not declare for socialism. But a socialism that is not confused with absolutism. This leaves the government in the awkward position of having to forbid these people to publish in their own language. Awkward because it is doubtful that so total a silence was enforced even by the czars or Hitler himself. Yet the present regime is certainly anti-czarist and violently opposed to Hitlerism.

And so the writer and his wife and their dog wish us all a Happy New Year. Needless to say—but possibly advisable to say to the Czech police—all these interpretations are entirely my own and not those of the subjects in the photograph, who were doubtless moved by their very Czech sense of humor to send out such a New Year's card, whose symbolism, in all fairness, applies to many other countries, and not all of them Eastern or socialist. It's simply that in certain countries at certain times a rather universal condition is more palpable and clear. Where, after all, are the waters not rising? Who does not feel, as he positions himself to speak his mind in public, a certain dampness around his ankles? In the days of his glory, did not the United States president propose to dismantle the television news organizations in order to get himself a still more silent majority? Was he not setting in place a secret police force responsible only to himself?

All this photo does is rather wittily inform us of how infinitely adaptable man is to whatever climatic conditions, firstly; and secondly, that—as the numbers on the life preserver make so terribly clear—the year is 1974 rather than, let's say, 1836, 1709, 1617, or 1237 in, for example, Turkey.

1974

The Limited Hang-Out:
The Dialogues of Richard Nixon
as a Drama of the Antihero

L et us begin with a few meaningless statements. The president is the chief law-enforcement officer of the United States. He also represents what is best in the American people, if not in his every action then certainly in his aims. These assertions were violated by Lyndon Johnson, John Kennedy, Dwight Eisenhower, and Franklin Roosevelt, not once but many times in each case. Johnson fabricated the Tonkin Gulf hysteria. Kennedy set the country on the rails into Vietnam even as he espoused humanistic idealism. Eisenhower lacked the stomach to scuttle Nixon despite his distaste, if not contempt, for Nixon's unprincipled behavior. Roosevelt tried to pack the Supreme Court when it opposed him and stood by watching the destruction of the Spanish republic by fascism because he feared the outrage of the Catholic hierarchy if he supported a sister democracy. And so on and on.

When necessity dictates, our laws are as bendable as licorice to our presidents, and if their private conversations had been taped an awful lot of history would be different now.

Yet Nixon stands alone, for he alone is without a touch of grace. It is gracelessness which gives his mendacity its shine of putrescence, a want of that magnanimity and joy in being alive that animated his predecessors. Reading the presidential transcripts, one is confronted with the decay of a language, of a legal system; in these pages what was possibly the world's best hope is reduced to a vaudeville, a laugh riot. We are in the presence of three gangsters who moralize and a swarming legion of their closely shaved underlings.

Let us, as the saying goes, be clear about it—more than forty appointed cohorts of Richard Nixon are already either in jail, under indict-ment, or on the threshold of jail for crimes which, as these transcripts demonstrate, the president tried by might and main to keep from being discovered. The chief law-enforcement officer could not find it in his heart to demand the resignation of even one of them for betraying the public trust. Those whom public clamor forced to depart were given sad presi-dential farewells and called "fine public servants."

This, to me, is the unexpectedly clear news in these transcripts—that, had he had the least civic, not to say moral, instinct, Richard Nixon could have been spared his agony. Had he known how to be forthright and, on discovering that the direction of the Watergate burglary came, in part, from his own official family, stood up and leveled with the public, he would have exalted his partisans and confounded his enemies, and, with a tremendous electoral victory in the offing, he would have held an undis-puted national leadership. Nor is this as naïve as it appears; it seems be-lievable that he need not have literally given the order to burgle Ellsberg's psychiatrist, was surprised by it, in fact. If, as also seems likely, he gave the nod to an intelligence operation against the Democrats at some previ-ous meeting, it would not have been the first such strategy in political his-tory, and he could have assumed the responsibility for that while disclaiming the illegal means for carrying it out. The nut of it all is that, even on the basis of self-survival, he marched instinctively down the crooked path.

So we are back with Plutarch, for whom character is fate, and in these transcripts Richard Nixon's character is our history. But to ask why he could not come forward and do his duty as the chief law-enforcement offi-cer is to ask who and what Nixon is, and there is no one we can ask that question. All one can really affirm is that these transcripts show certain at-tributes which now are evidentiary. Like a good play these dialogues spring from conflict surrounding a paradox: his power as president de-pends on moral repute, at bottom; therefore, one would expect him to go after any of his associates who compromised him. Instead, something en-tirely different happens. He sits down with Haldeman and Ehrlichman and proceeds to concoct a double strategy: first, to convince the public that he was totally ignorant of the crimes, which is an intelligent decision; and, second, to make it appear that he is launching an outraged investiga-tion of the facts in order to reveal them, when actually he is using his dis-coveries to keep his associates' infractions concealed. The latter objective is impossible and therefore stupid, and in short order he finds himself in possession of guilty knowledge, knowledge an honest man would have handed over to the requisite authorities. So the crux is always who and what he is. Another man need not have been swept away by events.

In the face of the sheer number of his appointees and their underlings who turn out to be unprincipled beyond the point of criminality, the issue is no longer whether he literally gave the orders for the burglary and the other crimes. The subordinates of another kind of man would have known that such despicable acts were intolerable to their patron and leader simply by their sense of his nature. That more than forty—thus far—are incriminated or in jail speaks of a consistency of their understanding of what this president was and what he stood for. Many of his staff members he barely knew personally, yet all of them obviously had caught the scent of that decay of standards emanating from the center, and they knew what was allowed and what was expected of them. The transcripts provide the evidence of the leader's nature, specifically his near delusionary notion that because he was "the president" he could not be doing what it was clear enough he was, in fact, doing.

At one point he and Haldeman and Ehrlichman are discussing the question of getting Mitchell to take the entire rap, thus drawing the lightning, but they suddenly remember John Dean's earlier warning that the two high assistants might well be indictable themselves.

> NIXON: We did not cover up, though, that's what decides, that's what's [*sic*] decides . . . Dean's case is the question. And I do not consider him guilty . . . Because if he—if that's the case, then half the staff is guilty.
> EHRLICHMAN: That's it. He's guilty of really no more except in degree.
> NIXON: That's right. Then [*sic*] others.
> EHRLICHMAN: Then [*sic*] a lot of . . .
> NIXON: And frankly then [*sic*] I have been since a week ago, two weeks ago.

And a moment later, Ehrlichman returns to the bad smell:

> EHRLICHMAN: But what's been bothering me is . . .
> NIXON: That with knowledge, we're still not doing anything.

So he knew that he was, at a minimum, reaching for the forbidden fruit—obstruction of justice—since he was in possession of knowledge of a crime which he was not revealing to any authority. One has to ask why he did not stop right there. Is it possible that in the tapes he withheld (as of this writing) there was evidence that his surprise at the burglary was feigned? that, in short, he knew all along that he was protecting himself from prosecution? At this point there is no evidence of this, so we must wonder at other reasons for his so jeopardizing his very position, and we are back again with his character, his ideas and feelings.

There is a persistent note of plaintiveness when Nixon compares Watergate with the Democrats' crimes, attributing the press's outcry to liberal hypocrisy. The Democratic Party is primarily corrupt, a bunch of fakers spouting humane slogans while underneath the big city machines like Daley's steal elections, as Kennedy's victory was stolen from him in Chicago. Welfare, gimme-politics, perpetuate the Democratic constituency. The Kennedys especially are immoral, unfaithful to family, and ruthless in pursuit of power. Worse yet, they are the real professionals who *know* how to rule with every dirty trick in the book. A sort of embittered ideology helps lower Nixon into the pit.

For the Republicans, in contrast, are naïve and really amateurs at politics because they are basically decent, hardworking people. This conviction of living in the light is vital if one is to understand the monstrous distortions of ethical ideas in these transcripts. Nixon *is* decency. In fact, he is America; at one point after Dean has turned state's evidence against them, Haldeman even says, "He's not un-American and anti-Nixon." These men stand in a direct line from the Puritans of the first Plymouth Colony who could swindle and kill Indians secure in the knowledge that their cause was holy. Nixon seems to see himself as an outsider, even now, in politics. Underneath he is too good for it. When Dean, before his betrayal, tries to smuggle reality into the Oval Office—by warning that people are not going to believe that "Chapin acted on his own to put his old friend Segretti to be a Dick Tuck on somebody else's campaign. They would have to paint it into something more sinister . . . part of a general [White House] plan"—Nixon observes with a certain mixture of condemnation and plain envy, "Shows you what a master Dick Tuck is."

This ideology, like all ideologies, is a pearl formed around an irritating grain of sand, which, for Nixon, is something he calls the Establishment, meaning Eastern Old Money. "The basic thing," he says, "is the

Establishment. The Establishment is dying and so they've got to show that . . . it is just wrong [the Watergate] just because of this." So there is a certain virtue in defending now what the mere duty he swore to uphold requires he root out. In a diabolical sense he seems to see himself clinging to a truth which, only for the moment, appears nearly criminal. But the *real* untruth, the real immorality shows up in his mind very quickly—it is Kennedy, and he is wondering if they can't put out some dirt on Chappaquiddick through an investigator they had working up there. But like every other such counterattack this one falls apart because it could lead back to Kalmbach's paying this investigator with campaign funds, an illegal usage. So the minuet starts up and stops time after time, a thrust blunted by the realization that it can only throw light upon what must be kept in the dark. Yet their conviction of innocent and righteous intentions stands undisturbed by their knowledge of their own vulnerability.

And it helps to explain, this innocence and righteousness, why they so failed to appraise reality, in particular that they were *continuing* to act in obstruction of justice by concealing what they knew and what they knew they knew and what they told one another they knew. It is not dissimilar to Johnson's persistence in Vietnam despite every evidence that the war was unjust and barbarous, for Good People do not commit crimes, and there is simply no way around that.

Yet from time to time Nixon senses that he is floating inside his own psyche. "If we could get a feel," he says, "I just have a horrible feeling that we may react . . ."

HALDEMAN: Yes. That we are way overdramatizing.
NIXON: That's my view. That's what I don't want to do either. [A moment later] Am I right that we have got to do something to restore the credibility of the Presidency?

And on the verge of reality the ideology looms, and they scuttle back into the hole—Haldeman saying, "Of course you know the credibility gap in the old [Democratic] days." So there they are, comfortably right again, the only problem being how to prove it to the simpletons outside.

Again, like any good play, the transcripts reflect a single situation or paradox appearing in a variety of disguises that gradually peel away the extraneous until the central issue is naked. In earlier pages they are merely worried about bad publicity, then it is the criminal indictment of one or another of the secondary cadres of the administration, until finally the heart of darkness is endangered, Haldeman and Ehrlichman and thus Nixon himself. In other words, the mistake called Watergate, an incident they originally view as uncharacteristic of them, a caper, a worm that fell on their shoulders, turns out to be one of the worms inside them that crawled out.

So the aspects of Nixon which success had once obscured now become painfully parodistic in his disaster. He almost becomes a pathetically moving figure as he lifts his old slogans out of his bag. He knows now that former loyalists are testifying secretly to the grand jury, so he erects the facade of his own "investigation," which is nothing but an attempt to find out what they are testifying to, the better to prepare himself for the next explosion; he reverts time and again to recalling his inquisitorial aptitude in the Hiss case, which made him a national figure. But now he is on the other end of the stick, and, after a string of calculations designed to cripple the Ervin committee, he declaims, "I mean, after all, it is my job and I don't want the Presidency tarnished, but also I am a law-enforcement man," even as he is trying to lay the whole thing off on Mitchell, the very symbol of hard-line law enforcement, the former attorney general himself.

Things degenerate into farce at times, as when he knows the Ervin committee and the grand jury are obviously out of his control and on the way to eating him up, and he speaks of making a "command decision." It is a sheer unconscious dullness of a magnitude worthy of Ring Lardner's baseball heroes. There are scenes, indeed, which no playwright would risk for fear of seeming too mawkishly partisan.

For example, the idea comes to Nixon repeatedly that he must act with candor, simply, persuasively. Now, since John Dean has been up to his neck in the details of the various attempts to first discover and then hide the truth, should Dean be permitted by the president to appear before a grand jury, eminently qualified as he is as the knower of facts? The president proceeds to spitball a public announcement before Ehrlichman's and Ziegler's sharp judgmental minds:

NIXON: Mr. Dean certainly wants the opportunity to defend himself against these charges. He would welcome the opportunity and what we have to do is to work out a procedure which will allow him to do so consistent with his unique position of being a top member of the President's staff but also the Counsel. There is a lawyer, Counsel . . . [it starts breaking down] not lawyer, Counsel—but the responsibility of the Counsel for confidentiality.

ZIEGLER: Could you apply that to the grand jury?

EHRLICHMAN: Absolutely. The grand jury is one of those occasions where a man in his situation can defend himself.

NIXON: Yes. The grand jury. Actually, if called, we are not going to refuse for anybody called before the grand jury to go, are we, John?

EHRLICHMAN: I can't imagine (unintelligible).

NIXON: Well, if called, he will be cooperative, consistent with his responsibilities as Counsel. How do we say that?

EHRLICHMAN: He will cooperate.

NIXON: He will fully cooperate.

EHRLICHMAN: Better check that with Dean. I know he's got certain misgivings on this.

ZIEGLER: He did this morning.

NIXON: Yeah. Well, then, don't say that.

Refusing himself his tragedy, Nixon ends in farce. After another of many attempts at appearing "forthcoming" and being thwarted yet again by all the culpability in the house, he suddenly exclaims, "What the hell does one disclose that isn't going to blow something?" Thus speaketh the first law-enforcement officer of the United States. Excepting that this government is being morally gutted on every page, it is to laugh. And the humor of their own absurdity is not always lost on the crew, although it is understandably laced with pain. They debate whether John Mitchell might be sent into the Ervin committee but in an executive session barred to the public and TV and under ground rules soft enough to tie up the Old Constitutionalist in crippling legalisms.

NIXON: Do you think we want to go this route now? Let it hang out so to speak?

DEAN: Well, it isn't really that . . .

HALDEMAN: It's a limited hang-out.

DEAN: It is a limited hang-out. It's not an absolute hang-out.

NIXON: But some of the questions look big hanging out publicly or privately. [Still, he presses the possibility.] If it opens doors, it opens doors . . .

As usual it is Haldeman who is left to interpolate the consequences.

HALDEMAN: John says he is sorry he sent those burglars in there—and that helps a lot.

NIXON: That's right.

EHRLICHMAN: You are very welcome, sir.

(Laughter), the script reads then, and along with everything else it adds to the puzzle of why Nixon ordered his office bugged in the first place, and especially why he did not turn off the machine once the magnitude of Watergate was clear to him. After all, no one but he and the technicians in the secret service knew the spools were turning.

As a nonsubscriber to the school of psychohistory—having myself served as the screen upon which Norman Mailer, no less, projected the lesions of his own psyche, to which he gave my name—I would disclaim the slightest inside knowledge, if that be necessary, and rest simply on the public importance of this question itself. Watergate aside, it is a very odd thing for a man to bug himself. Perhaps the enormity of it is better felt if one realizes that in a preelectronic age a live stenographer would have had to sit concealed in Nixon's office as he exchanged affections with a Haldeman, whom he admired and whose fierce loyalty moved him deeply. At a minimum, does it not speak a certain contempt even for those he loved to have subjected his relationship with them to such recorded scrutiny? Can he ever have forgotten that the record was being made as count would show he has more broken speeches by far than anyone in those pages. He is almost never addressed as "Mr. President," or even as "sir," except by Henry Petersen, whose sense of protocol and respect, like—remarkably enough—John Mitchell's, stands in glaring contrast to the locker-room familiarity of his two chief lieutenants. He can hardly ever assert a policy idea without ending with, "Am I right?" or, "You think so?" It is not accidental that both Ehrlichman and Haldeman, like Colson, were so emphatically rough and, in some reports, brutal characters. They were his devils and he their god, but a god because the Good inhabits him while they partake of it but are his mortal side and must sometimes reach into the unclean.

To turn off the tapes, then, when an elementary sense of survival would seem to dictate their interruption, would be to make an admission which, if it were made, would threaten his very psychic existence and bring on the great dread against which his character was formed—namely, that he is perhaps fraudulent, perhaps a fundamentally fearing man, perhaps not really enlisted in the cause of righteousness but merely in his own aggrandizement of power, and power for the purpose not of creativity and good but of filling the void where spontaneity and love should be. Nixon will not admit his share of evil in himself, and so the tapes must go on turning, for the moment he presses that STOP button he ends the godly illusion and must face his human self. He can record his own open awareness that he and his two bravos are quite possibly committing crime in the sun-filled, pristine White House itself, but as long as the tapes turn, a part of him is intrepidly recording the bald facts, as God does, and thereby bringing the day of judgment closer, the very judgment he has abhorred and dearly wants. For the hope of being justified at the very, very end is a fierce hope, as is the fear of being destroyed for the sins whose revelation and admission will alone crown an evaded, agonized life with meaning. The man aspires to the heroic. No one, not even his worst enemies, can deny his strength, his resiliency. But it is not the strength of the confronter, as is evidenced by his inability to level with John Mitchell, whom he privately wants to throw to the wolves but face to face cannot blame. It is rather the perverse strength of the private hero testing his presumptions about himself against God, storming an entrance into his wished-for nature which never seems to embrace him but is always an arm's length away. Were he alive to a real authority in him, a true weight of his own existing, such a testing would never occur to him. There are leaders who take power because they have found themselves, and there are leaders who take power in search of themselves. A score of times in those pages Nixon refers to "the President" as though he were the president's emissary, a doppelgänger. Excepting in official documents did Roosevelt, Eisenhower, Kennedy, even Truman, so refer to himself? Surely not in private conversation with their closest friends. But to stop those tapes would mean the end of innocence, and in a most cruelly ironic way, an act of true forthrightness.

If such was his drama, he forged the sword that cut him down. It was a heroic struggle except that it lacked the ultimate courage of self-judgment and the reward of insight. Bereft of the latter, he is unjust to himself and shows the world his worst while his best he buries under his pride and the losing hope that a resurrected public cynicism will rescue his repute. For it is not enough now, the old ideology that the Democrats are even more corrupt. The president is not a Democrat or Republican here, he is as close as we get to God.

And if his struggle was indeed to imprint his best presumptions upon history, and it betrayed him, it is a marvel that it took place now, when America has discovered the rocky terrain where her innocence is no more, where God is simply what happens and what has happened, and if you like being called good you have to do good, if only because other nations are no longer powerlessly inert but looking on with X-ray eyes, and you no longer prevail for the yellow in your silky hair. The most uptight leader we have had, adamantly resisting the age, has backhandedly announced the theme of its essential drama in his struggle—to achieve authenticity without paying authenticity's price—and in his fall. The hang-out—it is a marvel, is unlimited; at long last, after much travail, Richard Nixon is one of us.

1974

Rain in a Strange City

A rainy day out there does it. Paris in rain, Budapest, London. Also Leningrad, Stockholm and Vienna. And Rome, Rome, yes. Oh, and Amsterdam. Yes, Amsterdam especially. Yes, and New York, come to think of it, and Mexico City. And of course Dublin. Oh definitely Dublin, and almost any suburb in this chill but not freezing late morning. Even Moscow. The heads-down people, indrawn and all thinking of shelter, everywhere alive below the incoherent languages, alive to the drizzle and the gray, the plans that must be changed are everywhere the same plans. The oneness of all the countrysides is the same, the dank short grass is always making the same remark, it is all Holland, swept and dripping from the eaves of the sheet metal sheds of the businesses outside Maria Enzersdorf and Meaux and the steelyards north of Philadelphia and outside Ljubljana and Graz, this rain allows these, all these, to gather in a rough circle like men with turned-up collars and soaked shoes around a fire in an oil drum, silent and tolerant of one another. This rain anywhere brings the girl to the curb where calculating the width of the puddle she makes the leap with her pointed galosh describing an arc underneath her as her feet come down splashing the inside of her thigh, and the girl everywhere having had her hair done by appointment when the sun was shining, she is also crossing Mount Street or Knightsbridge or Dorottya Utca behind the dank Pest café, miraculously springing from a taxi on Gorki Street her head huddling in wet fur.

It is perhaps that nothing can be done. Without any thought of remedy all must simply endure, and without a cure for it there can be no manipulating the cure for other purposes. There can be no interference with it in any city, neither a technique nor a refusal of it, but only the same receiving of it everywhere in all cities, the act of being given something, a condition which all must recognize and submit to, the Emperor Rain, soft humiliator who feminizes and gentles, halts the thief in his own doorway turning him back to wait it out, forces the farmer to sit and rest his back and talk, for once, to his thin-faced daughter who has taken a dead wife's place, grounds the plane, turns armies from attack to letter writing and empties slum boulevards whose very windows glisten under the grit of their blind bitterness until all gleams and glistens, even filth and garbage cans.

Things that must be hidden from rain are heavily made-up clowns' faces, mascara and magazines, felt, wool blankets, very small infants, malt, good hay and photographs, bedroom slippers, diplomas, lecturers and violins, poets reading and much more regardless of zone or language area. Things which rain won't harm are naked girls and boys, grass, glass, galoshes and trees, spectacles, nonelectric typewriters, autos and boats, pens and pots and bald heads. For these rain is good or neutral and this is a division true in all cities, two groups of consequences whether in Beirut or New York or Gaza and Prague; wherever rain falls men and women go about blinking the drops off their eyelashes, in all places everywhere thinking of shelter in the wet cities and smelling of damp, in all places, all cities everywhere. Beyond my window now it is raining on the two bare young cherry trees, the crab apple, the pruned branches lying on the ground, and overhead the gray, rainloaded sky stretches away toward the east, the Atlantic, Ireland and England, Norway and Holland, France and Germany and Poland, all in this drizzle, collars turned up, the hiss of taxi tires on all their avenues, the hatless Sorbonne student peering through the fogged café window for his friends on Boul' Mich or Third Avenue, King's Road, Dorottya Utca. Rain. Gray. Nothing whatsoever to be done about it. Can't be helped.

1974

On True Identity

Frances Knight, for a generation in charge of deciding who is worthy enough to receive a United States passport and who not (I was not for several interminable years), has now conceived an awesome idea. She proposes that every American be required to carry a card of identity. It would be issued, inevitably, by the federal government, which "owes every American citizen a true, recorded national identity to protect him from criminal impersonations," Miss Knight says.

That a person might really be identified by a government-issued card is a breathtaking thought whose clear simplicity brings to nought the labors of philosophers and poets from Socrates to Freud and back to Shakespeare who, aside from eating, spent their time doing nothing but trying to identify people. Personally, it would end the waste of a good half of my day during which, it seems to me, I am in one way or another trying to nail down who I am. With Miss Knight's card I shall merely have to pat my wallet and get on with my business. People who presently clog analysts' offices and mental clinics will simply have to stop by long enough to drop their cards off. Having read them, the doctors will merely have to nod and say something like, "Oh."

What baffles me is why nobody ever thought of this before, especially when the procedure has been so stunningly successful in other countries. Under the czars, who, I believe, invented the idea in the first place, and under the Soviets now, the government is so adept at identifying each and every citizen by his card that he hardly dares go downstairs to get the mail in his pajamas. In South Africa, or so I read, no black can enter or leave any area without his passbook, which any policeman is at liberty to require he produce on command. In Nazi Germany the internal passport, which is what an identity card is, took on a positively metaphysical importance. Since you could not get a ration card without it, should the authorities confiscate your card for whatever reason, you lost your identity and your legal right to eat in the bargain.

One assumes, inevitably, that like every other privilege the government distributes to the population, the internal passport will also be revocable or simply canceled. In fact, Miss Knight refused to renew my own passport in the early Fifties, when I wanted to go to Brussels in response to a Belgian invitation to attend the European premiere of *The Crucible*. My trip, it seems, was not then in the country's best interests.

I have searched my mind, and I can see no reason why the government couldn't decide that a man's internal passport could be lifted because traveling from Brooklyn to Jersey City is not in the country's best interests. For there is no law of life more unbreakable than that which decrees the right of the government to take away that which it giveth.

But why stop at limiting travel? There are untold possibilities. With no effort at all I can imagine a card of what might well be called Limited Identity. This might dis-identify anybody once he has crossed the borders of his own neighborhood. Indeed, I can see Green Cards, Yellow Cards and Red Cards (after all, the passport issued me after my four passportless years was limited to six months instead of the customary three or five years).

In truth, Miss Knight told her interviewer for *U.S. News & World Report* that her idea was "loaded with political dynamite" because it "touches on the sensitive issues of personal privacy and a free society." But not necessarily, I think; provided everybody were identified *properly*. For example, the suspension of a sixth of the Bristol, Conn., police department for pilfering from local stores some years ago was made possible by the fact that they were loading the goods into squad cars early in the morning, while in uniform. Now both the cars and the uniforms were manifestly identifiable. But the point, I think, is that their possession of certified identity cards would have revealed only that they were perfectly ordinary policemen.

So we shall have to do more than identify people with these cards. We shall have to characterize them. On such cops' identity cards there would have to be a coded number, or probably a dot, which, translated into

Miss Knight's files, would tell her that Officer Blue "Has Tendency to Pilfer."

But who is to make these characterizations? Who, in short, is to supply the new identities—the government or the citizen? Take Richard Nixon. If he were to fill in his card without interference, it would doubtless read, "Pres. of U.S." If "true" identification is to be the standard, however, the government would have to stamp his card "Pardoned Pres. of U.S.," but would that really be fair? In years to come, when Watergate is totally forgotten, ought Mr. Nixon be forced to show his card and to explain to some ignorant postal clerk that he was not pardoned for having been president but for felonies? So, self-identification is bound to lead toward flattery, while if left to the government it is likely to be a constant humiliation; but which is true?

No, I'm afraid that telling us who we are still leaves *what* we are a matter for divination, the psychoanalyst, the insightful clergyman, or the friendly bar buddy. And if these seem inadequate, as they surely are, they can't be any worse than those in the Passport Office—which, according to Miss Knight's interview, has been unable to prevent a rise in passport frauds from 501 in 1970 to 791 in 1974. In fact, Miss Knight gives as a reason for the new cards this very rise in passport frauds. This would seem a small number of fakers in comparison to the hordes of passport-holders, but to Miss Knight it is frighteningly large. In short, because a few have succeeded in evading spouse, police, the tax man—indeed, the government itself—we who have failed must be doubly punished now with yet another mark of identification.

But even on the most practical level the notion needs more work, it seems to me. For example, it is impossible to imagine that a man with nerve enough to rob a bank or rip off an apartment would faint at the idea of forging an identity card. I have the sinking feeling that the honest people, those who have scruples about forgery, would end up being the most controlled. In fact, if I were living under a government which had shown even the very slightest tendency toward repression, this would seem the very heart and soul of the proposal.

So let us pray together that Miss Knight's proposal dies aborning. Oh, I know how shaky things are, and undefined. Surely no earthly pleasure beats that crystalline clarity of mind and soul by whose light the enemy among us is revealed. But the real evil, if one may use a drastic word, is that the urge to "identify" is the urge to freeze and fix forever what in truth is fluid and flowing. Indeed, if a "true identity" is needed in this country it is the government's; every poll shows that the people don't know what it stands for anymore, yet it takes more of their substance from them than all the con artists put together. If a "minority" is opposed to an internal passport, only another minority will benefit from it—the manufacturers of wallets.

1975

A Genuine Countryman
(*from* In the Country)

Three hours from New York City in those days and, with superhighways, an hour closer now, the area in the late Forties still had farmers who recalled shoveling a path through snow for miles cross-country, followed by the team and wagon filled with milk cans. In a district settled since the 1700s they lived in houses like the one I live in; without a closet, and in a lifetime had never traveled farther than forty miles from home. I still have the arched-lidded trunks in which generations kept their few good clothes and the linens. One of these people, a fellow named Bob Tracy, was born in that first house I bought, but it was something he never mentioned until we had known each other for two or three years.

In fact, it had as little significance for him as the fact that his family name showed up on deeds of thousands of acres of land, while he lived now on an acre down in a gully where the postmaster, a part-time mason with an enormous wen on the left hinge of his jaw, had built him a cinder-block cabin. "Well," he explained one time, "I had six sisters, don't y'know, and whenever one of 'em wanted a new hat they'd sell twenty acres." Now he did odd jobs for farmers, spelling them with the chores when they were sick or lazy or had to go off to a wedding or funeral, and mowed lawns for the few professional people around the township.

The interior of his cabin smelled, as the saying goes, like a bachelor on Friday, the atmosphere a mixture of kerosene, body sweat, and dog. More than once I had come on him asleep in his cot beside his dozing coonhound, Ella, the last remaining of three that he believed hunters from Waterbury had stolen. Awakened, he would clump out of bed pulling up his suspenders and, pretending the decency of surprise, would yell at the bitch to get out of his bed. She would open one eye and move a leg and go back to sleep and he would shake his head and say for the hundredth time, "Well, they stole my *good* dogs, don't y'know," and glare back at Ella as though it were her fault.

He must have been in his late fifties then, a thin but hard-bodied man with crinkly eyes and a mum mouth that he could press shut when listening with skeptical amusement. He first stopped by on hearing a city man had bought a house, to ask if I had any junk I wanted to discard. Quickly catching on to my penchant for never throwing anything away if I can help it, he conceded, "Well, waste not, want not," and from then on we got along fine, for the profligate habits of the few city people he knew left him confused about their characters, and character for Bob and his kind was something like what television was later to become for millions of people—the most delicious amusement, a source of infinite interest, the chief escape from humdrum existence. Thinking of him now, and of the others of his generation, it seems to me that this sets them apart from those who followed them into a quite altered time. When you came by for a visit they sat back, and with a certain appetite, an eagerness born of much silence and few interruptions, seemed to wait like an audience for the curtain to rise and reveal something wonderful. With none of them did I ever sense that they feared. It had nothing to do with bravery or nobility, but was simply a confidence that the man before them had an existence worth looking into.

Every item in Bob's cabin had either been given to him as junk or rescued from the town dump. Except, of course, for his rifle and three shotguns standing on their butts against a wall, shining and clean. On an upended crate stood a two-burner kerosene stove and an iron frying pan with a deep layer of yellow grease that had probably not been disturbed since the first Roosevelt administration. The longer I knew him, the more likely it seemed that if he were to wake one morning and find himself living at the turn of the eighteenth century, he would have needed less than ten minutes to feel at home, and much more so than he did now, as the 1950s were beginning. For one thing, he could never understand why people discarded cars, refrigerators, furniture, pots and pans that were still perfectly usable, reminder of an age when people spent a large amount of time repairing things. Once, inspecting a new car I had just bought, he turned to me and asked, "How long you going to keep it?" The question was pure, without irony; he was trying to understand what objects meant to people like me, for in his mind we sort of rented what we possessed.

Useless as a carpenter, he would nervously consent to steady one end of a board while I nailed the other. Once when I stood back to admire my work, and asked for his opinion, which I hoped would be positive, he asked, "How long you going to keep this place?" It bewildered him that people bought places, rushed about for two or three years redoing them, planting new trees and shrubs, and suddenly one morning were loading everything into a moving van—divorced, or changing states on orders from their companies. Finally he thought he understood the rationale: "It improves the countryside anyway."

One day early in our acquaintance when he was helping me to set posts for a fence around the new vegetable garden, he said, "I hear you write movies."

"Not movies, plays. For the stage."

Oh! those old-fashioned shows. Where they put them on?"

"New York."

"Well now—I didn't know they still had them."

At the approach of any female he removed his hat and pressed it against his chest, and his face turned pink. He would wash the outsides of windows but not the insides and the cellar stairs only to the top step, past which point he might find himself trapped inside a house with a woman. Anyway, inside a house was "woman's work," which he did not so much disdain as fear he would be criticized for doing badly, and to face a woman criticizing him was as close to dying as a man could come this side of the grave itself.

Through his eyes I saw the countryside emerging from its anonymity. Not far from his cabin, the one-room schoolhouse still stands, surrounded with old lilac bushes, a space twenty by thirty feet where he had gone to school as a boy along with the children of nearly every family for miles around. So they came to know each other's kinks and habits from the beginning and what to expect from them as adults.

"This Donald Price. When he grew up he come to run the general store. Old Donald was always on the lookout for a trick to play on y'. Well, there was this Mrs. Croker used to have him deliver everything, never would carry a bag out of the store herself. This one time he delivered the groceries and she says to him, 'I forgot a spool of white thread, Donald, would you bring it by if you don't mind.' Well, Donald thought about that and says to her, 'You want one spool of white thread delivered?' And she says that is what she wanted.

"So he goes back to his store, and they had this great big wagon for delivering lumber and a team pullin' it. So he hitches up the team, and sets this spool right on the bed and drives over to Mrs. Croker's and knocks on the door and she opens up and he says, 'I have your thread, where do you want it?' And he goes back to the wagon and pulls out these two heavy planks they used to roll down barrels on, and sets them on the tail of the wagon, and doesn't he roll that spool down the planks and picks it up on his shoulder like it weighed two hundred pounds and staggers up to her porch and sets it carefully right next to her feet. And that was that."

The World War II years were the best in his life. If he had a profession, it was hunting red fox, worth a dollar a pelt, if it had not yet been destroyed by rabies. Walking a dirt road he would point to the crotch of a tree where twenty-five years earlier he had rested his gun and gotten three big ones. His mind was filled with pictures of encounters on the roads.

"About midnight once, I's coming down this road looking for fox, and off ahead I hear this sound, *zoo, zoo, zoo*, like somebody sawing. No wind at all, and a full moon you could read your paper by. Well, I stood still listening, and sure enough it sound just like somebody sawing up ahead in the middle of night. So I come around the turn and there's this Pollack—they used to live in your house—and he's sawing this horse's head off right there in the middle of the road. It'd dropped dead there that afternoon and he was taking him apart to feed the pigs. They'd cut a hole in the kitchen floor and'd drop food down to the pigs in the cellar when it was winter. They certainly were peculiar people."

He parted the brush beside a road one day to show the remains of a stone foundation where he claimed an inn once stood, and beside it a blacksmith shop. "All the kids'd come and sit right here and watch the people getting out of the stage from Litchfield. This was the busiest spot around." I doubted a stage was still running in what must have been the nineties, but he insisted. "One time two robbers held them up and ran off with a bag of gold from the bank. They caught them, but they never found the money. It's buried up back on your land if you ever want to go look for it." I said I'd go half with him if he looked for it, and he burst out laughing, but it was still hard to tell how much of a spoof it was. Keeping a straight face was one of life's pleasures, and like his friends he cultivated a talent for Yankee one-liners.

Albert, the local state trooper, had been repeatedly warning Bob that it was illegal for him to be selling junk without a license. The weeds around his cabin were studded with burned-out vacuum cleaners, rusted gears, refrigerators, lawn mowers, and the first thing he did each morning when he came out the door on his way to the brook where he took his bath was to run his eye over his treasures to see if anything had been stolen during the night. Paying the license fee, about ten dollars, was bad, but his real reluctance was to have his name written down on any government register. This was why he refused a job as a grounds keeper at a nearby private school. "They make you put in for that social security, you know, and you got to sign for that. Next thing they'll be after me for the income tax." So he took care to cover whatever he was taking to the junkyard with burlap bags until someone gave him a derelict truck. Piece by piece he transported the vehicle to the junkyard, but at last he was down to the long rear axle housing, which there was no way to conceal—the end of it stuck out several feet from under his trunk lid.

He decided to take the chance, however, and set out with it for Waterbury. On his way he stopped off for bread, and coming out of the store he saw Albert standing behind his car staring down at the protruding axle. Selling auto parts without a license is especially frowned on. "So I knew I was in for it now. Well, I couldn't do much about it and I walk over to him and he looks at me and says, 'Hi, Bob.' And I says, 'Hi, Albert.' And he says, 'Nice day.' And I says, 'It was.'"

His class consciousness was stubborn, a reminder of a long-gone populism very much at odds with the new wisdom of the Fifties, when the intellectual centers were busy announcing the end of ideology and the imminent disappearance of the American poor. The system's only remaining problem, they said, was to save itself and the world from communism, while internally we need only rely on the automatic spreading of infinite riches to everybody. Bob read the only available local newspaper with its prideful Republican slant, never missing the local newscasts on his radio, a Thirties model shaped like a cathedral. He ended up supporting Henry Wallace for President, a candidate favored by the Left who piled up a full one million votes against Truman. "He's the only one I can understand," he would say, but the real reason was that most people hated and feared Wallace as a menace. In his mind these were the same kinds of people who kept pushing for stricter zoning regulations requiring three-acre lots around any new house. "They just don't want the workingman living around here," was his interpretation. From where he sat, the prospect was weird; "You be turning it all into a park." The land, he meant, which had always been a place of work and workingmen.

Through his vision of the land, the picturesque tended to disintegrate into long-forgotten purposes that had once created its aesthetic. The New England landscape is partitioned by patterns of stone walls, lichen-painted and enduring. Originally, they were convenient dumps for the rocks cleared from the fields they enclose that otherwise could not be planted. I was dismantling a section of wall one day when he came by in his bouncing Olds that stalled a few yards away. Its gasoline pump had died a year or so earlier and above the engine he had hung a Mazola can with a rubber tube from an enema bag leading to the carburetor. We got to talking about walls.

"My grandfather built your wall. A man and a team of oxen could do a rod of fence a day. That's the fence that nearly got him in the Civil War."

"How come?"

"Well, he was a real small man, and he's out here building this wall, and this squad of cavalry come riding down the road here conscripting men for the army, and they catch sight of him working here. But my grandmother was out behind the house, and she heard the horses and came running. She was a tremendous woman, and don't she pick up my grandfather and set him on her hip and says, 'You can't take my boy!' That saved him cause they wouldn't take boys helping their mothers."

Talking of war, he was reminded of Ben Fitzer. Fitzer was in his nineties during World War I, a farmer in this secluded valley who rarely even came into town. "But this one time, he come in for some reason, and this fellow come over to him and says, 'Isn't it awful all those men killing each other by the millions?' It was the first beautiful day of spring and old Fitzer says, 'What men you mean killing each other?' And the fellow says, 'Over in Europe, Ben. There's a terrible big war going on over there.' 'Well,' says Fitzer, 'they got a nice day for it.'"

Speaking of isolated people reminded him of the two unmarried brothers who had once lived in my house. "They were real churchgoers, don't y'know, went down there every Sunday. And around about January or so they didn't show up. Then next Sunday come and they're not there either. Finally, after they hadn't been for three Sundays, a committee was appointed to go up and see if there's anything wrong. Well, they come up the house and knock, and the door opens, and there's one of them, and they goes inside and asks why they hadn't been to church all month. And he says his brother'd died and he didn' feel he ought to leave him. 'Ought to leave him! Why? Where is he?' 'In the front room,' he says. And sure enough, they go over to the parlor, and there he's got him laid out on two sawhorses and a board. 'I'm waitin' for the thaw,' he says. That'll give you an idea how cold those houses were."

He would go through seizures of business acumen, especially on hearing how somebody had gotten thousands of dollars for a few acres. In the late Forties when I arrived, land was sold with a wave of the arm indicating the bounds, and it was so cheap, around forty dollars an acre, worth three or four thousand fifteen years later, that the "more or less" on the contract could often leave the purchaser with fifteen acres when he had paid for ten. By the Sixties, when the farms were being transformed into residences, ledgy back pastures that had hardly had a money value were discovered to have a view, and surveyors were popping up in the brushy woods with their transits and stakes, marking off lines as though an inch either way mattered greatly. Bob would suddenly show up in my yard trying to incarnate himself into a canny businessman. "Sell y' my whole place including the house for six thousand dollars," he said one day.

"What the hell would I do with it?"

"Sell it. Make yourself a profit. My cabin's *quiet,* it's *secluded*"—he had picked up the real estate jargon by now but spoke it uncertainly, as if it were some foreign language—"nice running brook, too."

"In August?"

"Well hell, *nothin'* runs in August." I expected the usual mock-innocent spoofing look, but his humor was no longer in his eyes. Instead, he actually seemed to be waiting for me to begin dealing about his miserable house and his damp and weedy gully, and his face showed an avidity I had never seen in him before. It was as though suddenly we were adversaries—he wanted what I had, and I was refusing what he had to offer. Our bantering connection was over with; he was trying to clamber aboard the great American train and resenting me as though I were stamping on his fingers.

We would meet on the road after that but he hardly paused. He sold his place and moved in with a retired bachelor, Dr. Steele, whose estate he tended, a miserly watcher of oil stocks, and they argued a lot, I heard. Years passed. I had forgotten about him entirely, when from my car window I spotted him mowing a lawn in front of the home of Mrs. Tyler, a divorced nurse. He had occasionally worked for her years before when we were still friends, and one time she had left a note for him on her door listing his chores, all of them to be accomplished in the two hours she paid him. "Dear Bob," it read, "please mow the lawn, put up the storm windows, clean out the flower beds, sweep out the garage, and take the garbage to the dump." Bob studied the list, then took out the stub of a pencil from his shirt pocket and carefully inscribed below, "Dear Mrs. Tyler, my ears are not that long, yrs, Bob," and never went back.

I stopped my car and called to him. It was good to see the grin that broke out on his face when he looked up. He stopped the mower, came over, and stood beside the car. It was hot, and his shirt was off, and it was a shock to see hanging flesh on his once tight-skinned body. His Irish blue eyes seemed to be shrouded by an unhealthy gray wetness. The old shyness seemed like shame now. Our paths had been crossing for nearly twenty-five years, and this was the first time in his presence that the thought of failure struck my mind. He was grinning, but his impishness had gone to bitterness in the curl of his mouth. As he came close, I could smell beer. He had never drunk enough to smell in daytime. His swollen-knuckled hands, the fingers arthritically curved, the faint wheezing of breath in his chest all sent me back to the day long ago when, teaching me to scythe, he had grasped the snath, and, trading his weight from leg to leg, his eyes fixed in a pleasurable gaze, he had circled half an acre, leaving behind a swath of smooth lawn, and returned to me hardly winded.

"You working for her again?"

"Well, she's not too bad."

"How's it going with Dr. Steele?"

"Oh, he's dead."

"I hadn't heard. When'd he die?"

"Oh it's over a year now," he said, and then he glanced carefully up and down the empty road and leaned down to me, and lowering his voice, he confided, "Won't be missed."

The mum, mock-proper mouth and the wicked eye were suddenly there again, and we laughed, and for an instant we were back the way it had been before he had learned caution, before all the land had become real estate and when his own kind were still on the farms around him and he was at home and free to savor whatever flew from his mouth.

He died a few months later, alone in a room he had taken over a tavern in town facing the railroad tracks. It was surprising to learn he had reached eighty. Then it was possible that he had sat by the inn as a boy to watch the passengers dismounting from the stage.

1978

The Sin of Power

It is always necessary to ask how old a writer is who is reporting his impressions of a social phenomenon. Like the varying depth of a lens, the mind bends the light passing through it quite differently according to its age. When I first experienced Prague in the late Sixties, the Russians had only just entered with their armies; writers (almost all of them self-proclaimed Marxists if not Party members) were still unsure of their fate under the new occupation, and when some thirty or forty of them gathered in the office of *Listy* to "interview" me, I could smell the apprehension among them. And indeed, many would soon be fleeing abroad, some would be jailed, and others would never again be permitted to publish in their native language. Incredibly, that was almost a decade ago.

But since the first major blow to the equanimity of my mind was the victory of Nazism, first in Germany and later in the rest of Europe, the images I have of repression are inevitably cast in fascist forms. In those times the communist was always the tortured victim, and the Red Army stood as the hope of man, the deliverer. So to put it quite simply, although correctly, I think, the occupation of Czechoslovakia was the physical proof that Marxism was but one more self-delusionary attempt to avoid facing the real nature of power, the primitive corruption by power of those who possess it. In a word, Marxism has turned out to be a form of sentimentalism toward human nature, and this has its funny side. After all, it was initially a probe into the most painful wounds of the capitalist presumptions, it was scientific and analytical. What the Russians have done in Czechoslovakia is, in effect, to prove in a Western cultural environment that what they have called socialism simply cannot tolerate even the most nominal inde-

pendent scrutiny, let alone an opposition. The critical intelligence itself is
not to be borne and in the birthplace of Kafka and of the absurd in its subtlest expression absurdity emanates from the Russian occupation like
some sort of gas which makes one both laugh and cry. Shortly after returning home from my first visit to Prague mentioned above, I happened to
meet a Soviet political scientist at a high-level conference where he was a
participant representing his country and I was invited to speak at one session to present my views of the impediments to better cultural relations
between the two nations. Still depressed by my Czech experience, I naturally brought up the invasion of the country as a likely cause for American
distrust of the Soviets, as well as the United States aggression in Vietnam
from the same détente viewpoint.

That had been in the morning; in the evening at a party for all the conference participants, half of them Americans, I found myself facing this
above-mentioned Soviet whose anger was unconcealed. "It is amazing,"
he said, "that you—especially you as a Jew, should attack our action in
Czechoslovakia."

Normally quite alert to almost any reverberations of the Jewish presence in the political life of our time, I found myself in a state of unaccustomed and total confusion at this remark, and I asked the man to explain
the connection. "But obviously," he said (and his face had gone quite red
and he was quite furious now), "we have gone in there to protect them from
the West German fascists."

I admit that I was struck dumb. Imagine!—The marching of all the War-
saw Pact armies in order to protect the few Jews left in Czechoslovakia! It is
rare that one really comes face to face with such fantasy so profoundly believed by a person of intelligence. In the face of this kind of expression all
culture seems to crack and collapse; there is no longer a frame of reference.

In fact, the closest thing to it that I could recall were my not infrequent
arguments with intelligent supporters or apologists for our Vietnamese invasion. But at this point the analogy ends, for it was always possible during the Vietnam war for Americans opposed to it to make their views
heard, and, indeed, it was the widespread opposition to the war which finally made it impossible for President Johnson to continue in office. It certainly was not a simple matter to oppose the war in any significant way, and
the civilian casualties of protest were by no means few, and some—like
the students at the Kent State University protest—paid with their lives.
But what one might call the unofficial underground reality, the version of

morals and national interest held by those not in power, was ultimately expressed and able to prevail sufficiently to alter high policy. Even so it was the longest war ever fought by Americans.

Any discussion of the American rationales regarding Vietnam must finally confront something which is uncongenial to both Marxist and anti-Marxist viewpoints, and it is the inevitable pressure, by those holding political power, to distort and falsify the structures of reality. The Marxist, by philosophical conviction, and the bourgeois American politician, by practical witness, both believe at bottom that reality is quite simply the arena into which determined men can enter and reshape just about every kind of relationship in it. The conception of an objective reality which is the summing up of all historical circumstances, as well as the idea of human beings as containers or vessels by which that historical experience defends itself and expresses itself through common sense and unconscious drives, are notions which at best are merely temporary nuisances, incidental obstructions to the wished-for remodeling of human nature and the improvements of society which power exists in order to set in place.

The sin of power is to not only distort reality but to convince people that the false is true, and that what is happening is only an invention of enemies. Obviously, the Soviets and their friends in Czechoslovakia are by no means the only ones guilty of this sin, but in other places, especially in the West, it is possible yet for witnesses to reality to come forth and testify to the truth. In Czechoslovakia the whole field is preempted by the power itself.

Thus a great many people outside, and among them a great many artists, have felt a deep connection with Czechoslovakia—but precisely because there has been a fear in the West over many generations that the simple right to reply to power is a tenuous thing and is always on the verge of being snipped like a nerve. I have, myself, sat at dinner with a Czech writer and his family in his own home and looked out and seen police sitting in their cars down below, in effect warning my friend that our "meeting" was being observed. I have seen reports in Czech newspapers that a certain writer had emigrated to the West and was no longer willing to live in his own country, when the very same man was sitting across a living room coffee table from me. And I have also been lied about in America by both private and public liars, by the press and the government, but a road—sometimes merely a narrow path—always remained open before my mind, the belief that I might sensibly attempt to influence people to see what was real and so at least to resist the victory of untruth.

I know what it is to be denied the right to travel outside my country, having been denied my passport for some five years by our Department of State. And I know a little about the inviting temptation to simply get out at any cost, to quit my country in disgust and disillusion, as no small number of people did in the McCarthy Fifties and as a long line of Czechs and Slovaks have in these recent years. I also know the empty feeling in the belly at the prospect of trying to learn another nation's secret language, its gestures and body communications without which a writer is only half-seeing and half-hearing. More important, I know the conflict between recognizing the indifference of the people and finally conceding that the salt has indeed lost its savor and that the only sensible attitude toward any people is cynicism.

So that those who have chosen to remain as writers on their native soil despite remorseless pressure to emigrate are, perhaps no less than their oppressors, rather strange and anachronistic figures in this time. After all, it is by no means a heroic epoch now; we in the West as well as in the East understand perfectly well that the political and military spheres—where "heroics" were called for in the past, are now merely expressions of the unmerciful industrial-technological base. As for the very notion of patriotism, it falters before the perfectly obvious interdependence of the nations, as well as the universal prospect of mass obliteration by the atom bomb, the instrument which has doomed us, so to speak, to this lengthy peace between the great powers. That a group of intellectuals should persist in creating a national literature on their own ground is out of tune with our adaptational proficiency which has flowed from these developments. It is hard anymore to remember whether one is living in Rome or New York, London or Strasbourg, so homogenized has Western life become. The persistence of these people may be an inspiration to some but a nuisance to others, and not only inside the oppressing apparatus but in the West as well. For these so-called dissidents are apparently upholding values at a time when the first order of business would seem to be the accretion of capital for technological investment.

It need hardly be said that by no means everybody in the West is in favor of human rights, and Western support for Eastern dissidents has more hypocritical self-satisfaction in it than one wants to think too much about. Nevertheless, if one has learned anything at all in the past forty or so years, it is that to struggle for these rights (and without them the accretion of capital is simply the construction of a more modern prison) one has to struggle for them wherever the need arises.

That this struggle *also* has to take place in socialist systems suggests to me that the fundamental procedure which is creating violations of these rights transcends social systems—a thought anathematic to Marxists but possibly true nevertheless. What may be in place now is precisely a need to erect a new capital structure, be it in Latin America or the Far East or underdeveloped parts of Europe, and just as in the nineteenth century in America and England it is a process which always breeds injustice and the flouting of human spiritual demands because it essentially is the sweating of increasing amounts of production and wealth from a labor force surrounded, in effect, by police.

The complaining or reforming voice in that era was not exactly encouraged in the United States or England; by corrupting the press and buying whole legislatures, capitalists effectively controlled their opposition, and the struggle of the trade union movement was often waged against firing rifles.

There is of course a difference now, many differences. At least they are supposed to be differences, particularly, that the armed force is in the hands of a state calling itself socialist and progressive and scientific, no less pridefully than the nineteenth-century capitalisms boasted by their Christian ideology and their devotion to the human dimension of political life as announced by the American Bill of Rights and the French Revolution. But the real difference now is the incomparably deeper and more widespread conviction that man's fate is *not* "realistically" that of the regimented slave. It may be that despite everything, and totally unannounced and unheralded, a healthy skepticism toward the powerful has at last become second nature to the great mass of people almost everywhere. It may be that history, now, is on the side of those who hopelessly hope and cling to their native ground to claim it for their language and ideals.

The oddest request I ever heard in Czechoslovakia—or anywhere else—was to do what I could to help writers publish their works—but not in French, German or English, the normal desire of sequestered writers cut off from the outside. No, these Czech writers were desperate to see their works—in Czech! Somehow this speaks of something far more profound than "dissidence" or any political quantification. There is something like love in it, and in this sense it is a prophetic yearning and demand.

1978

The Pure in Heart Need No Lawyers
(from Chinese Encounters)

In Peking only four days, I feel the intense need to talk to someone about the law, a subject in which no one in China seems to have the least interest. (In fact, however, within two weeks of our departure from China there were demands voiced in demonstrations and on wall posters that the leadership adopt a new attitude of respect for legality.) Surely if I were Chinese and did not wish to see my country losing another decade or two to anarchy, and more important, did not wish to be unjustly charged and punished for nonexistent crimes, I would look to the law for at least some reassurance that the past would not return. But China has still not yet passed a legal code. The Party has the power to punish or let pass whatever it deems harmful or helpful to its rule, and worse yet, can change back and forth at will. It is government not by law but by political resolution, something understandable in a revolution's early stages but questionable, to say the least, after nearly thirty years of existence. There is a constitution, of course, but this cannot be more than a guide if beneath it there exists no body of laws designed to make its provisions universally applicable.

Sid Shapiro came to China in the early Forties, has lived here since, and is a Chinese citizen. In his sixties now, he translates from English and is fluent in Chinese. He studied at "the subway law school," St. John's University in Brooklyn, and was raised a few blocks from my family home in the Midwood section. His house, in a quiet part of Peking, is close by an artificial lake, and the neighborhood is rather suburban in its somnolence this midmorning. As is the case in some parts of Brooklyn, it is hard to find a passerby who knows where his street is, though we are only three blocks away, and as our driver squeezes down one narrow lane after another I find myself staring out at the mamas and babies and grandmas and grandpas padding around the neighborhood—carrying a chair or a package or looking for a key on the ground—just being people, and I experience a vain longing for the day when it will be possible, perhaps a thousand years hence, to govern people by leaving them alone.

As Inge talks with his Chinese wife (Shapiro Tai-tai), a former actress and now a drama critic, my fellow Brooklynite corrects my vision of things here. "No, they don't need lawyers," he explains. "At least only very rarely, hardly ever at all." He is a man who is as comfortable with his ideas as he is with his Hopje candy (it has a Chinese name here), reminding me of Brooklyn where this formerly Dutch, coffee-flavored sweet was the dentist's best friend.

"Where the hell'd you get Hopjes?" I ask.

"They don't know they're Hopjes," he confides, "they just make them. But aren't they terrific?"

We sit there chewing away in his rather somber living room. He recently went back to Brooklyn to see his family, but after an absence of thirty years all he found impressive in America was the fear of crime. "They were worried as hell that I was going back to Manhattan on the subway at midnight. I couldn't believe it; imagine being afraid to go out of your house!"

"No fear here?"

"Not for a minute. These people are members of society."

"But don't they *ever* get out of line?"

He settles back and I realize we are into his favorite topic. We both unpeel paper from our Hopjes. I can see him clearly in Depression Brooklyn, cramming his courses, getting good grades, turning his face from a failed economy and feeding his soul on the communist ideal of effortless justice. For injustice is not an inclination of humanity but something imposed by unjust conditions. Man is not only by nature good, he is most often Chinese.

Sid got out of the United States before McCarthyism took over, no doubt because he had analyzed the future and found nothing but American crisis and decline while China was climbing upward and building the world he dreamed of.

"As Mao said, there are two kinds of contradictions: among the people, and between the people and the enemy. The courts don't involve themselves with the first kind of trouble . . ."

"Let's say a kid smashes a window, a guy beats up his wife."

"That kinda stuff never gets into a court."

"What about cops?"

"Rarely get near it. What happens, the neighbors lean on the kid and his parents to straighten him out. The peer pressure can weigh fifty tons."

"Like in Brooklyn."

Shapiro hesitates to agree—there should be nothing in China like anything in America.

"I mean," I continue, "that families were really the main source of discipline in those times."

"Well, in a way," he agrees, politely rather than actually, "but here the pressure is not just sentimental, it's based on political principle."

"To beat your wife is anticommunist." And I suddenly think of a line in a Depression play by Clifford Odets: "A man who beats his wife is the first step to Fascism."

"You could put it that way, sure. But beating a woman is political, since it cuts across the Party's position on women's equality; it's a feudal throwback."

"Gotcha."

"Stuff like that."

We both laugh at the revival in us of our ancient speech. "But what do they do with hard cases?"

"There aren't that many."

"But there have to be some."

"Well, in that case he goes before a judge and two laymen who know the defendant. And they struggle with him to reform his ideas. Crime is basically political, the result of reactionary ideas."

"Give me an example. Take theft."

"Okay. Theft is the attempt to consume goods without working or producing, so it is antisocialist and therefore a political act."

"That's very good." I am impressed.

"So political means are the only ones that can cure it."

"In other words, instead of moral inhibitions . . ."

"Which mostly don't work," he quickly adds.

"Why don't they work?"

"Because under capitalism you've got enormous crowds that don't have anything, while a few have a lot."

"So, in a sense," I say, "it is politically correct to steal under capitalism."

"And even morally correct. They are righting injustice. But," he cautions, "you can't graft the Chinese system onto America because it is based on a just economy. You can blame a man for stealing when he has a job and the chance to eat, but you can't if he's unemployed and starving."

It is the socialist lesson I first learned in Depression Brooklyn days, but Sid clearly delivers it like late news, and I find myself both marveling and irritated at the windless space he occupies, where in truth nothing has penetrated in forty years. "But you really don't feel anyone needs to be defended once he's in trouble?"

There is a certain smidge of defensiveness, though not enough to tip over his rice bowl. "But why? Before anybody's accused, the investigation is absolutely fair and thorough, and it goes on for weeks. Believe me, people who aren't guilty are never accused. The problem is never guilt, it's how to reform a person."

"There can't even have been a case of mistaken identity?"

"Well, maybe one in ten thousand, but that's not a real problem to the point where you'd have to introduce lawyers into the system."

"But, Sid," I say, trying to smooth the anger out of my voice, "from my first minute in this country I have heard nothing but the crimes of the Gang of Four, the thousands jailed without charges, without appeal, unjustly . . ."

"Yes, but that was not the system, it was the *breakdown* of the system! The Gang of Four *disrupted* the system!"

I am surprised that this particular kind of childishness can still start anger flowing into me. But there are millions like him all over the world who have managed to convince themselves that revolution cannot and should not make men freer. Every eighteenth- and nineteenth-century revolution at least declared the rights of the person to be the centerpiece of society and sought to draw a line beyond which the state could not reach into the individual's life. Now only the state has rights and powers, and the person, like his property, belongs to the collective, with no recourse or appeal if fools or factions should decide on his ruin.

With our disagreement in the open, Sid Shapiro does not look contented any longer, but that is life and cannot be helped. What occurs to me, however, is that this moment is emitting the same opaque quality as frequently arises with Chinese when any principle is up for discussion. Shapiro must surely be disturbed, if only remotely, by a society in effect without law, but a revolutionary cannot display his own uncertainties, let alone allow them to be part of a discussion. So it is once again not so much a cultural barrier I feel warding me off in China—Shapiro and I could not be more alike culturally—as a political creed whose fundamentals must not be so much as examined, most especially in the presence of those not of the faith.

As we drive away down the quiet Peking back streets, mazelike and narrow, the thought returns that hardly more than ten percent of Chinese live in cities, and that "out there" is the vast majority, bent to the earth as it has been forever. Is Marxism, with its nearly religious expectation of the human community reborn, the true successor system of capitalism or feudalism? The distance to post-Renaissance parliamentary capitalism is truly vast, but to feudalism it is amazingly close. Feudal man "owed" much to the group; everything, in fact. Under the Chinese kind of socialism he cannot move his residence without higher permission, for he is "part" of his commune, his factory, his social organization, and every single one of the nearly billion Chinese, like the Russians, is a member of what in feudal times was called a guild and here is called a collective—of doctors, dentists, workers, peasants. Looked at this way, there is indeed no place for lawyers, for the very concept of an individual standing apart from the group is no longer possible for the mind to entertain.

And it has happened, too, I recall, in another place and another time. The Puritans also forbade lawyers; I even gave to Judge Danforth in *The Crucible* a response to the very mystery I am now turning around in my head. "The pure in heart need no lawyers," he assures the complainants who come to beg him for lawyers to defend their loved ones against the charge of witchcraft.

And there, as here, it was not mere cynicism that drove intelligent men to embrace and celebrate their own vulnerability before injustice. It was the age-old dream of unity, of sonship and daughterhood, of the trustingness of family transposed into social relations. And all of it by virtue of a high belief in the state's sublimity, in the Society of Saints in Massachusetts and in socialism here in China. One may smile at its naïvetés, but not at the morale it so often imbues its believers with, and the feats in war and construction it rallies them to perform.

The Puritan theocracy lost its monopoly when surpluses of food and goods undermined the earlier need for a near military unity and the justification for the suppression of conflicting ideas. Has the time approached for China when suppression, for analogous reasons, no longer appears as justified as it did when the Japanese army still occupied the country, and a feudal Chiang Kai-shek had yet to be pushed into the sea?

A Sid Shapiro, in a word, persists in his warm bondage to the sublime, the very same condition from which the Chinese are cautiously emerging, for the first time daring to judge their leaders on a human scale.

1979

After the Spring

I have never understood why we keep a garden and why, thirty-five years ago when I bought my first house in the country, I started digging up a patch for vegetables before doing anything else. When you think how easy and cheap, relatively, it is to buy a bunch of carrots or beets, why raise them? And root crops especially are hard to tell apart, when store-bought, from our own. There is an atavism at work here, a kind of backbreaking make-believe that has no reality. And besides, I don't particularly like eating vegetables. I'd much rather eat something juicy and fat. Like hot dogs.

Now hot dogs and mustard with some warm sauerkraut—if you could raise *them* outside your window—you'd really have something you could justify without a second's hesitation. Or a hot pastrami vine.

As it is, though, I can't deny that come April I find myself going out to lean on the fence and look at that cursed rectangle, resolving with all my rational powers not to plant it again. It's not even economical any more with the price of seed so high now, and if I calculate what I have invested in a tiller and other tools, fertilizer, wire fence, and all the rest, it becomes ludicrous. I don't dare speak of my time and my wife's—which would figure out to be about six or seven thousand dollars per tomato—in good years.

But inevitably a morning arrives when, just as I am awakening, a scent wafts through the window, something like earth-as-air, a scent that seems to come up from the very center of this planet. And the sun means business, suddenly, and has a different, deeper yellow in its beams on the carpet. The birds begin screaming hysterically, thinking what I am thinking—the worms are deliciously worming their way through the melting soil. But it is not only pleasure sending me back to stare at that plot of soil, it is really conflict. The question is the same each year—what method should we use? The last few years we unrolled thirty-six-inch-wide black plastic between the rows and it worked perfectly, keeping the soil moist in dry times and weed-free, and when we go off for a few days it's not hard to find our garden again, as it has been when we used to cultivate.

But, here we go again—black plastic looks so industrial, so unromantic, and probably gives cancer of the fingertips from handling it. And of course some people think it unfair to use black plastic because it does work so efficiently. Like the early opposition to the large tennis rackets. Anything that reduces suffering has to be a little evil. Nevertheless, I have gradually moved over to hay mulch, mostly because we cut a lot of hay and it does improve the soil's tilth as it rots, looks lovely, and comes to us free. But it needs to be very heavily laid on or you will have planted a hayfield, which we did one year, long ago. No less than six inches deep, unless you buy salt hay, but that costs so much you might as well eat salad in a restaurant.

Keeping a garden makes you aware of how delicate, bountiful, and easily ruined the surface of this little planet is. In that fifty-by-seventy-foot patch there must be a dozen different types of soil. Parsley won't grow in one part but loves another and the same goes for the other crops. I suppose if you loaded the soil with chemical fertilizer these differences would cease to affect growth, but I use it sparingly and only in rows right where seeds are planted rather than broadcast over the whole area. I'm not sure why I do this beyond the saving in fertilizer and my unwillingness to aid the weeds between the rows.

I never spray anything principally because insect damage and fungi have never affected more than a scant proportion of plants in this garden. I am not sure why it is spared except that it lies in the midst of a former hayfield where there is heavy grass growth, and maybe insects get enough to eat out there beyond the fence.

The attractions of gardening, I think, at least for a certain number of gardeners, are neurotic and moral. Whenever life seems pointless and difficult to grasp, you can always get out in the garden and *get something done.* Also, your paternal or maternal instincts come into play because helpless living things are depending on you, require training and discipline and encouragement and protection from enemies and bad influences. In some cases, as with squash and some cucumbers, your offspring—as it were—begin to turn upon you in massive numbers, proliferating more and more each morning and threatening to follow you into the house to strangle you in their vines. Zucchini tend to hide their fruits under broad leaves until they have become monster green phallic clubs to mock all men and subvert the women.

Gardening is a moral occupation, as well, because you always start in spring resolved to keep it looking neat this year, just like the pictures in the catalogues and magazines, but by July you once again face the chaos of unthinned carrots, lettuce, and beets. This is when my wife becomes— openly now—mistress of the garden. A consumer of vast quantities of vegetables, she does the thinning and hand-cultivating of the tiny plants. Squatting, she patiently moves down each row selecting which plants shall live and which she will cast aside. Tilling and planting having been completed, I excuse myself from this tedious task, for one thing because the plants have outgrown their grassy look and show signs of being lettuces. (Although on certain days unaccountably I like lettuce.)

At about this time my wife's eighty-five-year-old mother, a botanist, makes her first visit to the garden. She looks about skeptically. Her favorite task is binding the tomato plants to stakes. She is an outspoken, truthful woman, or she was until she learned better. Now, instead of saying, "You have planted the tomatoes in the damp part of the garden," she waits until October when she makes her annual trip to her home in Europe; then she gives me my goodbye kiss and says offhandedly, "Tomatoes in damp soil tend more to get fungi," and toddles away to her plane. But by October nothing in the garden matters, so sure am I that I will never plant it again.

The psychology of gardening, obviously, is quite complicated. In my experience far more educated city people who move to the country bother with gardens than do people born in the country. The latter take immense pleasure in being well enough off *not* to have to work that hard to eat lettuce. City people feel they have to work off their sins, perhaps, or are convinced they are being poisoned by sprays on their vegetables. Country people, being generally more conservatively business-oriented, spray everything in sight, perhaps to show their faith in chemical companies.

I garden, I suppose, because I must. It would be intolerable to have to pass an unplanted fenced garden a few times a day. But if it makes little economic sense to plant it, and a very debatable taste advantage, there are certain compensations and these must be what annually tilt my mind toward all that work. There are few sights quite as gratifyingly beautiful as a vegetable garden glistening in the sun, all dewy and glittering with a dozen shades of green at seven in the morning. Far lovelier, in fact, than rows of hot dogs. In some pocket of the mind there may even be a tendency to metamorphose this vision into a personal reassurance that all this healthy growth, this orderliness and thrusting life must somehow reflect similar movements in one's own spirit. Without a garden to till and plant I would not know what April was for.

As it is, April is for getting irritated all over again at this pointless, time-consuming hobby. I do not understand people who claim to "love" gardening. A garden is an extension of oneself—or selves, and so it has to be an arena where striving does not cease, but continues by other means. As an example: You simply have to face the moment when you must admit that the lettuce was planted too deep or was not watered enough, and *cease hoping* it will show itself tomorrow, and *dig up the row again.* But you will feel better for not standing on your dignity. And that's what gardening is all about—character building. Which is why Adam was a gardener. (And we all know where it got him, too.)

But is it conceivable that the father of us all should have been a mason, weaver, shoemaker, or anything but a gardener? Of course not. Only the gardener is capable of endlessly reviving so much hope that this year, regardless of drought, flood, typhoon, or his own stupidity, this year he is going to do it *right!* Leave it to God to have picked the proper occupation for His only creature capable of such perpetual and unregenerate self-delusion.

I suppose it should be added, for honesty's sake, that the above was written on one of the coldest days in December.

1983

Suspended in Time

I began living on Brooklyn Heights in 1941 in an old apartment house overlooking Montague Street and the bay. That was long before the Promenade cut off the Heights from the waterfront and the life of the piers. You descended Montague on a long steep cobbled grade, and if you turned to the right, you saw the bridge. It seemed, as indeed it was, of the same vintage construction and the same verdigris and silvered patina as the pier structures and the warehouses down there. You were conscious of treading the stones of the nineteenth century and even in some places the eighteenth, for it had not been improved or changed since Whitman's and in some cases Melville's time.

So the bridge, before it was renovated in the Fifties, was ironically less remarkable than it seems now, less an artwork and more a normal element of a venerable neighborhood, conceived by an obsessively caring industrialist-engineer. Now that newer structures line its approaches, and probably also because of a greater awareness of such things in the press, it seems to stand out as a work of art. I must have walked or biked across the bridge a hundred times without once thinking I was passing along a work of art; it was simply the bridge, the most challenging and at the same time tension-relaxing object in my world.

Born in New York, in Harlem, as a matter of fact, I have never been without a certain background apprehension about crime, but before World War II there was not the current air of doom. In good weather one crossed the bridge and found people on the benches on the pedestrian path watching the sunset as though suspended in a park over the glistening river. There was a trolley that took you in both directions for the same nickel.

The motorman would get out at either end and push the car around a turntable to start his run again. I don't think I ever saw more than three or four people on that trolley, but they ran it anyway, no differently than it had been run since fourteen years after the bridge was opened. I remember the pink stub they gave you when you bought your ticket, which was good for one day.

It had really not changed since my father as a very young man used to hire a horse and gig and drive from the Lower East Side over the bridge to Coney Island for a Sunday's outing. He fell asleep on the way back and always found himself waking up in the stable on Rivington Street.

To walk the bridge then without thinking of Hart Crane's poem was an impiety, and it came to one's lips the way grace does to the devout at dinner. But unlike grace at dinner, it somehow defined the object being blessed more vividly than even one's own eyes could.

> *How many dawns, chill from his rippling rest*
> *The seagull's wings shall dip and pivot him,*
> *Shedding white rings of tumult, building high*
> *Over the chained bay waters Liberty—*

and

> *O harp and altar, of the fury fused,*
> *(How could mere toil align thy choiring strings!)*
> *Terrific threshold of the prophet's pledge,*
> *Prayer of pariah, and the lover's cry,—*

Through that poem, "To Brooklyn Bridge," your vision rippled under sunbeams broken by the cables and did indeed "descend/ And of the curveship lend a myth to God." The poem by a poet not celebrated, not even widely known, a broken and suffering man who died at thirty-two, seemed to confirm the sublimity of an architecture that alone of all the stoneworks in the city moved the heart as an unaggressive structure made to ease people on their way rather than to exploit or rule them. In the city, which was and is really a bazaar, a market, a place for exchange and a striver's arena, where proofs are given of victory and the self's magnitude, this walk across air and water asked of you only that you breathe in the sea scents and see the sky through those altarlike harp strings—in a word, to enjoy and yet to recall with some surprise that the thing was, above all, useful, a structure born of commercial need.

The more remarkable, then, that it has always been a poet's bridge, a dreamed bridge. Possibly because it seemed to have sprung not so much from the calculations of an engineer but the imagination of a dreamer. And because its feasibility from its inception had been surrounded with so much hardheaded doubt. So entirely the idea of a single man, it came to life not unlike an artwork does, a poem, in fact, which is always launched with bated breath, in fear and with something like a prayer that it will live. It was never a bridge that was ordered, so to speak, for its concept had little precedent. John A. Roebling, after all, was not primarily a bridge builder but a maker of cables. And so it seemed a kind of amateur bridge, a craftsman's oddity with its unheard-of span and almost total steel construction. And indeed, the mistakes made, the accidents, the failures and victories were not unlike the moves and revisions and backtrackings of artists feeling through the confusion of mind to the original image that first evoked the energy of creation. Above all, perhaps, for artists it meant the challenge thrown against the elements and naysaying against the antipoetic sludge of the threatening commercial civilization that seemed unable to aspire, to celebrate the spirit rather than the body alone. The bridge, astonishingly, unified them both.

But like many things of beauty it could be dangerous, and there was a night in the early Fifties when the bridge nearly killed me. In those pre-renovation times, two narrow roadways carried the cars and they were still paved with cobbles made of wooden blocks. Worse yet, they were a car and a half in width, making passing impossible.

At about one o'clock one morning I started across from the Manhattan side and saw the banks of fog rising up from the river. I slowed to a crawl at once, knowing that this much moisture would turn the old wooden, grease-covered blocks into butter. But at that hour, I figured, there would not be many other cars to contend with, and so I mounted the crest and started the ride down to the Brooklyn side in fairly good cheer when far ahead I thought I saw the glow of a pair of taillights. I tested my brakes. The car simply continued moving at a nice five-mile-an-hour clip as though it were sliding down a long hill of mud. Horror began to move into my spine when it became clear that those taillights were not moving; the car was doubtless stalled down there, and I had no possibility of getting around it. Now the final idiocy—I could faintly make out human figures behind the car. They would have to die of their stupidity unless I could stop.

I had an almost new green Studebaker convertible with a beige top, the Raymond Loewy squared-off design that had revolutionized the looks of automobiles, the first of my trophies from the success of *Death of a Salesman*. Gritting teeth, I maneuvered the car to the edge of the roadway and gradually pressed the front left wheel against the stringer, a girder that ran a few inches above the entire length of the road, hoping the friction would slow me down to a stop. But a break in the girder grabbed my tire, and the car spun completely about and came to a stop facing Manhattan. But at least it had stopped, and I could slowly back down to Brooklyn once the other car was gone. I peered through the rear window, and naturally it had now departed and the way was clear.

Then, inevitably, I saw a pair of headlights rising over the crest at the bridge's center and coming down toward me. I knew this driver could no more stop than I had been able to. There had to be a crash, and my momentary sympathy went out to the poor guy facing my headlights. I slid out from behind the wheel (it would have been even worse to get out of the car and be vulnerable to flying debris that might well knock me into the river) and rolled up in a ball on the floor on the driver's side, wedging myself against the seat.

A few seconds, and the crash came. Then silence. I got out and nearly slipped on the cobbles. My headlights were still on, throwing light on a highly polished but wet Ford, both of whose front wheels lay flat on the road, its headlights popped out, its radiator crushed and bleeding. A stout man with a tiny porkpie hat stood facing me with the angry fright of a solid workingman whose dearest possession had been not only wounded but also humiliated.

"What da hell yiz doin'? Yiz're goin' the wrong way!" Only his suspicion that I was drunk or insane held him in place, and I quietly explained how my car had gotten turned around. But once again he repeated, "But yiz're goin' the wrong *way!*"

And there we stood in the drifting fog, the blinded ships below bawling through their horns, the bridge dripping on our heads, while for the tenth time I explained my car's unorthodox position. Exchanging licenses, I saw his name—Rudy Zizzo. It all ended with my driving him around for half an hour searching for a cop—there was supposed to be one cruising the bridge at all times but he was off on some private business. And when finally we did flag down a cruiser, Zizzo, still stunned by the apparition that had confronted him as he had come over the crest of the roadway, almost cried to the cop, "He wuz goin' the wrong *way!* And I just this afternoon got my car out of the shop!"

So along with Hart Crane's lyric, the bike rides across and the walks, the people watching sunsets, the trolley and much else, I have Mr. Zizzo's awestruck face under the glare of headlights and a glistening gauze of fog and my new green Studebaker to remember when I glance at that bridge. Plus one thing more. In the early Fifties there bloomed on walls and the stone buttresses of the bridge, scrawled in white chalk, "Dove Pete Panto?" (Where is Pete Panto?). The rains washed off these words, but they were soon redone by unseen hands. I discovered that Panto, a young longshoreman, had risen from the ranks to challenge the corrupt leadership of the union and that the common idea was that he had been murdered. I would ultimately write a movie about him and the abortive movement he had started, but it would never see the screen for reasons that are another story for another time.

It was also the ironic contrast between its clean and airy span, with the tides of mindless traffic flowing back and forth, and the fury of the life in its shadow below that brought me the title and the angle of vision of *A View from the Bridge.*

What millions of such human connections must be caught in its lacy steel mesh over this century! It is a veritable myth, a kind of speech to the city's endless forgetting.

1983

The Night Ed Murrow Struck Back

Fear, like love, is difficult to explain after it has subsided, probably because it draws away the veils of illusion as it disappears. The illusion of an unstoppable force surrounded Senator Joseph McCarthy of Wisconsin at the height of his influence, in the years from 1950 to 1954. He had paralyzed the State Department, cowed President Eisenhower, and mesmerized almost the entire American press, which would in all seriousness report his most hallucinatory spitballs as hard front-page news. His very name struck terror not only in the hearts of the several million Americans who in the previous decades of the Forties or Thirties had had a brush with any branch or leaf of the Left, but also those who had ever expressed themselves with something less than a violent hatred of the Soviets, Marx, or for that matter cooperatives—or even certain kinds of poetry. At my own hearing before the House Un-American Activities Committee, a flank of the McCarthy movement, a congressman from Cincinnati asked me with wild incredulity, "You mean you believe that a man has the right to write a poem about *anything?*" When I confirmed this opinion, he turned to his fellow committeemen and simply threw up his hands.

How this vaudevillelike absurdity could have been taken in dead seriousness by vast numbers of Americans is hard to explain in retrospect. The Fifties' Red hunt not only terrified people but drove some few to suicide. It is not easy to conceive of Harry Truman, ex-artilleryman and quintessential small-town American, being labeled a traitor to his country, yet Senator Joe McCarthy and his fellow Republican leaders blithely went about pronouncing Truman's and Roosevelt's administrations "twenty years of treason." Never was this greeted with scorn or laughter. How to explain it?

Of course, an outrageous mixture of viciousness and naïve provincialism is endemic to the political extremes. Stalin awoke one morning and decided that all the Jewish doctors were in a plot to poison the party leadership, and nobody laughed then either. I had known an outlandish tap dancer who in desperation was touring Europe in the Thirties with his little troupe; in Berlin he found himself to his amazement the idol of the newly risen Nazi establishment, and soon of Hitler himself. Tap dancing so delighted Hitler that he spoke of ordaining it the *echt* German dance, which all the *Volk* must begin learning at once—a veritable nation of tap dancers was to spring forth, with my friend to be the head teacher. One morning a uniformed "race expert" showed up at his hotel prepared to measure his cranium, nose, mouth, and the spatial relationships of his face to make sure he was the Aryan type. My friend, a Jew, explained that he had an urgent appointment and took the next train out of the country.

By 1953 it was common talk in Europe that America had at last met her own native dictator in Joe McCarthy; but if a great many Americans agreed, they were in no position to say so safely, especially if they worked in government, or as teachers, or in the larger corporations. Another dreamlike element, moreover, was that McCarthy's Senate investigating subcommittee, whose claimed intent was the rooting out of communists hidden in the government, never seemed to find any actual Reds, let alone one who might be guilty of betraying the United States. To his critics, however, McCarthy would reply, "It isn't the number of communists that is important; it's the general effect on our government," one of his more candid statements.

He rose like a rocket to his power in a matter of weeks once he had stood on a podium waving a piece of paper and declaring, "I hold in my hand the names of . . ." I have since forgotten whether it was sixty-two or thirty-nine "card-carrying communists" inside the State Department, but it hardly matters because in subsequent months he himself kept changing the count and of course could never produce one name of an actual person. Yet his fraudulence, which had perhaps seemed so obvious to me because I had uncles like him who shot off their mouths in argument and said anything that came into their heads, was frighteningly persuasive to a lot of Americans, including some important newsmen. One half understood why the country was still in shock at having "lost" China to Mao, whose revolution had swept into Peking in 1949. How could this mucky peasant horde have won fairly and squarely against a real general like Chiang Kai-shek, whose wife, moreover, was the graduate of an American college and so beautiful besides? It could only be that worming their ways through our State Department were concealed traitors who had "given" the country to the Reds. In the light of Vietnam, we have perhaps come to understand the limits of our power, but in the early Fifties any such concept was unimaginable. Henry Luce, for example, was confidently propagating "the American century," when we would lead the grateful human race into baseball, private enterprise, eight-cylinder Buicks, and, of course, Christianity; and for a fact, the Swiss franc aside, the American dollar was truly the only nonfunny money in the world. Before he had finished, Joe McCarthy would have "named" the revered ex-general of the U.S. Army, George Catlett Marshall, as a communist.

McCarthy had struck gold with the point of a syllogism; since he was totally and furiously against communism, anyone who opposed him had therefore to be in favor of communism, *if only by that much.* This simply numbed the opposition or backed them into futile defensive postures. For example, when Senator Millard Tydings, having investigated McCarthy's charges that the State Department was full of Reds, reported that they were "a fraud and a hoax perpetrated on the Senate of the United States and on the American people," McCarthy, for revenge, then went into Maryland and, charging Tydings with being "soft" on communism, helped defeat him for reelection! His was a power blessed by Cardinal Spellman, a power that the young John F. Kennedy would not bring himself to oppose any more than did Eisenhower until 1954, near the end of McCarthy's career. For myself, I believed McCarthy might well be on his way to the presidency, and if that happened an awful lot of Americans would literally have to take to the boats.

When it was announced in 1953 that Edward R. Murrow would be devoting the entire half hour of his prestigious weekly TV commentary to an analysis of McCarthy, my own joy was great but it was mixed with some skepticism. Murrow had been the brightest star at CBS for more than a decade and remains to this day the patron saint of anchormen for his judiciousness and devotion to the truth. It was during the London blitz that he had seared our minds with the unique sound of his voice, a gravelly baritone that had rolled out to us across the Atlantic each night from the fog and blast of London under bombardment, his quiet toughness a reassurance that the great beleaguered city was still alive.

But all that anti-Nazi wartime gemütlichkeit was long gone now; indeed, CBS in the past couple of years had cooperated with the unacknowledged blacklisting of radio and TV writers, actors, and directors who had or were accused of having too much enthusiasm for the Left by newly sprouted self-appointed guardians of the airwaves like *Red Channels,* a broadsheet listing the names of purported subversives. In true private-enterprise style they were always ready to "clear" you for a fee plus your signed anticommunist declaration, or preferably an ad in *Variety,* which you paid for, with some similarly edifying and spontaneous patriotic locution. Still, it would be fascinating to see how far Murrow and CBS would want to go against the snarling senator from Wisconsin whose totally missing scruples had made him murderously effective as a debater. I was not at all sure it would be far enough.

There was such a widespread feeling of helpless paralysis before the McCarthy movement by this time that one questioned whether any mere journalist, whatever his wit and courage, could stay on his feet with him.

In such apocalyptic gloom, very nearly convinced that my days as an American playwright were numbered even as I was generally thought to be a great success, I adapted Ibsen's *An Enemy of the People* with the hope of illuminating what can happen when a righteous mob starts marching. But despite a brilliant performance by Fredric March as Dr. Stockmann, the critics batted the play right back at my feet. For one thing, it was a post-Odets and pre-Brecht time, when things artistic were supposed to deal with sentiments and aspirations, but never with society.

The failure of that production only deepened the sense of a mass mythic shadow dance, a ritualized, endlessly repeated consent to a primitive anticommunism that could end only with demagogues in power over the country. In the Salem witch hunts of 1692, a story I had known since college, I thought I saw nakedly unveiled something like the immemorial psychic principles of what we were once again living through. There too people had been at odds with a reality that indeed was sawing straight across their conception of themselves and nullifying the omnipotent powers of their society. There too men had been seized with paranoid terrors of dark forces ranged against them. It is hardly accidental that apart from *The Crucible* our theater would mount no other reply to a movement that surely meant to destroy its freedom. So feverish, so angry, so fearful had people become that any mention of the senator's name on a stage, or even an allusion to his antics, would have generated an impacted silence in the majority, and open rage in his partisans.

In *The Crucible* a public hysteria, based upon economic, sexual, and personal frustrations, gathers the folds of the sublime about itself and destroys more than twenty lives in the village of Salem, Massachusetts, in 1692. Between its heroes and villains stands a timeless hunger for mythic solutions to intractable moral and social dilemmas—particularly the myth of a hidden plot by subterranean evil forces to overwhelm the good. But *The Crucible*, too, would fail; either mistrusted as a "false analogy"—there had never been witches but there certainly were Reds, quite as though McCarthy had really uncovered a Soviet plot utilizing highly placed Americans—or regarded as a "cold" play, a charge partially justified by its direction as a disinterred classic. Interestingly, within two years, a new Off-Broadway production would succeed, judged hot stuff now by many of the same critics who theorized that I had more warmly revised the script. But the only revision had been the relaxation of society after McCarthy's quick decline and death—which, I suppose, permitted a longer view of the issues raised in the drama.

Shortly before Murrow's broadcast was announced, I had had my own personal little brush with a McCarthyite State Department. The Belgo-American Association, a business group, had invited me to come over to Brussels for the European premiere of *The Crucible* in the National Theatre, and I applied for a renewal of my outdated passport. A new passport was quickly denied me. "Not in the best interests of the United States," they said. So at the end of the opening performance, the audience, believing I was in the house, the papers having reported I had accepted to attend, began calling for the author, who, of course, was still in Brooklyn. The roar of the audience would not cease—to Europeans *The Crucible* at the time was reassurance that fascism had not yet overwhelmed Americans—and the United States ambassador had finally to stand and take my bow for me, a scandal in the papers the next morning when the imposture was revealed. (But who knows if he had stood up in sympathy for me or in silent protest at his department's stupidity in denying me a passport?)

All in all, by the time of Murrow's broadcast, I had only a small capacity left to believe that he would really do more than remonstratively tap McCarthy's shoulder. The broadcast was coming somewhat late in the game, now that an occasional soft murmuring of common sense was being heard in the press—although that, too, was still in danger of being suppressed once the senator got around to blasting its authors. For me, there was little reason anymore to expect a meaningful resistance to McCarthyism when I knew that, myself not altogether excepted, people were learning to keep a politic silence toward idiocies that a few short years before they'd have derided or laughed at.

An unsettling experience at a cocktail party shortly before the broadcast had stayed with me. I had overheard a TV producer assuring a circle of guests that he was free to hire any actor or produce any script he chose to and that no blacklist ever existed. Since I had friends who had not been hired in over a year despite long careers in TV and radio, and two or three who had suffered mental illness as a result, and I knew of at least two suicides attributable to the despair generated by blacklisting, I walked over to the producer and offered him the television rights to *The Crucible*. He laughed, assuring me and his listeners that he would of course be honored but his budget would never stand for what such rights would doubtless cost. So I offered them to him for a dollar. He went on laughing and I went on persisting, growing aware, however, that our little audience, many of them in television and the theater, was turning against me for a display of bad manners.

Leaving that party, I exchanged glances with people who I was certain shared my knowledge and views but who showed nothing in their faces. It was an experience that would be useful to me in future years when writing about the life of the artist in the Soviet Union, China, and Eastern Europe, where what might be called a permanent state of McCarthyism reigns, at times more virulently than others, but always warning artists—who, after all, are the eyes and voices of the society—that their souls ultimately belong to Daddy.

Edward R. Murrow appeared on the screen that night of the much-anticipated broadcast, as usual a picture of classy Bogartian straightforwardness, the cigarette between the fingers with the lethal smoke coiling up around the peaked eyebrows and the straight black hair, unsmiling as ever, his voice nasal and direct. I did not yet own a set, so I was watching this at my poet-friend Leroy's house a couple of blocks from my own in Brooklyn Heights. Leroy believed he was blacklisted in TV and radio, but a few producers occasionally gave him scriptwriting work because they loved him. People also gave him old but usable cars, trips to Florida, and more or less shared a mystic belief that Leroy must not die of want, with which Leroy agreed. He had once found a new can of anchovies on the sidewalk and a month later, on a different street, the key. Leroy had even graver doubts than I about what Murrow would be able to do.

Murrow could often affect an airy confidence and even sentimentality, rather like Cronkite talking about Vermont farmers, but not tonight; tonight he had his chin tucked in like a boxer and apprehension tightened the corners of his eyes with the knowledge, no doubt, that if some back talk against McCarthy had squeaked up recently in the press, his partisans were still passionate, religiously devoted to him, and numerous. Watching Murrow appear on the tube we were all aware of those millions out there who must hate him now for spoiling their god, or trying to; and even in that poet's snug and remote living room with its in-laws' cast-off furniture, the American violence charged the air. Tina, Leroy's wide-cheekboned blonde wife, who usually could never see a TV set switched on without turning away and launching a new topic of conversation, now stared in silence at Murrow's familiar face blossoming on the black and white tube.

To her and Leroy this broadcast was of far more than academic or abstract interest. Two of Leroy's closest relatives had gained some fame as American volunteers fighting for the Spanish loyalists against Franco. This, combined with his having the usual Left views of a Thirties survivor, was enough of a taint on Leroy to damage his right to sign his own name on the occasional radio script he was able to sell. On the slim proceeds of such fitful commerce he pressed on with writing his poems. And Tina pressed on with her winsome complaints that Leroy was stubbornly immune to the American Dream of wealth and fame. Thus she stared at Murrow like a woman in love with a fighter climbing into a ring.

I think it only dawned on us as he started to speak that Murrow was the first man to challenge McCarthy out in public rather than into his sleeve, and I think we were scared for him now, although we were still pretty sure that establishment politesse would gentle his confrontation with the senator. And indeed, Murrow's introduction was not at all belligerent. But this was television, not print, and it quickly became clear what his strategy was going to be—McCarthy was going to hang himself before the whole country by reruns of his own filmed performances. And there now unwound pictures of him hectoring witnesses before his Senate subcommittee, railing against a bespectacled author of an obscure college textbook with the accusation that this man was a member of the American Civil Liberties Union, "listed as a front doing the work of the Communist party." But the stinger was the speech before a mass rally during the recent Eisenhower–Adlai Stevenson contention for the presidency.

A cold and windy day, and McCarthy behind the podium, hatless, a burly and handsome man in a saturnine way, quick to laugh through a clamped jaw—more of a tight-assed snicker really, as though not to overly warm his icy ironies. Watching him again in these reruns was even scarier than seeing him the first time, in the previous months, for now somehow he was there to be studied and he was indeed villainous, almost laughably so. Now one saw that his great wish was for a high style, his models might well have been Oscar Wilde or Bernard Shaw, epigrammatists of the cutting Irish persuasion who could lay the opponent low with a jibe impossible ever to erase. Oddly, though, it was hardly ten minutes into the program when one knew it was the end of McCarthy, not altogether for reasons of content but more because he was so obviously handling subjects of great moment with mere quips, empty-sounding jibes, lumpy witticisms; it had not seemed quite as flat and ill-acted before.

At one point, as the applause of his audience died down he gave them his little knowing grin and said, "Strangely, Alger . . . I mean Adlai . . ." and a sweep of appreciative roaring laughter sent him into a helpless giggling spell and redoubled his audience's big-decibeled recognition for this association of Adlai Stevenson with Alger Hiss, an accused communist with whom Stevenson had no connection whatsoever. Now, with the election over and settled and its passions gone, the sheer vileness of this man and his crummy tactic was abstracted from its original moment and there he stood in all his mendacity, appearing joyfully immune to all moral censure or the most minimal claims of decency.

The Murrow broadcast was a deep, if not mortal, wound for McCarthy. At least it seemed so to me at the time. By the end of the half hour all our debt to Murrow came clear and my skepticism toward him had gone. But McCarthy was given his own half-hour rebuttal period three weeks later, and we gathered again to hear what he would have to say. Now live in the studio, a subdued McCarthy seemed to know he had been badly hurt by the Murrow broadcast. A plaintive tenor line lifted his voice into the doubtlessly authentic plaint of a persecuted man. "If there had been no communists in our government, we would not have given China to the communists!" This was one of his standards, but under attack now he knew he had to get more specific, and so maps appeared on the screen, showing how the dark stain of communism had spread from Russia over China, engineered by a tiny secret group of schemers, their agents, and their dupes like—yes, like Edward R. Murrow. In his rebuttal, McCarthy, left to himself, undid himself. Unaccustomed to anyone confronting him with his lies, he seemed unable to use elementary caution. Murrow, he blithely said, was a member of the terrorist organization the Industrial Workers of the World; Harold Laski, "the greatest communist propagandist in England," had dedicated his last book to Murrow. Now snarling, he attempted the ultimate unmasking of Murrow with his by-then familiar horror words: "Edward R. Murrow, the cleverest of the jackal pack which is always found at the throat of anyone who dares to expose individual communists and traitors; Murrow, who served the communist cause as part of the transmission belt from the Russian secret police into the American home." McCarthy's desperate appeal ended something like "The Communist Party opposes me; Murrow opposes me; Murrow is a transmission belt of communist propaganda." Such was his counterattack.

But Murrow, unlike others, had a network to allow him the last word. And he had easy pickings: the ACLU had never been "listed" by any agency as a front; Murrow had simply never belonged to the IWW; and Laski, a rather confused on-and-off-again Marxist professor, had dedicated his book to Murrow for his valiant broadcasts from bombed London in the late war. As for the communists supporting Murrow, this consisted of a notice in the *Daily Worker* that his upcoming McCarthy telecast was a "Best Bet."

Oddly, one lacked the urge to applaud Murrow at the end. He had been so persuasive because he had said what everyone had always known, that Joe McCarthy had merely been the master of the rhetorical style of lawyer-talk, an actor in love with the sound of his voice and his capacity to hold an audience in astonishment.

What ultimately undid McCarthy was hubris, his attacks on the patriotism of the leadership of the Army, on General George Marshall and Eisenhower himself. He may have gone mad with his power and too much booze. But Murrow's broadcast had cut the bag open and it was empty. How could one applaud our having striven so long after wind? Still, there was no doubt that night that Murrow's was the voice of decency, and if he and CBS had not struck at McCarthy until his decline had begun—if it was less a dragon slaying than a coup de grace—it still demonstrated, and would continue for years to come, the persistence of scruple as a living principle, one that had for so long been defied and doubtless would be again, and yet would live.

Murrow, in his summing up, said, "We are not a nation of fearful men," and one knew that there are things that do have to be repeated as fact even when they are only hopes. But for that kind of hope this nation is in Murrow's eternal debt.

1983

Excerpt from Salesman in Beijing

March 31

On arriving this morning I discover a dozen or so bewigged dummy heads standing in rows on some tables pulled together, the cast trying them on with the fervent advice and aid of four or five women and one man from the theater's own wiggery. These specialists are all, of course, dressed in the standard blue trousers and plain jackets, the man wearing his blue cap as befits wigmakers in a workers' theater. Ying is trying on a scraggly mouse-colored wig with a receding hairline; a hairdo like that would get anybody fired from his job for sheer neglect. To my amazement he is studying himself in a mirror with serious deliberation. Worse yet, I spot two platinum-blonde wigs that are undoubtedly intended for the two women in the restaurant scene whom Happy picks up. In other words, they are intending to "whiten" themselves for the play even though I had stated in my first day's lobotomized speech, without any demurral, the principle of their not trying to imitate Americans but to play as Chinese doing an American work. Admittedly, this places them in a never-never land, ethnically speaking, but at a minimum it is a more beautiful sight to see than Chinese with blonde hair, something that can only convince an audience that the actor is capable of wearing a wig. Of course I am leaving out their conventions, but I am doing so purposely since I cannot honestly judge by a taste I do not share or even understand. In any case I have a gut conviction that Westernizing the cast will vitiate the production.

Ying asks my opinion of the wig and I tell him it is all wrong, and he is easily convinced. In his case a wig is necessary to help age him and that is all. But it must have a pre-Beatles look, unlike the long hair he had been trying on. It has to be reminiscent of the fairly close-cropped businessmen of the 1950s, 1940s, and earlier. If a salesman can be ruined, as Charley says in the Requiem, by a couple of spots on his hat, a scraggly haircut would have sunk him without a trace.

From nowhere—we are now a milling mob of actors, wiggers, technical people with opinions, the sweet and aged doorman with his point of view, and me in the middle with bewigged Ying walking around and looking as if he could frighten bats—a small wigger woman appears with a fat illustrated book of Great Movies, which I open to a picture of Jimmy Steward in *Mr. Deeds Goes to Washington.* Stewart has the standard American haircut of the period. "That's it!" I yell. Whereupon I find myself facing a large, jolly, rather overweight, cherry-cheeked man—a wigger—in his late fifties who is just taking off his blue cap to scratch his head.

"*There's* your hair, Ying!" I call, and at a glance Ying is taken with it: dense, silvery-white hair clipped short all over but in a distinctive, efficient-looking way that is not quite conventional and yet could be. Immediately, of course, all the wiggers object that it is too short for Weelee. It is the old story—if you can make a wig, make a big one, something that *looks* like a wig, or why else bother? And so I must fight off wigs for Biff and Happy, whose own haircuts are perfect, with Biff's rather short cut quite right for an athlete, and Happy's about the style of Adolphe Menjou, very black, carefully shaped, and natty. My suggestion that Biff shorten the length of his sideburns, which are halfway down to his jaw, arouses his instant defensive indignation—"My jaws are so wide I must have these sideburns to make my face narrower!"—and I give up quickly without argument. And he does, I admit, tend to bulge toward the jaw hinges in rather a pear or punching-bag shape.

Speaking of which, as we finally settle down to begin running a scene, and everyone is getting back to his tea or taking position on stage, the tall doors to the outer corridor open and a monstrous shape begins moving into the room, its gait shuffling, its progress a few inches with each shove from the rear. The entire cast turn, as I do, transfixed by this apparition. It appears to be brown leather, about six feet in height, and as big around as a large culvert, with great brass grommets set around its open top through which a veritable hawser could have been threaded before it was separated from whatever might have been its normal abode. It is with sinking heart that I slowly realize that this is supposed to be the punching bag that

Willy bought for his boys in Boston and brought home as a surprise in the trunk of his little Chevrolet.

The thing now ceases to shuffle into the room, and around from its rear appears a small man in the usual blue, his cap and shoulder whitened with the dust of the bag that he has, incredibly, been pushing single-handed, God knows from what distance and over what boulevards and even mountains. "I think that's the punching bag," Ying says with typical Manchu understatement, staring up at me with his thick lenses, doubtless aware— at the least—of a slight awkwardness in my coming attempts to stage the moment when Happy will rush onstage carrying this object in one hand. The man now comes forward, I suppose to claim his credit from the great star and the Foreign Expert for having accomplished the impossible. I refuse even to imagine what they must have gone through even to locate this thing in Beijing. An ordinary punching bag, of course, is about the size of a lengthened basketball, and a sandbag is about four feet in height and perhaps a foot in diameter. This thing could only have been fabricated in prerevolutionary times, probably from a description of one seen in a New York or London gymnasium by a Chinese businessman who was extremely small.

But I know that Chinese are tough in the face of discouragement— how else could they have endured their history of suffering? "That is not the right punching bag," I tell the man, as quietly and forthrightly as possible, and draw him a picture of a light bag suspended from a round board. The stage manager suddenly recognizes this and explains it to the moving man, who, looking stunned, nods vaguely as he is led out of the hall into the corridor. Another day another dollar, as my father would say.

1984

Tennessee Williams' Legacy: An Eloquence and Amplitude of Feeling

So long as there are actors at work in the world, the plays of Tennessee Williams will live on. The autocratic power of fickle taste will not matter in his case; his texture, his characters, his dramatic personality are unique and are as permanent in the theatrical vision of this century as the stars in the sky.

It is usually forgotten what a revolution his first great success meant to the New York theater. *The Glass Menagerie* in one stroke lifted lyricism to its highest level in our theater's history, but it broke new ground in another way. What was new in Tennessee Williams was his rhapsodic insistence that form serve his utterance rather than dominating and cramping it. In him the American theater found, perhaps for the first time, an eloquence and an amplitude of feeling. And driving on this newly discovered lyrical line was a kind of emotional heroism; he wanted not to approve or disapprove but to touch the germ of life and to celebrate it with verbal beauty.

His theme is perhaps the most pervasive in American literature, where people lose greatly in the very shadow of the mountain from whose peak they might have had a clear view of God. It is the romance of the lost yet sacred misfits, who exist in order to remind us of our trampled instincts, our forsaken tenderness, the holiness of the spirit of man.

Despite great fame, Williams never settled into a comfortable corner of the literary kitchen. It could only have been the pride born of courage that kept him at playwriting after the professional theater to which he had loaned so much dignity, so much aspiration, could find no place for his plays. But he never lost his humor and a phenomenal generosity toward other artists. A few months before his death, I had a letter from him about a play of mine that had had some of the most uncomprehending reviews of my career. I had not seen Tennessee in years, but out of darkness came this clasp of a hand, this sadly laughing voice telling me that he had seen and understood and loved my play, and in effect, that we had both lived to witness a chaos of spirit, a deafness of ear and a blindness of eye, and that one carried on anyway.

His audience remained enormous, worldwide. Hundreds of productions of his plays have gone on each year—but not on the Broadway that his presence had glorified. He would end as he had begun, on the outside looking in—as he once put it, scratching on the glass. But of course, past the suffering the work remains, the work for which alone he lived his life, the gift he made to his actors, his country, and the world.

1984

The Face in the Mirror:
Anti-Semitism Then and Now

Some part of the genesis of this novel, *Focus,* must lie in the Brooklyn Navy Yard where I worked the night shift in the shipfitting department during World War II, one of some 60,000 men and a few women from every ethnic group in New York. It is no longer possible to decide whether it was my own Hitler-begotten sensitivity or the anti-Semitism itself that so often made me wonder whether, when peace came, we were to be launched into a raw politics of race and religion, and not in the South, but in New York. In any case, whatever the actual level of hostility to Jews that I was witnessing, it was vastly exacerbated in my mind by the threatening existence of Nazism and the near absence among the men I worked with fourteen hours a day of any comprehension of what Nazism meant—we were fighting Germany essentially because she had allied herself with the Japanese who had attacked us at Pearl Harbor.

Moreover, it was by no means an uncommon remark that we had been maneuvered into this war by powerful Jews who secretly controlled the federal government. Not until Allied troops had broken into the German concentration camps and the newspapers published photographs of the mounds of emaciated and sometimes partially burned bodies was Nazism really disgraced among decent people and our own casualties justified. (It is a fiction, in my opinion, that national unity around the war reached very deep in a great many people in those times.)

I cannot glance through this novel without once again feeling the sense of emergency that surrounded the writing of it. As far as I knew at the time, anti-Semitism in America was a closed if not forbidden topic for fiction—certainly no novel had taken it as a main theme, let alone the existence within the Catholic priesthood of certain militants whose duty and pleasure was to stoke up Jew-hate. When one is tempted to say that everything in the world has gotten worse, here is one shining exception.

I was reminded of this only recently when, quite by chance, I happened to tune in on a local Connecticut radio station and heard a Catholic priest trying to reason with an obviously anti-Semitic man who was laying the blame for several bombings of Jewish homes and synagogues in the Hartford area on the Jews themselves. There was a widespread search going on for the perpetrators, so the man had called in to the priest's talk program to offer his ideas as to who might have been responsible. He had no doubt it was somebody whom a Jew had mistreated, either one of his employees, or somebody who had bought some defective item from him, or someone he had bilked out of money. Or maybe it was the work of the client of a Jewish lawyer outraged at having been defrauded. There were, he thought, all sorts of interesting possibilities since the Jews, as everyone knew, have a habit of defrauding and exploiting their workers, and in general have no respect for right and wrong and feel responsible only to one another. (The arsonist was caught some weeks later—a mentally disturbed young Jew.)

I had not heard this litany since the 1930s and early '40s. But here it was again, as though freshly minted, brand new discoveries which the caller was supremely confident everyone knew perfectly well but thought it bad manners to talk about in public. And such was the confidence of his manner that he soon had the poor priest on the ropes, and could assert with utmost self-assurance that he was simply being factual and not anti-Semitic.

The differences now, of course, are that no Hitler stands at the head of the greatest armed force in the world vowing the destruction of the Jewish people, and there is an Israel which, notwithstanding all the futility of much of its present vision, is still capable of defending the right of Jews to exist. *Focus,* in short, was written when a sensible person could wonder if such a right had reality at all.

It is inevitable that one should wonder whether anything like the situation in this novel could recur, and it is a question no one can answer. In the Fifties and Sixties I might have persuaded myself that its recrudescence was not likely, and I would have based such reasoning on what had begun to seem a truly profound shift in the world's conception of the Jew. For one thing, anti-Semitism, linked as it was to totalitarianism, was being viewed as one of the keys to the dismantling of democracy and at least in its political forms was no longer an option for people who, whatever their private grievance against Jews, were still committed to the liberal state. By the end of World War II, anti-Semitism was no longer a purely personal matter.

But there was also the shift, however paradoxical, in the perception of the Jew as a consequence of the first successful decades of Israel's life as a state. In a word, the Jew was no longer a shadowy, ghettoized mystery, but a farmer, a pilot, a worker. Throwing off the role of victim, he stood up and was suddenly comprehensible as one of the world's dangerous peoples—dangerous in the conventional military and characterological sense. He was like everybody else now and for a time it would be difficult to imagine the traditional anti-Semitic attitudes feeding themselves on warriors rather than passive victims. For a time, Israeli technical and military missions were spread across Africa and her example seemed about to become an inspiration for any poor country attempting to enter this century.

This exemplary condition was not to last. By an irony so gigantic as to sweep the mind into the explications of mysticism, Israel has turned in the world's perception from a land settled by pastoral socialists and internationalist soldier-farmers into a bellicose armed camp whose adamant tribal defensiveness has inevitably hardened against neighboring peoples to the point of fanaticism. Jewish aloneness is back, but now it is armed. One more impersonation has been added to the long historic list that supplied so many contradictory images; Einstein and Freud and/or Meyer Lansky or another gangster; Karl Marx and/or Rothschild; the Prague communist chief Slansky running Czechoslovakia for Stalin and/or the Jew Slansky hanging by the neck as tribute to Stalin's paranoid anti-Semitism.

Focus is much involved with impersonations. Its central image is the turning lens of the mind of an anti-Semitic man forced by his circumstances to see anew his own relationships to the Jew. To a certain degree, it seems to me that Newman's step toward his human identification with some part of the Jewish situation has indeed occurred, at least in sectors of the democratic world, since the mid-Forties, and so the projection of such a change as occurs in this story was not altogether romantic and unlikely.

But in the four decades since I wrote *Focus*, new perspectives on the Jewish situation have opened up from surprising angles. In particular, the attitudes of some Asian peoples toward certain successful strangers settled in their midst, for example the Chinese in Thailand and the Vietnamese in the Cambodia of Sihanouk before the Vietnamese occupation of that country. It used to amuse me to hear descriptions in Bangkok of the local Chinese which were so exactly similar to what people used to say about Jews, and doubtless still do in the West: "The Chinese really have only one loyalty, to one another. They are very clever, study harder in school, always try to be first in their studies. There are lots of Chinese bankers in Thailand, too many; in fact, it was a real mistake to give Chinese Thai citizenship, because they have secretly taken control of the banking system. Besides, they are spies for China, or would be in time of war. Actually, what they are after is a revolution in Thailand (despite their being bankers and capitalists), so that we would end up as dependents of China."

Many of the same contradictory things were said about Vietnamese who had been settled in Cambodia for generations. The similarities in these two instances were striking—the Chinese in Thailand and the Vietnamese in Cambodia were very frequently visible as merchants, landlords of stores and small houses, peddlers, and an inordinate number of them were teachers and lawyers and intellectuals, enviable in a peasant country. They, so to speak, visibly administered the injustices of life as far as the average Thai or Cambodian could see, since it was to them that one paid the rent or the limitlessly inflated prices of food and other necessities of life, and one could see with one's own eyes how soft a life they led as intellectuals.

It is important also that the host people characterized themselves as somehow more naïve than these strangers, less interested in moneymaking, and more "natural"—that is, less likely to become intellectuals. In the Soviet Union, and the lands ruled by her arms and culture in Eastern Europe, the same sort of accusations are made openly or implicitly. *Focus* is a view of anti-Semitism that is deeply social in this particular sense: the Jew is seen by the anti-Semitic mind as the carrier of that same alienation the indigenous people resent and fear, the same conniving exploitation. I would only add that they fear it because it is an alienation they feel in themselves, a not-belonging, a helplessly antisocial individualism that belies fervent desires to be a serving part of the mythic whole, the sublime national essence. They fear the Jew as they fear the real, it often seems. And perhaps this is why it is too much to expect a true end to anti-Semitic feelings. In the mirror of reality, of the unbeautiful world, it is hardly reassuring and requires much strength of character to look and see oneself.

1984

Thoughts on a Burned House

In the weeks that followed, I would be surprised at the dimness of my re-action when our daughter called us in China to say that the house had burned. "But a lot of it is okay. My room is pretty much gone, but yours is only sort of half. And the dining room is just smoked up, and the front par-lor. But the living room is pretty much sort of disappeared, but the kitchen's okay. . . ." None of this registered; it simply dropped into my velvet-lined shock pocket.

Some ten days later, driving up to the house with my wife, I still won-dered at the way I had so quickly canceled the place out of my heart, so it seemed, a place I had lived in for nearly thirty years, a home full of our liv-ing and our junk. How strange; all the second- and third-floor windows nailed shut with plywood sheets, and long smoke stains on the white paint above them. The house looked blinded, the victim of an attack by a wild maniac who had thrown everything out the windows. Piles of bedding, window frames, doors, broken glass, lay vomited out on the front lawn. The garage was stuffed with burned couches, chairs, cushions, trunks; piled high with boxes, which turned out to be filled with books, an old pipe rack hung from a lawnmower handle, a couple of partially burned dolls, steel file drawers with their contents obscenely displayed. The fire department had done a fine job saving paintings and anything else that could be quickly moved outside, but my mind said to forget it all, truck the whole mess to the dump.

Inside, the silence of death in the black stench of ashes and the damp of water-soaked leather and woolen carpet. The back veranda, with its view of endless hills, was buried under mounds of our scorched clothes, silk scarves, brocaded jackets, evening gowns, shoes curled by water. From the edge of the vast hole in the living room floor, I looked down at the dark cellar where it had all started—in a failed oil burner cut-off valve. Overhead, the great ceiling beams were cooked, charred black. The floor varnish, according to the firemen, had bubbled in 1800-degree heat. The hi-fi had melted; I looked at its littered insides, thinking of all the music that had come out of it, and thought of the word *garble*. It had been a fine-sounding set, bought in the Sixties. The TV cabinet had imploded into a Daliesque hourglass with a square dead eye. How silly to treasure things. I had no link to this charred ruin of a room; the house I had known had swiftly receded into memory.

It was black dark on the second floor, with all the windows covered by plywood, and the water smell was stronger, ashen. Our bed stood on edge, spring coils melted, the fibers all gone. My flashlight caught flecks of our life here. The wrath of fire had simply eaten up my wife's closetful of clothes, leaving nothing but a few wire hangers and shreds of the shoulders of garments, soles of shoes. In one of the side tables, though, I found amid the trash a leather box in which I had kept a gift, a gold watch thin as a quarter. Surprisingly, the box opened, and there was the watch, and I wound it and it ticked. Leather and wood, it turned out, protect better than steel, which conducts heat.

The house would have to be gutted back to the frame itself, the timbers sandblasted to remove the char, and a special paint sprayed on the inside of the clapboards to kill off the smoke smell. Now, each day, two masked men with crowbars and sledges smashed the place apart and threw it out the windows. Trim installed two hundred years ago groaned as it was pulled apart, panes of old glass with rainbow bubbles were ground underfoot, chestnut flooring screeched against the old square-cut nails as it was yanked up. In less than two weeks, two centuries had been dropped onto the lawn; an anonymous skeleton was left. Yet it was interesting to inspect the immensely weighty framing, which, by custom in those early days, was probably joined together on the ground, tenon into mortise, then raised in a single day by family and neighbors. Washington was still fighting the French then, at the borders of the Great Lakes. In some walls were corncobs for insulation; horsehairs stuck out of the plaster. How much labor has been bombed to pieces in this century! Slowly, over days, the mortal wounds of the house and its resurrection, rather than thoughts of our possessions, began to move within me.

I was unprepared for the shock I felt when the architect builder, in his offhand way, implied we ought to think about building a new modern house instead of restoring this one. The impulse to fill this frame with life again was more powerful than I would have imagined, especially when we really did not need so large a house anymore. Then it occurred to me, for the first time, that in some hidden sense we had been borrowing a history here and had unknowingly enlisted in its continuation. And it was not a question of sentiment, I thought, but of something else. Absurd as it sounded to me, I only now thought of the fact that I had spent more than a quarter of my life here. Still, I could not say precisely why I could not think of abandoning what now was little more than a framework of three boxes, set one on top of the other under a roof, with an immense chimney in the center supporting the whole thing.

The bachelor farmer I had bought the place from was the last of his long line stretching back to Washington's army. For some years I had lived down the road and envied the cool breeze that always seemed to blow through the line of grand maples in front of this house at the top of the rise. When the farmer's mother died, at the age of ninety-three, he wanted to sell right away and start enjoying life at sixty-four, and he immediately took off with my purchase money to Florida, to die of lung cancer six months later.

I began to wonder whether there were many left who would recall him anymore. Or the barn, so neglected and filthy, where I had discovered a faded slip of pink paper nailed up over the Monel milk tank, a typed note from the county inspector: "Your milk temperature is still too high. Floor has not been hosed down. Cobwebs still everywhere. What do you intend to do about this?" Underneath, scrawled with a blunt pencil, the reply, "Stick it up your ass." Ah, tradition! Up in the dark windowless attic I would find a wooden stool beside a large spinning wheel, and a great loom with a five-foot span, at which the women must have worked through the winters in a windowless darkness and freezing cold, unless the original chimney had had an opening up there. And then there was the shoebox full of postcards that turned up in the cellar.

They were posted by the farmer during World War I from his army camp in California. "Have just come back from Los Angeles. Pie 15 cents bread five per loaf milk five per qt. Yrson Lewis," said one. Another read: "Been to Los Angeles again. Yrson Lewis." Another: "Have been to nearby town. Very pleasant. Pie 10 cents milk ten" (up five from Los Angeles) "nice grapes cheap. Swam. Yrson Lewis." Another: "Am feeling fine now. Out of quarantine." (Quarantine? Had he been to Los Angeles once too often?) "Say we'll be home by November or there abouts. Yrson Lewis." Not a bad war.

One day we had to choose the new windows, and the most efficient for insulation and letting in light were the single-pane type. But they would undo the authentic colonial look of the house. And so I found myself recalling the house when I'd bought it. The great old baking oven–fireplace had been removed after World War I, when labor-saving kerosene heaters were the rage; a steep stairway had been plunked into the living room for access to the second floor, where the brother and his wife had an apartment—electric kitchen and all—while the bachelor lived below with Mother. A concrete front porch was stuck out the end of the house nearest the road, so that Mother could sit and watch the one or two cars and wagons passing each day, and indeed a whole kitchen wing had been added in 1881—I found the date in chalk on a beam exposed by our rebuilding nearly thirty years ago.

What exactly was the continuity in this so-American place? In my first weeks here I discovered, under a pile of old hay, four enormous giltframed family portraits, photographs of two stern, heavily bearded farmers and two Victorian, high-busted women, and I offered them to the farmer's elder brother, who lived in the next village. Stopping by one day, he looked at them and said, "Oh yes, there's Grandpa and Grandma, and Father and Mother. Yes, indeed." It did my heart good to see the warmth of recognition in his seventy-odd-year-old face, but when I offered to load them into the car for him, he gave me a look of surprise that was close to shock, and soon drove off, and I no longer recall exactly what I did with them.

I suppose what is continuous is change. At least in this instance, the only tradition is the memory of it. This place has gone through one more revision of many, and it is, I think, more beautiful than it ever was—certainly it is more efficient, which is a form of beauty. Nevertheless, nothing prevents one from imagining the unknown, unknowable generations who watched the same march of night across these hills and heard the same wind whispering under the eaves.

1984

Dinner with the Ambassador

In March, Harold Pinter and I went to Turkey for a week on behalf of the International PEN Club. We made the visit not primarily to conduct an investigation of human rights—an impossibility in so short a stay—but to demonstrate to the country's writers and artists and to its political prisoners that the outside world cares about what is happening to them. It was to be an act of moral solidarity by the members of International PEN, and we hoped it might also have an effect on the country's military government.

We had wanted to talk to people of all political views, including Prime Minister Turgut Ozal and the martial law commander of Istanbul, Gen. Necit Torumtay. The prime minister was in Saudi Arabia, however, and the commander declined to see us, saying that the government is now controlled by Parliament—nonsense, since the military runs the country. We did meet with publishers and editors of conservative newspapers, who more or less support the regime. All of them, however, said that under censorship the truth about touchy issues could not be printed. We also attended the trial of a lawyer who had defended the Turkish Peace Association, a banned group which used to lobby for nuclear disarmament and détente, and we spoke with people who have been jailed and tortured without being accused of any act. We went to a dinner in my honor at the American ambassador's residence. Apart from the government-imposed news blackout on our press conference at the end of the trip, that dinner turned out to be the climax of the week.

It is important to understand that the 1980 military coup in Turkey was preceded by two years of terrorism, which had piled up some five thousand dead. At times, as many as twenty people a day were killed, and by all accounts the country appeared to be on the verge of civil war. Justification for the military takeover rests on this fact, which no one seems to deny. But some observers, including Suleyman Demirel, the prime minister at the time of the coup, find it suspicious that although seemingly helpless to curb the violence for two years, the military brought an amazing peace within a matter of weeks after taking power. In Demirel's view, the generals deliberately allowed the chaos to expand until their intervention would be gratefully accepted. Support for the military government is still based on fears that the violence will return.

A former high-level government official told us that there are currently about two thousand political prisoners in Turkey. In addition, seven thousand people are said to have been arrested as terrorists; most of them are under the age of twenty-four, and some are as young as sixteen. Many of these young people were picked up on the street for scrawling slogans on walls or arrested for harboring others in their homes. It is generally believed that about forty-eight "terrorists" have been hanged and that seventy more are awaiting execution.

The Turkish Constitution permits the police under martial law to detain a citizen for forty-five days without notifying his family or lawyers, and most instances of torture take place during that time. We met a respected Turkish publisher who had been arrested with his brother and had seen him beaten to death. In spite of his anguish as he related the details, he insisted on conveying the horror to us step by step. He told how he and his brother had been put in a van and, on their way to the prison, had been struck repeatedly by four guards. He believed he had survived because he had been handcuffed with his arms in front of him, allowing him to use them to protect his head. His brother's hands were cuffed behind his back, so he was helpless. When they arrived at the jail, the guards pulled them out and kicked his brother as he lay on the ground until he stopped moving.

Because of his prestige, the publisher was able to sue the police for assault. He won the case, but the four guards were sentenced to a few years in jail. Their superiors, who had ordered the arrests, were not mentioned in the proceedings.

We had looked forward to meeting U.S. ambassador Robert Strausz-Hupe, if only to hear the official U.S. view on the situation in Turkey. The dinner took place the day after we spent a deeply moving evening with the fiancée of Aly Taygun, a young director whose innovative work had created much excitement at Yale University's drama school a couple of years ago, and the young wife of a painter who, like Taygun, is serving an eight-year jail sentence for his membership in the Turkish Peace Association. The second woman's hope that we might help her husband in some way prompted her to show us several sepia drawings he had handed her during the five-minute visits she is permitted every two weeks. The drawings, mostly portraits of her, were packed with an almost palpable sensuous power.

When I found myself momentarily alone with the ambassador, I immediately began telling him about the imprisoned artist and his wife. To my surprise and pleasure, he was at once caught up in the story. He wanted to know their names, implying he would inquire about them. It seemed a good beginning. The ambassador, a spry, diminutive man in his eighties, is famous for his absolute deference to the Turkish military, with whom he has completely identified American interests. All I knew about him was that he had worked as a campaign adviser to Barry Goldwater. I learned later that he had been a professor at the University of Pennsylvania and has been considered a leading thinker of the far right.

That night he displayed a cultivated, literary air, not at all the image of a fiercely militant right-winger. He is an Austrian, naturalized in 1938; his rosy complexion and full head of silver hair, his blue baggy eyes with their soft drooping lids, his natty gray suit and sharp intelligence all suggested Vienna and civilized coffeehouse discussions. As we moved toward the dinner table, he confided to me that there might well be a declaration of amnesty in Turkey in the near future, giving the impression of cautious liberalism. "We can't push them too far," he said of the military. "We don't want to lose them."

Taking my seat across the table from the ambassador and to the right of his wife, I thought how functional the elegance of the table was, as though to protect power by enforcing good manners and empty conversations. The image of the imprisoned painter would not go away, but could such an unpleasant thought be introduced at a dinner given by my country's ambassador in my honor?

Harold Pinter was seated on the same side of the table as I was, half a dozen places down. The soup had hardly been served when I heard his strong baritone above the general babble and caught in it the flow of a quickened mind. On my left, Mayrose Strausz-Hupe, a beautiful woman who looks less than half her husband's age (the daughter, she volunteered, of a Ceylonese Ford dealer), was drawing a map of her country on the tablecloth with her fingernail, showing the demarcations between the religious factions that had been tearing the country apart in the years since the British left.

As the roast veal was served, Pinter's voice rose higher, his British diction sprouting angry ratchets. I could hear that he was engaged in a cross-table discussion with Nazli Ilicak, a widely read columnist whom we had met at the offices of her husband's newspaper, *Tercuman,* some days earlier, and Frank Trinka, the American deputy chief of mission, an unsmiling, tight-bodied man, with tinted glasses and a knife-like self-assurance. I could not make out what Pinter was saying, but I could hear Ilicak and the deputy chief replying, "That's your viewpoint. We have to see it in the round. You are only seeing part of it . . ." The ambassador, forking his veal, did not even glance in Pinter's direction as the playwright's voice reached the volume of an M.P. in the House of Commons. Madame Ambassador continued with her geographical drawing, maintaining an admirable aplomb. Her husband was trying to engage his neighbor in conversation, when Pinter, with open rage, shouted across the table at Ilicak, "That is an insult and was meant as an insult and I throw it back in your face!" As I learned later, she had told Pinter that although the Turks would have to remain and face the realities of their country, he could go home and put it all into a profitable play.

The ambassador quickly tapped his crystal water glass with a silver spoon and brought silence. "I wish to welcome Mr. Miller as our honored guest," he said, and went on to extol my work in the theater. He ended with a glance around the table which came to rest only for a moment on Pinter. "This demonstrates that all viewpoints are welcome here," he said. And then, pointing to the floor of his residence, his voice thick with emotion: "Here is democracy. Right here, and we are proud of it. Imagine this happening in a communist country!" Whereupon he thanked me for coming.

I understood that it was up to me to respond to the toast. Protocol must be observed, and the ambassador had been an engaging host. But as we sat there in the brightly lit room, an image popped into my mind: the painter's wife staring at an empty pillow; her husband lying on his mattress hardly a mile away, with six more years of prison ahead of him, all for an offense that, had I been a Turk, I surely would have committed myself.

I began by quietly thanking the ambassador for the dinner and the welcome, at which he looked relieved. "Whatever our political differences," I said, "we share the same faith in democracy." The ambassador nodded appreciatively. I went on:

As democracy enhances candor, my speech being without fear, it
is impossible for us to ignore what we have witnessed in Turkey.
We are playwrights, and playwrights are different from poets or
novelists or perhaps any other kind of writer. We deal in the concrete. . . . An actor has to be moved from point A to point B, and
so you cannot act in general, only in particular. We do not know
what the situation in Turkey was last year, so perhaps it is better
now, as is claimed. We don't know what it will be in the future. We
do know concretely what we have seen, and what we have seen
has no tangency with any democratic system in Western Europe or
the United States. I wrote in *The Crucible* about people who were
jailed and executed not for their actions but for what they were alleged to be thinking. So it is here; you have hundreds in jail for
their alleged thoughts. We are told that Turkey is moving closer
and closer to democracy, and that may turn out to be so, no one
can say, but what it is now is a military dictatorship with certain
merciless and brutal features. We are helping Turkey, and I am
not saying we should not; but the real strength of a state in the last
analysis is the support of her people, and the question is whether
the United States is inadvertently helping to alienate the people
by siding so completely with those who have deprived them of
their elementary rights. Not a single action is alleged against the
hundreds of Peace Association people in prison.

As I continued, I thought I saw the eyes of the ambassador glaze with
astonishment or horror. But at the same time, he seemed to be listening to
a kind of news: not political news, for he knew better than I did the state
of affairs there, but news of an emotion, an outrage. After twenty minutes
I ended my speech:

There isn't a Western lawyer who could come to this country and
see what is happening in these military courts who would not
groan with despair. The American part here ought to be the holding up of democratic norms, if only as a goal, instead of justifying
their destruction as the only defense against chaos.

The ambassador turned, gazed at the faces around the silent table and
asked Erdal Inonu, son of a former president and prime minister and head

of a political party, if he would respond to my remarks. Inonu, sixty, balding and squinting, a man with a gentle face and long hands which he softly clasped above the table, said that in general he could not help agreeing with my views and wanted to add his welcome to that of the ambassador. I could hardly believe this apparent victory. The ambassador gestured toward Ilicak; she simply shook her head, her eyes rounded in shock. A bearded journalist was then invited to comment; he chose simply to rub his hands together, smile and welcome me to Turkey (though Pinter later revealed that this man had exchanged approving glances with him while I was speaking). And so, with no more takers, we all rose, as the ambassador said something to the effect that it had been a fascinating dinner. Before I could stop myself, I added, "This is one you won't forget soon," to which the ambassador responded with an uncertain smile.

The company adjourned to the sitting room for coffee, and I sought out the deputy chief, sensing that he occupied the center of power in the place. But I had hardly sat down when once again I heard the awesome baritone of Harold Pinter. Near the entry hall, Pinter was just turning away from the ambassador, who, half his size, was shouting something and walking abruptly toward an astonished guest. Pinter came directly to me and said proudly, "I have insulted your ambassador and have been asked to go."

Forced to be practical by Pinter's visible emotion, I wondered about transportation and found a guest whom we had met at a gathering of Peace Association supporters. He was happy to share his car, but the French ambassador intervened, at the risk of offending Strausz-Hupe, his colleague and friend, and offered to drive us to his residence. On the way out to the black Peugeot, Pinter explained that the ambassador had remarked that there can always be a lot of opinions about anything, and he had replied, "Not if you've got an electric wire hooked to your genitals." The ambassador had stiffened and snapped, "Sir, you are a guest in my house!" Whereupon Pinter had concluded he had been thrown out. Pinter was brimming with admiration for my peroration, as I was for his righteous indignation, without which I could not have launched my twenty-minute speech. We decided we ought to form a team that would visit American embassies around the world.

Throughout our stay we had declined interviews, promising instead to hold a press conference on our last day. It took place in the building of the Journalists' Association in Istanbul, and was attended by twenty-five or thirty men and women and a television crew from United Press International. What we said at the press conference was more or less what we had said at the ambassador's dinner. We understood that Turkish journalists would be forbidden to print more than scraps of such opinions, but we felt we had to speak candidly. The next day, in London, we learned that reporting about the press conference had been banned by the government and that an investigation was to be launched into the whole visit. But news of it has nevertheless penetrated the prisons, as we have indirectly learned, and has brought some hope that the world has not forgotten these people. Unhappily, Prime Minister Ozal could stand before the Washington Press Club a few weeks ago and declare there are no political prisoners in Turkey without causing a ripple in his audience. There is nothing farther away from Washington than the entire world.

1985

Ibsen's Warning

I don't suppose anything has given me more gratification than the success of *An Enemy of the People* in its recent Young Vic production. I have made no secret of my early love for Ibsen's work, and now to have been in some way responsible, along with some very fine young actors and a passionately perceptive director, for a new appreciation of one of his most central ideas, is something that puts a satisfying warmth in my belly.

It is a terrible thing to have to say, but the story of *Enemy* is far more applicable to our nature-despoiling societies than to even turn-of-the-century capitalism, untrammeled and raw as Ibsen knew it to be. The churning up of pristine forests, valleys and fields for minerals and the rights of way of the expanding rail systems is child's play compared to some of our vast depredations, our atomic contamination and oil spills, to say nothing of the tainting of our food supply by carcinogenic chemicals.

It must be remembered, however, that for Ibsen the poisoning of the public water supply by mendacious and greedy interests was only the occasion of *An Enemy of the People* and is not, strictly speaking, its theme. That, of course, concerns the crushing of the dissenting spirit by the majority, and the right and obligation of such a spirit to exist at all. That he thought to link this moral struggle with the preservation of nature is perhaps not accidental. After all, he may well have found enough examples of moral cowardice and selfish antisocial behavior in other areas such as business, science, the ministry, the arts or where you will.

It is many years now since I looked into an Ibsen biography but I seem to recall that the genesis of *Enemy* was usually thought to be a news report of the poisoning of the water supply at a Hungarian spa. If there was a Dr.

Stockmann prototype who vainly protested against keeping the public ignorant of the truth, I cannot recall it. But whether or not this was the overt stimulus behind the play the question still remains why Ibsen should have seized upon it so avidly—he wrote this play in a remarkably short time, a few weeks.

Thinking about his choice throws me back to Henry David Thoreau who likewise found in nature's ruin the metaphor of man's self-betrayal. And Thoreau, I think, stood within an intellectual tradition of distrust of progress, one that goes back to the Roman poets, and the concomitant age-old view of the city as inevitably decadent and the unspoiled country as noble. Where it comes to nature even radical artists are likely to be very conservative and suspicious of change; perhaps nature takes on even more of a pure moral value where religion itself has vanished into skepticism. The sky may be empty but to look out on untouched forest or a pristine lake is to see if not God or the gods, then at least their abandoned abode. Ibsen needed an absolute good for evil to work against, an unarguably worthy brightness for dark mendacity to threaten, and perhaps nature alone could offer him that. And, of course, this is even more effective in our time when people have to go to the supermarket to buy clean water.

I am sure that few in the first New York audience of the early Fifties were terribly convinced by the play's warnings of danger to the environment. The anticommunist gale was blowing hard and it was the metaphor that stood in the foreground; moreover, in that time of blind belief in rational, responsible science, any suggestion that, for example, we might be building atomic generating plants that were actually unsafe would have simply been dismissed as dangerous obscurantist nonsense. And given my own identification with the Left, the metaphor was widely suspect as a mere ploy, an attempt to link the Reds, then under heavy attack, with Ibsen's truth-bearer. So neither the story nor the metaphor could carry the credibility that they do now when both have been revalued as alarmingly prophetic instinctual conceptions—it often does indeed take moral courage to stand against commercial and governmental bureaucracies that care nothing for the survival of the real world outside their offices. It is but one more evidence that the artist's powerful desire to penetrate life's chaos, to make it meaningfully cohere, has literally created a truth as substantial as a sword for later generations to wield against their own oppression.

1989

Uneasy About the Germans:
After the Wall

Do Germans accept responsibility for the crimes of the Nazi era? Is their repentance such that they can be trusted never to repeat the past? When people worry about the unification of Germany, these are the usual questions. But for me there is a deeper mystery, and it concerns the idea of nationhood itself in the German mind.

Three attempts to create a successful state have been smashed to bits in the mere seventy-two years since Germany's defeat in 1918. And although we are now in the presence of a great victory of a democratic system over a one-party dictatorship, it is not a democratic system of German invention. The nation about to be born is one that never before existed. And in apprehension over what this may mean, the Jews are by no means alone. The British are concerned and so are the French, not to speak of the Russians and numerous others whose lives were ruined by German aggression.

I have more than the usual contact with Germans and German-speaking people. My wife, Austrian by birth, spent the war years in Germany, and her family is involved in German industry; I have German journalist friends, as well as colleagues in the German theater and the film and publishing industries. If I were to announce that I am not too worried about unification and have confidence in the democratic commitments of the younger generation, my friends would doubtless be happy to hear it—and proceed to worry privately on their own.

No one can hope to predict what course any country will take. I believe that for Germans, including those who are eager for unification, the future of German democracy is as much of an enigma as it is for the rest of us. They simply don't know. More precisely, they are almost sure it will turn out all right. But that's a big almost.

Several weeks ago in West Berlin, one of my wife's high school friends, a woman in her late sixties who never left Germany through the rise of Nazism, the war and reconstruction, had some conflicted, if not dark, things to say about the question. "In Germany it will always be the same," she said. "We go up very high, but in the end we come down. We are winning and winning and winning, and then we lose. And when we are in trouble we turn to authority; orders and work make us happiest."

She is using a cane these days, after a fall on the ice. She has a broad-beamed peasant air, thinning hennaed hair, ruddy cheeks. A survivor of a battered generation, she seems to refer to her own observations rather than to things she has read. "We must go slowly with unification," she said. "It is all darkness in front of us." And if the future is murky to West Germans, she wondered: "What is in the minds of the East Germans? We don't know. For us it was bad enough. We had twelve years of dictatorship, but after that we have had nearly fifty years of democracy. They have had nothing but dictatorship since 1933. To become democratic, is it enough to want a good job and a car and to hate the left?"

She has come to visit, despite her injury, because in her circle it is hard to find an open-minded conversation. "I fear it is all very artificial," she said. "It is the same old story, in one sense. We are not like the French, the British, the Americans. We never created our own democracy, or even our own regime, like the Russians; ours was handed to us by the Allies, and we are handing it to the DDR people. But we had a memory of democracy before Hitler. Even their fathers have no such memory now. Who will influence whom—we over them or they over us?"

She talks about the Republicans, a far-right extremist party that won ninety thousand votes in the last West Berlin election after only a few months of existence. "People say they are nonsensical, a tiny minority," she said. "I remember the other tiny nonsensical minority and how fast it took over. And mind you, we are prosperous now. What happens if we run into hard times and unemployment?"

That conversation could be repeated as many times as you like in Germany. But it is entirely possible that two-thirds of the Germans—those under 50, who can barely recollect Nazism—have only the remotest connection with the woman's sentiments and underlying worry. So hostile are they to any government intrusion in their lives that some of them made it nearly impossible to conduct a national census a few years ago because the questions being asked seemed to threaten them with regimentation from on high. Questions had to be altered, and some census takers were even accompanied by inspectors to make sure more personal questions than those prescribed were not asked.

Nevertheless, the Berlin woman's apprehensions do leave a nagging suspicion. Does the Federal Republic of Germany arouse lofty democratic feelings in its citizens' minds, or is it a system that is simply a matter of historical convenience invented by foreigners? To be sure, this system has helped the nation to prosper as never before, but the issue is how deep the commitment is to its democratic precepts, how sacred they are, and if they will hold in hard times.

I have often sensed something factitious about German society in the minds of Germans, regardless of viewpoint. Discounting the zephyrs—or clouds—of guilt and resentment that obscure conversations with foreigners, especially Jewish liberals like me, it seems that the very reality of the German state is still not quite settled in their minds. I have never, for example, felt that Germans have very transcendent feelings toward the Federal Republic; it does not seem to have imbued them with sublime sensations, even among those who regard it as a triumph of German civic consciousness risen from the ruins of war.

Nothing, at least in my experience, approaches the French emotions toward their republic, the British toward their confusing monarchy, the Swiss toward their multilingual democracy, or Americans' feelings toward their country (which at least once every quarter century is pronounced imminently dead from depression, war, racial conflict or corruption, and therefore requires the loudest avowals of patriotic fervor on the face of the earth).

In a word, the German ship, in the German mind, increasingly powerful and promising though it may be, seems to float slightly above the surface without displacing water. Again, I may get this impression because of the tendency of Germans to apologize for themselves implicitly, which in some is a form of secret boasting, given the incredible success of the German economy.

The Berlin woman's sense of the system as having been conferred on Germans rather than created by them—a routine enough idea in Germany—nevertheless expresses the insubstantiality or, as she put it, the artificiality of the society that is now being merely multiplied by unification.

It has sometimes seemed to me in Germany that there is a feeling of walking on Astroturf rather than natural sod. Or maybe it is simply a feeling that the other shoe has not yet dropped.

But when one recalls the polities they did unquestionably create on their own—Frederick the Great's Prussia, Bismarck's state and Hitler's—they were all dictatorial or at least heavily authoritarian and in their time remarkably successful. This is also what my wife's Berlin friend was trying to say to me, namely that as a German she does not quite trust her compatriots' civic instinct when it comes to constructing a free society. And I wonder whether, unspoken, this is the source of the distrust a great many people feel in and out of West Germany, especially now that its territory is to be reunited with the East.

Of course, for the foreigner, Germany's civic failure is most perfectly expressed by the Holocaust and military aggressions of Hitler. But I have wondered whether, foreigners and their accusing attitudes on these counts apart, a different and less obvious historical experience is not more active in creating an uneasiness in them, an experience uniquely German.

It has often been said that Germans alone among the major peoples have never won a revolution. Instead, Germany's intense inner integration of social services, economy and culture was conceived and handed down by kings, princes and great chancellors like Count Bismarck (who though elected was kingly and sternly paternalistic), then a ferocious dictator and, since 1945, by her wartime victors. It is as though George Washington had accepted the widespread demand that he be crowned king, and proceeded to carve out a new society with little or no contribution or interference by elected legislatures. America might well have emerged with a fine well-ordered society in which the rules were very clear and life deeply organized from cradle to grave.

Instead, the state's decisions became the American citizen's rightful business, a conception that destroyed the time-honored relationship in which he was merely the subject of the state's attentions and efforts. The image of himself as citizen was thus vastly different from that in other post-feudal societies of the time—and from that of most people of our time.

Besides a lack of revolutionary past, the Federal Republic is unique among the great powers in another way: it came to life without a drop of blood being shed in its birth. No German soldier can say, "I fought for democracy." It was not given him by history to do so. West Germany is the creation not of arms, but work. The Japanese system, also practically America's creation, is a quite different case, in that the monarchy and government were never destroyed as such; indeed, MacArthur took great pains to make its continuity with the past obvious to all.

The German break with Hitlerism, the last German-made system, had to be total and condign. And German society had to be started almost literally from a pile of bricks under which the shameful past was to be buried, put out of mind, deeply discredited.

If these observations are in fact operative, and I cannot imagine how they can be proved or disproved as such, then what Germans lack now is the consecration by blood of their democratic state. The torrent of German blood that has flowed in this era in the Hitler-launched wars was, in fact, to prevent any such state from coming into existence.

For me, this is what keeps sucking the life out of German protestations of a democratic faith and casts suspicion on the country's reassurances that its economic power is no menace to the world. The fact is, West German civic practice has been as democratic as any other society's for more than forty years and is less repressive and all-controlling than, for example, that of France, whose bureaucracy is positively strangulating by comparison.

I know Germans who are as certain as it is possible to be that democracy will hold; I know other Germans who do not believe that at all. The world, it seems to me, has no choice but to support the positive side of the split and to extend its hand to a democratic Germany. By giving it the recognition it deserves, German democracy can only be strengthened, but meeting it with endless suspicion may finally wither its hopes. A recent New York Times/CBS News poll shows a large majority of Americans in favor of reunification, a vote of confidence with which I agree. At the same time, no German should take umbrage at the reminder that his nation in a previous incarnation showed that it had aggressive impulses that brought death to forty million people. This memory should not vanish: it is part of democratic Germany's defense against the temptation to gather around some new extreme nationalism in the future.

It does not really do any good to remind Germans of those horrendous statistics if the purpose is simply to gratify an impulse to punish. But it is necessary never to forget what nationalistic blood lust can come to, so that it will never happen again.

Likewise, German resentment at such reminders has to be understood. No one can live in a perpetual state of repentance without resentment. In the scale and profundity of its degradation Nazism has no equal in modern time, but each country has had some level of experience with contrition, some taste of it, as a repayment for oppression of other people. What if every nation guilty of persecution were to own up? Are we really prepared to believe in their remorse? And while penitence in the persecutors may be a moral necessity for those who survived victimization, it will not bring back the dead. So is it not infinitely more important that the descendants of persecutors demonstrate something more than contrition, namely political responsibility?

What do I care if a Nazi says he's sorry? I want to know what the constitution and educational system of Germany are doing to defend democracy under possibly difficult future circumstances. That is important to me and to my children. It is equally important that democracy live not only in institutions but in the German heart. But in all candor how are we ever to know that it does, except as crises are faced in a democratic spirit?

The world has a right—its World War II dead have earned it the right—to reproach and criticize and make demands of Germans if and when they seem to revert to bad habits. For a long time to come, the Germans are going to have to face the legacy of their last attempt to dominate other nations.

But there is another Germany—the Germany of high aspirations. It does truly exist, and it must be welcomed wholeheartedly in the hope that one day its permanent dominion over the country will be unquestioned by any fair-minded person. In short, the time has come to look the worst in the eye but to hope for the best.

A German journalist in her mid-forties, typical of many of her generation despite an upper-class Black Forest origin, has struggled with her country's past all her life and by turns is in despair and hopeful. "The problem," she says, "or part of it, is that the world is still thinking of Germany as it was in the Nazi time or shortly after. But a lot has happened in Germany in the last forty years!" As her voice rises, I am struck by an odd resemblance to the attitude of the Berlin woman. They both seem to doubt that they are *registering;* it is as if events were wild horses flying past with no one really pondering how to tame them. "For example," she goes on, "the impact of the 1968 French students' rebellion. It overturned Germany's educational system and for the first time made it possible for German workers to go to universities, the way it happens in America. Until then, we had a very narrow elite system. In fact, ours is now far more democratic than the French or the English, and we are now paying people to go to university, eight hundred marks a month if their parents together earn less than fifteen hundred a month. University education is free. This has had good and bad results—a lowering of standards, actually—but socially it has broken the class system."

Slim, elegantly dressed and a stubbornly heavy smoker, she is unable to come psychologically to rest. "This generation cannot be confused with the stupid, lumpen people who flocked to Hitler," she said. "Moreover, there is an immense amount of travel by this generation. They are not the parochial, isolated mass that Hitler poisoned so easily with antiforeign propaganda. This is not in any sense the pre-Hitler German people."

Then, hardly a moment later: "The problem with the German, the one great weakness of his character, is his worship of loyalty. Loyalty! Loyalty! It's the supreme virtue, the chain around his heart. . . ." And she is quite suddenly angry, and, for a few minutes, blue and uncertain and perhaps fearful.

In short, the uneasiness about national character is subjective, difficult to catch in the nets of rationality, but it may turn out to be more decisive than any other.

The anxiety shown by the journalist and my wife's Berlin friend transcends political viewpoints, I believe. Nor is it purely a product of the catastrophic last war and the Holocaust. I know some liberal Germans, a couple of radicals and some very conservative business types, and from all of them I have felt a similar emanation of uncertainty as to what, in effect, the German is—and consequently what kind of society fits him, expresses his so contradictory nature. And this is what I think the perplexity comes down to.

The Federal Republic is not a nation like others, born of self-determining revolution. Paradoxically, perhaps, West Germany is the first great society born of peace; if it is to achieve a deep sense of identity it will have to be real, not slyly apologetic, an identity reflecting the evil past and the present resurrection together.

If Germany remains implicitly on trial for a long time to come, release must come through good works and a demonstrated devotion to democratic ideals and practice. The past cannot be changed, but the future of democracy is in the nation's hands. Perhaps Germany can one day even stand as an example to other new societies of how to win a place in the world by work and the intelligent use of science rather than arms.

There is now a generation that cannot remember the war or Nazism, and in fact finds it difficult to understand them, especially what to it is the incredible degree of Nazi regimentation to which Germans submitted. Maybe it is time for Germans to take a look at how and why their society began, not for the sake of cosmetizing an image, but to make themselves more real in their own eyes. If I may quote *Incident at Vichy*, when the Jewish psychoanalyst confronts the self-blaming Austrian prince, "It's not your guilt I want, it's your responsibility." That is to say, to relinquish denial and take to heart the donations of history to one's character and the character of one's people, the most painful but rewarding job a people can undertake.

1990

The Measure of the Man

What struck me strongly about Nelson Mandela in his American public appearances, as well as our Soweto interview for BBC TV, was the absence in him of any sign of bitterness. After twenty-seven and a half years with his nose against the bars he seemed uninterested in cursing out the whites who had put him there for the crime of demanding the vote in a country where his people outnumber their rulers by about six to one.

I suppose his rather majestic poise, unmarred by rancor, lowered white defensiveness to the point where reactionaries could join with liberals in applauding his speech to Congress. But such unanimous appreciation is bound to be suspect when an honest man can hardly please everyone with his views; after all, with all his charm and civility he was still the man who had organized the African National Congress's guerrilla force, for one thing.

Watching from a distance I had found him extraordinarily straightforward in his persistent refusal to pulverize his history to suit current American tastes, crediting communists for being the first whites to befriend his movement, sometimes at the risk of their lives. Likewise, he criticized Israel and in the same breath reminded us that the overwhelming majority of his earliest supporters had been Jews.

In short, he allows himself to remain complicated; with a grandson named Gadafi (which was not his idea, however), he has written that the highest expression of democracy is the British House of Commons and the best legal system the American, with its written Bill of Rights. To me in our interview he would say that he had never joined the Communist Party. He did not add that he had never been a Marxist, but whether or not he thought he had been, I judge that he sees people in all their variety of character and deed in the foreground of events, rather than as shadowy creatures manipulated by forces, as a Marxist usually must.

I agreed to a conversation with Mandela after much hesitation, lasting a couple of weeks. The whole thing had begun with a London phone call from one Beverly Marcus, through whose South African English I discerned that she had proposed to the BBC that they film Mandela and me talking about life rather than politics, and that Mandela was receptive to the idea because he had called a halt to any more interviews in which the same simple-minded questions would inevitably be asked.

Lacking a reporter's killer instinct or investigative techniques I was simply very curious about the roots of this man's unusual character. How does one manage to emerge from nearly three decades in prison with such hopefulness, such inner calm?

But my main impulse came out of my background in New York, a racially splintered city with more than 2,000 people murdered last year. It has next to no inspiring black leadership, and so Mandela's success or failure seemed far from an academic question for me. If he can lead his riven country into a multiracial democracy the ripples could rock New York, Chicago, Detroit—and London and Europe and Israel, where the most explosive social problem is ethnicity and its unmet, often incoherent demands.

South Africa was full of surprises, the first being the fact that Beverly Marcus's younger sister, Gill, is Nelson Mandela's veritable right hand and a spokesperson for the ANC, and that their father was his accountant. I suppose I should have felt my integrity put at risk by this news, but I had never had any intention of drawing and quartering Mandela. I sought only a pathway into his nature and that of his movement. Gill, with her inside knowledge of the movement and unabashed admissions of its amateurish failings, as well as of the constantly shifting so-called tribal conflict, turned out, in fact, to be of great help in my grasping this situation.

Cape Town and the Cape area, which Beverly suggested my wife, Inge Morath, and I visit for a few days to unwind from the fourteen-hour plane trip, is an unlikely place to begin preparing for a talk with a revolutionary leader, since it is as close to Beverly Hills and the California littoral as you can get without tripping over a movie studio. Balmy air, a lazy Atlantic surf lapping white beaches, swimming pools and very good fish restaurants—I felt myself beginning to sink into its lovely lethargy.

But then one climbs a dune a hundred yards across a beach road in Hought Bay that fronts some extremely lavish homes and their tennis courts—and from the dune's ridge one looks down into a squatter town of hundreds of cardboard and tin shacks thrown one against the other right up to the edge of the sea. Don't the rich who live nearby object? Not all do—some happily sell drinking water to the blacks here who have no supply of their own. But of course this shantytown will have to go, for the view of the sea is superb here and the sand as white as sugar, a piece of prime real estate that will not be denied its promise forever.

One can drive around the Cape and Cape Town and indeed South Africa end to end without the slightest awareness that this sanitized prosperity involves only five million of its thirty million inhabitants. The famous South African schizophrenia is not hard to understand. To be sure, the back pages of the papers display ads for razor wire with which to surround one's home, and the walls surrounding most whites' homes show a metal sign reading "Instant Armed Response," and in many areas you are instructed not to stop at red lights at night lest your car be hijacked. But you quickly get used to this palpable fear, just as we have in New York, where as a child in Harlem I always carried my belongings with me to the blackboard or they'd be gone when I got back to my seat.

But South Africa is unique; it has state socialism for the whites—until very recent privitizations, sixty percent of all jobs were in state enterprises—and fascism for the blacks. Still, by the time we got back to Johannesburg after five days in the country I felt the place strange but comprehensible as merely one more kingdom of denial, unusual mainly for the immense proportion of its majority ghettoized and stripped of all civil rights.

Mandela's new house in the middle of Soweto has been criticized by some as one of Winnie Mandela's ostentations, standing as it does in the midst of the Soweto slum. Actually, donations built it. And there is a scattering of other quite good middle-class homes in the midst of the squalor, since the few successful middle-class blacks have been barred from white areas along with the poor. It is all part of a hopeless muddle of a modern technological state trying to sustain the most primitive, chest-pounding, Nazi master-race dogmas. So surrealism looms at every turn—a BMW dealership, black-owned, stands at the center of Soweto, a glass cube showroom exploding beams of white light toward houses yards away that have neither water nor sewers and whose occupants are no doubt unemployed and probably illiterate.

From the outside the Mandela house seems less elaborate than odd, a large chesty configuration of obliquely angular brick walls, an impromptu sort of construction until one is inside and realizes that it is a kind of fortress, its vulnerable dining and living rooms with their glass doors protected by a deep brick veranda extending outward some thirty feet. One drives into a receiving yard surrounded, as with so many other homes in this scared country, by a high wall with a steel, electronically controlled sliding door. And the doors of the main rooms are double-hinged to support a steel inner gate painted a discreet ivory to match the walls. Presumably these are barriers to an invading force.

Mandela's daughter, Zindzi, came into the living room pursuing her three-year-old son, both of them handsome, round-faced and no doubt accustomed to crowds of strangers in the place. Our crew was stringing its cables out; Gill Marcus was already on the phone; the floors and walls seemed covered with gifts, trophies and bric-a-brac; and now Winnie was here, explaining that she would not be eating with us because Nelson kept watching her calories and she liked to eat what she liked. Whereupon Mandela appeared, making a round gesture with both hands referring to her weight and saying "Africa!," both of them laughing while she bent to lift her rampaging grandson, whom she handed to a nurse. Even in his quick glances at her one saw his overwhelming love for his still-young wife, and she clearly basked in it. But her indictment in a murder case and impending trial seemed to hang in the air despite her tired jocularity.

Mandela was not wearing one of his formal London suits but a collarless short-sleeved African blouse with a gold-embroidered yoke—a chief's blouse, it looked to me. Gill hoped he would relax with me, and after a while he did come quite close. But he is by nature a formal, conservative man who in a peaceful country would have been chief justice of its Supreme Court or perhaps the head of a large law firm. My first question to him—after we had walked out on his veranda and looked down at Soweto, the dumping ground for human beings—was how he had been raised.

At first he sat pressed against the back of his couch, somewhat on guard, having been cornered by interviewers who find it impossible to believe that he simply means what he says. He was the son of a chief, and one could see how serious it was to be a chief's son; he had been taught early on that he would have the responsibilities of governing and judging. Even now he straightened a bit as he told with pride how, when he was ten and his father died, an uncle had taken over his education and his life. "My father occupied a position equivalent to that of prime minister in the tribe. . . . To me as a child the Transkei was the center of the entire world. . . . The missionaries tried to destroy the belief in custom and they created the perception that we have no history or culture." And with an amused grin: "When the 1939 war began we felt we were loyal subjects of the British monarch. That was the atmosphere in which we were brought up."

"And what went on inside you when the missionaries told you you had no history?"

"I'm not so sure I knew that I had a history." And later, "I must confess that Africa remained a dark continent in that I knew very little about it and I knew better about Europe, especially Britain."

This meticulous specificity, and his staid, almost Victorian structure of speech and demeanor suddenly had a root and expressed an innate authority which no doubt helped to keep him together through his prison decades. Mandela, to put it simply, *is* a chief.

And this may help explain why it has been so difficult for him to deign to confer with Mangosuthu Buthelezi of the Zulus, who have recently been on the attack against the ANC Xhosa people. Buthelezi, it is felt, helped to justify apartheid by accepting the headship of a concocted homeland where his people were dumped. It is the equivalent of a French maquisard guerrilla accepting political equality with a Vichy collaborator; there is not only a moral issue but his pride. Nevertheless, when Mandela did appear at a recent press conference with Buthelezi, the latter's people so threatened him that he was forced to leave the area.

The tribe, he insists, is basically an extended family. And in modern times there is no "natural" conflict between tribes, which are largely urbanized now, living side by side and intermarrying, joining the same unions and attending the same schools. It was the British and then the apartheid government that had always tried to tribalize Africa, pitting one against the other, setting up so-called homelands, newly founded territories that had never existed before. "There is one Africa and there will be one," Mandela said, creating a ball with his two hands.

The present conflict is "simply a conflict between two political organizations," a conflict that has failed to make headway in Soweto, as one example, because Soweto is more politically sophisticated rather than because the people are mainly Xhosa. "But when Zulus attack they never ask whether you are Zulu or something else, like the recent attack on people in the train, who do not sit according to tribes. They attack anyone."

And who would be interested in orchestrating these attacks?

He pauses before his answer, which goes to the heart of his hopes. "My belief is that Mr. de Klerk wants South Africa to take a new direction, and it is therefore difficult . . . to say that the government itself is orchestrating this violence."

De Klerk still has Mandela's confidence, it seems, but the miasma remains dense and impenetrable where some of his government's lower officials are concerned. Last July Mandela's people had gotten information that an Inkatha (Buthelezi's political organization) attack on a township was being planned and had notified the police and higher officials. The attack came off, thirty were murdered, and the police did nothing to prevent it. "I immediately went to see de Klerk. . . . Why were they allowed to enter the township when we told you beforehand that this attack was coming? . . . Mr. de Klerk is a very smart man, a strong leader. He was unable to give me an answer." However, on the day of Mandela's visit to the scene of the slaughter de Klerk personally sent four helicopters and five hundred police to protect him. And besides, "When you discuss with Mr. de Klerk he seems to have a genuine sense of shock, unlike others."

And finally, "They have either lost control over certain elements of their security forces or those elements are doing precisely what the government wants. . . . They want to negotiate with a weakened ANC. . . . You are not dealing with tribal people from the countryside but people who are sophisticated in the use of weapons, who know how to move very swiftly with military precision. . . . There are efforts now to start the Renamo movement in South Africa." (Renamo was the Rhodesian-organized mercenary outfit that murdered thousands in Mozambique.)

I turned to a discussion of his prison time. He and his comrades had originally been assured by a prison officer that they'd be out in five years because the world was so outraged by their life sentences. But five years came and went. Winnie could visit only twice a year; his children were growing up with no father. Here his face showed pain at his inability to protect his family—the helplessness desecrated his chiefly role.

Government harassment of Winnie was driving her out of one job after another until "there were certain moments when I wondered whether I had taken the correct decision of getting committed to the struggle. But at the end of these hesitations with myself I would feel that I had taken the right decision. . . . The certainty of our final victory was always there. Of course I sometimes became very angry when I thought about the persecution of my wife and that I could not give her the support she needed. I felt powerless. And also my children were hounded out of one school after another."

His vulnerability was plain here, but over it his hardness flared. This was as close as he was able to come to acknowledging what must have been the loss of hope for release before he died; instead he preferred to find something positive to emphasize. When the world began to forget him and all black movements were suppressed, the government restated that a life sentence meant life, "but in the English universities they came all-out to oppose these harsh measures. . . . People tend to forget the contribution that was made by the National Union of South African Students, which was a white organization."

This was not an opportune, upbeat recollection but his ultimate vision of a nonracial South Africa. I am convinced it is more than a tactic to recognize the absolute future need for whites who have advanced education and business prowess. It was striking how he never seemed to categorize people by race or even class, and that he spontaneously tended to cite good men even among the enemy.

"That came from my prison experience. It gets very cold on Robben Island and we had no underwear. Some warders went strictly by regulations—you were allowed two blankets. But another warder would slip you an extra one. I made some good friends among the warders; some of them visit me now."

In fact, toward the end of his imprisonment he ran "Mandela University" on Robben Island, and white warders were among his pupils. But there wasn't time to talk about this. We'd scheduled two sessions and at the last minute had to settle for one because he had to rush off to deal with the murders going on all over the place and the government's inability—or unwillingness—to keep order.

On the way back to Johannesburg that night, Gill Marcus pressed the driver on no account to stop at red lights and to drive as fast as possible through the darkness.

1991

Get It Right: Privatize Executions

The time has come to consider the privatization of executions.

There can no longer be any doubt that government—society it-self—is incapable of doing anything right, and this certainly applies to the executions of convicted criminals.

At present, the thing is a total loss, to the convicted person, to his family and to society. It need not be so.

People can be executed in places like Shea Stadium before immense paying audiences. The income from the spectacle could be distributed to the prison that fed and housed him or to a trust fund for prisoner rehabilitation and his own family and/or girlfriend, as he himself chose.

The condemned would of course get a percentage of the gate, to be negotiated by his agent or a promoter, if he so desired.

The take would, without question, be sizable, considering the immense number of Americans in favor of capital punishment. A $200 to $300 ringside seat would not be excessive, with bleachers going for, say, $25.

As with all sports events, a certain ritual would seem inevitable and would quickly become an expected part of the occasion. The electric chair would be set on a platform, like a boxing ring without the rope, around second base.

Once the audience was seated, a soprano would come forward and sing "The Star-Spangled Banner." When she stepped down, the governor, holding a microphone, would appear and describe the condemned man's crimes in detail, plus his many failed appeals.

Then the governor would step aside and a phalanx of police officers or possibly National Guard or Army troops would mount the platform and surround the condemned. This climactic entrance might be accompanied by a trumpet fanfare or other musical number by the police or Army band, unless it was thought to offend good taste.

Next, a minister or priest would appear and offer a benediction, asking God's blessing on the execution.

The condemned, should he desire, could make a short statement and even a plea of innocence. This would only add to the pathos of the occasion and would of course not be legally binding. He would then be strapped into the chair.

Finally, the executioner, hooded to protect himself from retaliation, would proceed to the platform. He would walk to a console where, on a solemn signal from the governor, he would pull the switch.

The condemned man would instantly surge upward against his bindings, with smoke emitting from his flesh. This by itself would provide a most powerful lesson for anyone contemplating murder. For those not contemplating murder, it would be a reminder of how lucky they are to have been straight and honest in America.

For the state, this would mean additional income; for the audience, an intense and educational experience—people might, for example, wish to bring their children.

And for the condemned, it would have its achievement aspect, because he would know that he had not lived his life for nothing.

Some might object that such proceedings are so fundamentally attractive that it is not too much to imagine certain individuals contemplating murder in order to star in the program. But no solution to any profound social problem is perfect.

Finally, and perhaps most important, it is entirely possible that after witnessing a few dozen privatized executions, the public might grow tired of the spectacle—just as it seizes on all kinds of entertainment only to lose interest once their repetitiousness becomes too tiresomely apparent.

Then perhaps we might be willing to consider the fact that in executing prisoners we merely add to the number of untimely dead without diminishing the number of murders committed.

At that point, the point of boredom, we might begin asking why it is that Americans commit murder more often than any other people. At the moment, we are not bored enough with executions to ask this question; instead, we are apparently going to demand more and more of them, most probably because we never get to witness any in person.

My proposal would lead us more quickly to boredom and away from our current gratifying excitement—and ultimately perhaps to a wiser use of alternating current.

1992

Lost Horizon

I must confess that I am not a proper estimator of theater in America because I see too few productions. But I have my own experience as reference as well as reports I get from writer, actor and director friends.

It seems clear, now in 1992, that we are at the end of something. Without indulging in overblown praise for theater in the Forties and Fifties, I do think that on the whole theater had far greater importance than it does now, not least for actors. Television held much less promise then of either fame, steady work or income for actors. And the movies, while always attractive to them for obvious reasons, did not gobble them up as they have since.

Judging from my own experience and that of several very active director and writer friends, theater now is a minor adjunct of the film media. It is basically a training ground for movies and television, the ultimate evidence of success. The people eager to play in theater are for one reason or another not wanted in TV or the movies. This doesn't mean they are lesser talents necessarily, merely that as types they do not attract roles in film or TV. To be blunt about it, the mature actors, people who have learned the trade and in other eras would be ready for the great roles, are not interested in theater. The money is ludicrously low compared to the film media, the work is much harder, and the chances of being blasted out of the water by critics immeasurably higher. What is the point?

When a well-known actor, not to speak of a "star," accepts a stage role now it is almost always for a limited time, three months or perhaps four or five, at most. And when a young actor who was previously unknown makes an impression in a play and is offered TV or film work, he is gone before he has practically learned all his lines. A director I know, who is probably a typical example, had a big Off-Broadway (really near-Broadway) hit recently in which the cast was replaced three times in a matter of months. The man kept directing the same play for a quarter of a year, and he does this all the time.

Can you blame the actors? I used to years ago, when, for instance, after a few months on Broadway, Lee Cobb quit the part of Willy Loman to gallop off as a movie sheriff. That cannon of an actor was using himself as a peashooter when he had a talent that could have developed into a major force in world theater. Of course he never did.

The waste of people is what bothers me. That and my own inconvenience, of course, when it is so bloody hard to find mature people for my own plays, old and new. Theater is the fifth wheel of a wagon that only really needs four.

This is not only an American dilemma, of course. Actors in London are not eager to tie themselves up for the run of play on the West End, for fear they will lose a TV series or a great film role. But what they have in London, and we don't have here, is a subsidized group of theaters which keeps alive—and sparkling so—both the old repertoire and new plays that need big and mature acting. As for France, Germany and Italy, commercial theater is barely extant, the main work being done by either tiny Off-Broadway–type theaters or the main subsidized houses.

I daren't look too far ahead for fear I will see only a downward slope for us. I think it a miracle even now when something really first-class is done, and there are a very few such productions still. It seems to me our level of work is barely acceptable most of the time, and lower than that too much of the time. And how could it be otherwise with the kind of insecurity, cynicism and haphazardness we live with? I could be wrong, but I think this country is bursting with talent—and it is being wasted like so much else that is human among us, when it is not brought up at its first youthful bloom, and then is too often tossed aside. It seems to me we don't have an American theater but only the shards of one, some of the broken pieces reflecting lights, others covered with the dust where they have fallen.

Theater is not an end only because so many people want desperately to act and write and direct and design. "Always the young strangers," as Carl Sandburg wrote. But our system is simply kicking them in the teeth most of the time. It's a pity. The vision of a prideful theater, with art rather than cynical greed at its center, is still beyond the horizon.

1992

The Good Old American Apple Pie

What a strange irony it is that at the very moment when all over Europe and Latin America repressive regimes have been driven out of power and with them their censors from office, that we Americans should be increasingly discovering the uses of censorship over our own writers and artists. The devil, as was once said, has many disguises; defeated in one place he pops up somewhere else.

Evidently there are many Americans who still do not understand why censorship and democracy cannot live happily together. What so many seem to forget is that a censor does not merely take something out, he puts something in, something of his own in a work that does not belong to him. His very purpose is to change a work to his own tastes and preconceptions.

Many forget that when they read a work that has passed through censorship, they are putting themselves in the hands of an anonymous person whose name appears nowhere and cannot be held responsible for what is published.

Perhaps we can appreciate what censorship really means by looking at a strange story that took place in Britain at the end of the eighteenth century.

A teenager named William Henry Ireland, illegitimate son of a wealthy London antique dealer, desperate to get into his father's good graces, came home one day claiming to have been given various papers in Shakespeare's hand, as well as a lock of hair of Shakespeare's wife, by a stranger whose carriage had nearly run him down on the street. Following the near accident, he and this stranger had become friends, according to young William, and as a token of the man's regard for him he had been given these invaluable papers and the lock of hair.

The elder Ireland immediately had the handwriting on the papers checked by the authorities who pronounced it Shakespeare's, and the ink and paper were without question of the Elizabethan period, nearly two centuries old. All London was agog, and the boy and his father became overnight sensations. Naturally, young Ireland, until now utterly ignored by everyone, got enthusiastic and announced that his new friend had a whole trunkful of Shakespeare's original manuscripts which he promised he might let the boy have one day.

After producing various forged snippets of Shakespeare's love notes, and a few of the Bard's "lost" verses, young Ireland (would-be poet and idolizer of the late Thomas Chatterton, another young forger-poet) proclaimed that his benefactor had decided to give him nothing less than the original manuscript of *King Lear,* but only in due time. And sure enough, after some weeks young Ireland showed up with that very manuscript. A gathering was instantly convoked in the Ireland living room where the new discovery was read to a dozen of the most authoritative literary critics, noble patrons of the arts, and cultural leaders of the time.

At the end, James Boswell, the famous biographer of Samuel Johnson, fell to his knees before the manuscript to thank God that at long last the true Shakespeare had been revealed to the world, a Shakespeare who was positive and cheerful rather than brooding and dark and defeatist, a Shakespeare who scorned foul language and never brought up sex or bodily functions, a Shakespeare who was clearly a true Christian gentleman rather than the barbaric, foul-mouthed rotter whose works had always embarrassed decent people with their obscenities and blood-covered view of mankind and the English nation.

Of course what young Ireland had done was to clean up *King Lear* to suit the narrow middle-class tastes of his time. It was a time when revolution was gathering in France, threatening to British stability, if not the idea of monarchy itself. Ireland's major fix was to brighten up the end so that the aged king, rather than raving on the heath, swamped in his madness and abandoned by the world, was reunited with his daughters in a comforting sentimental scene of mutual Christian forgiveness, whereupon they all lived happily ever after. The paper on which this version was written was indeed authentic, the young forger having snipped off sheets of it from the blank ends of Elizabethan wills and deeds in the files of the London law office where he worked as a clerk. The antique ink he had produced himself after months of lonely experiment.

Only one critic, Edmund Malone, saw through the forgery, but he did not expose the fraud by analyzing ink or paper but rather the mawkishness of the "newly discovered" alterations, the shallow naïveté behind their versification. But as important as any technical doubts was his conviction that the spirit behind this "new-found authentic *King Lear*" was pawky, narrow-minded, fearful of sexuality and the lustiness of the English tongue, and fearful too of the play's awesome image of human judgment's frailty, and the collapse of the very foundations in reason of government itself. The real *King Lear* reduces man to his elemental nature, stripping him of rank and money and his protective morality, in order to present a vision of the essence of humankind with no ameliorating illusions. In place of these challenges the "newly discovered" play was a story of reassurance fit for family entertainment, one that offers comfort by turning a far-ranging tragedy into a story of misunderstandings which are pleasantly cleared up at the end.

In a word, young William Ireland did what censorship always attempts to do—force a work to conform to what *some* people want life to look like even if it means destroying the truth the work is written to convey.

Had the Ireland forgery been left uncontested, we can be sure that *King Lear* as a play would never have survived the hour. Many critics then and since have thought it a nasty work with an improbably black estimate of humanity, but succeeding generations have come to treasure it precisely for its truthfulness to life's worst as well as its best.

What Ireland did was erase the doubts about life that were in the original play and were so discomforting to the upper class of Britain at the time.

Censorship is as old as America. The Puritans forbade the reading of novels—or, indeed, anything but scripture—as one of the condemned "vain pursuits." A reader nowadays would find it impossible to recognize in those novels what could possibly have aroused the Puritan fathers to such fury against them. But closer to our time, there is hardly a master writer who has not felt the censor's lash, from James Joyce to Gustave Flaubert to D. H. Lawrence to Hemingway and Fitzgerald, to William Faulkner and a long, long list that just about comprises the roster of world literature. Someone somewhere could doubtless find reasons for moral outrage in a McDonald's menu or a phone book.

Of course there is no denying that there are people who misuse freedom to appeal to the sinister in us, our brutality, scorn for justice, or concealed violence and lust. By exploiting our suppressed feelings people with no interest in anything but making an illicit buck can prosper, for example, by exploiting human sexual curiosity even if it victimizes children.

But the problem, clearly, is that when we legitimize censorship of what we agree is antisocial art we come very close to legitimizing it for real art. For example, right now some three hundred and fifty lines of *Romeo and Juliet* are customarily removed from American school textbooks because they are about sex. There is a similar emasculation of the two other most commonly taught Shakespeare plays, *Julius Caesar* and *Macbeth*. In other words, lines of very high poetry are forbidden American students who, it is assumed, will think that much less often about sex. Of course this is ridiculous; all this censoring does is deprive them of realizing that there is something sublime and beautiful in sex and that it is not merely dirty. It throws them entirely to the mercies of suggestive videos and rock lyrics and really raw pornography which apparently nothing will stop, and will certainly not be slowed by censoring *Romeo and Juliet*.

The purported aim of censorship is always to preserve public morality but we ought not forget that for those who advocate censorship pornography is by no means necessarily the only kind of immoral communication. If it becomes established policy that blotting out certain sexual images in art is acceptable, then there is nothing in principle to stop the censoring of other "immoral" expression.

I have had some experience with "moral" censorship myself. In 1947, my play *All My Sons* was about to open in the Colonial Theatre, Boston, for its first performances before coming to Broadway. The Catholic Church at that time exercised censorship over the Boston theaters and threatened to issue a condemnation of the play unless a certain line were eliminated from it. I should add that the raunchiest burlesque shows in America were playing on the Boston "Strip" at the time, but these apparently were not bothersome to the moral authorities. What troubled them terribly was the line, "A man can't be a Jesus in this world!" spoken by Joe Keller, a character who has knowingly shipped defective engine parts to the Air Force resulting in twenty-odd fighter planes crashing and who is now pleading for his son's forgiveness. The name of Jesus was forbidden utterance on the Boston stage, no matter that in this case it was used to indicate Jesus' high moral standard. I refused to change the line, as much because I could not think of a substitute as anything else, but the hypocrisy of the complaint was painful to contemplate, given the level of entertainment of the Boston "Strip" a few blocks from my theater.

In 1962, when my film *The Misfits* was previewed by religious censors, the gravest displeasure was expressed with a scene in which Marilyn Monroe, in a mood of despair and frustration—fully clothed, it should be said—walks out of a house and embraces a tree trunk. In all seriousness this scene was declared to be masturbation, and unless it was cut the picture would be classified as condemned and a large part of the audience barred from seeing it. Once again it was necessary to refuse to oblige a censor, but I would not have had that privilege had I lived in a different kind of country. Experiences like these have helped me to stand against censorship.

Life is not reassuring; if it were we would not need the consolations of religion, for one thing. Literature and art are not required to reassure when in reality there is no reassurance, or to serve up "clean and wholesome" stories in all times and all places. Those who wish such art are welcome to have it, but those who wish art to symbolize how life really is, in order to understand it and perhaps themselves, also have a right to their kind of art.

I would propose to censors and their supporters that they write the stories and paint or shoot the pictures they approve of, and let them offer them to the public in open competition with the stories and pictures of those whose works they want to suppress.

Let them write a new *Romeo and Juliet* that is wholesome and unoffending and put it on a stage and invite the public to come and enjoy it as millions have enjoyed Shakespeare's play for three hundred years. Who knows?—maybe they will win out.

But of course they cannot accept this challenge; censorship is an attack on healthy competition. It comes down to a refusal to enter the arena and instead to wipe out the competitor by sanctions of suppressive writs and the police power.

I write this as one who is often disgusted by certain displays that call themselves art and are really raids on the public's limitless sexual curiosity, purely for the purpose of making money. As an artist I sometimes wonder at my having to compete with this easy and specious way of attracting attention and gaining a public following. And I will not deny my belief that there may ultimately be a debasement of public taste as the result of the incessant waves of sexual exploitation in films and other media.

But bad as this is, it is not as bad as censorship, because the censor is given a police power no individual ought to have in a democracy—the power not only to keep bad art from the public, but good art, too; the power not only to protect people from lies but from uncomfortable truths. That way lies not wholesomeness, not community values, but the domination of the many by the few acting in the name of the many. Nobody said it was easy to be a free people, but censorship not only makes it harder, it makes it in the end impossible.

Probably because we in general enjoy freedom to express ourselves we are unaware of not only the power that a censor takes but the hypocrisy that inevitably accompanies it. In the winter of 1965 I interviewed a lady in her Moscow offices, one Madame Elena Furtseva, then head of all culture of the Soviet Union. In theory and often in practice this woman and the committee she headed had the power to shut down any play before or during its run in a theater, or to cancel a film or suppress a novel or book of poems or whatever. She could also promote certain books if she so pleased. She had been Khrushchev's special friend and when he was ousted she cut her wrists but was saved and restored to her job.

Behind her chair was a long table piled high with at least a hundred books lying on their sides. Each volume had a few slips of paper sticking out of its pages which I deduced marked passages of censorable writing which her assistants were submitting to her to decide upon.

She looked quite exhausted and I remarked sympathetically on this. "Well I have so much I must read, you see," she said, and gestured toward the possibly offending books behind her.

With nothing to lose—my U.S. passport snug in my pocket, I ventured: "You know, I have never met writers anywhere who are as patriotic as your Russian writers. Whatever their criticisms, they have a deep love of country. Why don't you make an experiment; don't tell anybody but let's say for one month just don't read anything. See what happens. Maybe nothing will happen. Then you won't have to be reading all this stuff every day."

She tried hard for a sophisticated smile but it came out looking hard and painful. And then she said something interesting: "The Soviet worker cannot be asked to pay for the paper and ink to print ideas that go counter to his interests and his moral ideas of right and wrong."

I can't help thinking of that statement when I hear people saying that the American taxpayers ought not be asked to pay for artworks that offend their tastes or their ideas of right and wrong. The fundamental fallacy in such a statement is quite simple and inexorable; how did Madame Furtseva know what the Soviet worker thought was right and wrong, moral or immoral? How *could* she know when no one but her and her assistants were allowed to read possibly offending works?

Indeed, for nearly three-quarters of a century Soviet writing has been kept remarkably chaste, with very strict rules about depicting sex, while at the same time the Soviet abortion rate was rising to the highest in the world. It was also very strict about barring negative pictures of Soviet conditions in all the media and forbade any genuine attack on the system. After three-quarters of a century of such censorship the Soviet system appears to have collapsed. Why? Because reality does not go away when a censor draws a line through a sentence or tears a page out of *Romeo and Juliet*.

If there is a way to curb pornography, if there is any possibility of preventing people from lathering after obscene material, it can only be the result of changing their tastes. If they don't want the stuff it won't be profitable and it will vanish. I doubt that day will ever come, no matter what, but surely cursing the darkness never brought light. Through education raising the intelligence level of the population, sensitizing people to real rather than cosmetic feeling, enhancing mutual respect between the sexes and between races—these are the paths to decency, not calling in the cops to drive out the bad guys.

There is an analogy here to the narcotics problem. We spend tens of millions on planes to spot smugglers, more millions to wipe out Peruvian coca crops, more millions on narcotics police; but of course the narcotics keep coming in because Americans want dope. Meantime, an addict who wants to get rid of the habit has to wait as long as a couple of years to get placed in a rehabilitation clinic because these are underfunded.

Censoring Shakespeare won't make us good and may possibly make us a little more stupid, a little more ignorant about ourselves, a little further from the angels. The day must come when we will stop being so foolish. Why not now?

1993

The Parable of the Stripper

The Yugoslav catastrophe raises, for me, an especially terrible and comical memory. In the 1960s I presided over the congress of International PEN that was held in Bled, a beautiful resort town built around a crystal-clear lake high in the lovely mountains of Slovenia. Bled had been the watering hole for generations of Europeans, a fairy-tale place. And it was already more than a decade since Tito had broken with Moscow.

Marxist intellectuals in Yugoslavia were remarkably open in their criticisms of the economy and politics of the country. That the system needed deep changes was taken for granted, and new concepts were being floated that would free individual initiative while retaining the social gains of the communist system. Worker ownership of factories was being tried, and identical consumer products, such as radios, were given different names in order to spur competition between factories, in the hope of raising quality and lowering prices. Yugoslavia was prodding the limits of socialism; and to come there from the dictatorships of Hungary, Czechoslovakia, East Germany, not to mention Russia, was to experience the shock of fresh air. In the Sixties Yugoslavia the place seemed filled with enormous energy. These were the proudest, friendliest people I had met in Europe, and the most frank and open.

There was one taboo, unmentioned but obvious: the ethnic nationalism that Tito had ruthlessly suppressed. I knew, of course, that Slovenians, Bosnians, Serbs, Croatians, Montenegrins and other nationalities made up the Yugoslav delegation to the PEN congress, but to me they all looked alike and conversed in a mutually understood language, so their differences might be no more flammable than those separating the Welsh and the English, or maybe even Texans and Minnesotans. And when I asked an individual, out of curiosity, if he was Croatian or Slovenian or whatever, and the question caused a slight uneasiness, it seemed minimal enough to be dismissed as more or less irrelevant in this rapidly modernizing country.

Then one evening a group of four writers, one of them a Serb journalist friend called Bogdan, invited me out for a drink after dinner. Two of my companions were poets, a Croatian and a Montenegrin, and one a Slovenian professor. We walked down the road to the local nightclub that usually catered to tourists. The room was very large, like a ballroom. There were maybe fifty bare, plastic-covered tables, only a few of them occupied by stolid, square-headed Alpine types. The cold night air was not noticeably heated. The place had the feeling of a big Pittsburgh cafeteria between meals.

Then a three-piece band took places on a platform up front and began tootling American jazz standards, and a woman materialized and stood unsmilingly facing the audience. Small and compact, she wore a matching brown skirt and jacket and a shiny white rayon blouse. In a businesslike way, she began undressing, in what I was informed was to be a delightful striptease. The scattered audience of men and their chunky women silently gulped beer and sipped slivovitz as the dancer removed her suit jacket, her shoes, her blouse and her skirt, until she stood looking out upon us in her pink rayon slip and bra. It was all done rather antiseptically, as if preparing for a medical examination. Each garment was tidily laid out and patted down on the piano bench, there being no pianist.

Then she stepped out of her slip, and in her panties did a few routine steps in approximate time to the music. She had very good legs. Things were heating up. From somewhere she picked up a heavy blue terry cloth robe and, wrapped in it, she slipped off her bra and flashed one breast. My fellow writers broke off their dying conversation. I don't know what got into me, but I asked a fatal question: "Can you tell from looking at her what her nationality is?"

My Serb friend Bogdan, depressed by his wife's absence in Belgrade, since it had left him for an entire week to the mercies of his melancholy mistress, glanced across the room at the stripper, and gave his morose opinion: "I would say she could be Croatian."

"Impossible!" the Croatian poet laughed. And with a sharpened eye and a surprising undertone of moral indignation, he added, "She could never be Croatian. Maybe Russian, or Slovenian, but not Croatian."

"Slovenian!" The mocking shout came from the Slovenian literature professor, a tall, thin fellow with shoulder-length hair. "Never! She has absolutely nothing Slovenian about her. Look how dark she is! I would say from the South, maybe Montenegrin."

The dark-skinned Montenegrin poet sitting beside me simply exploded in a challenging "Ha!" Just a few minutes earlier, he had been ethnically relaxed enough to tell a joke on his own people. Montenegrins are apparently famous for their admirably lethargic natures. One of them, said the poet, was walking down a street when he suddenly whipped out his revolver and, swiveling about, shot a snail on the sidewalk behind him. His energetic Serbian friend asked what the hell he had done that for. The Montenegrin explained, "He's been following me all day!"

When it came to the stripper, however, humor had noticeably evaporated, as each of the men kept handing her over to somebody else. And in the middle of this warming discussion of ethnic types, I noticed that the dancer had left the platform in her thick terry cloth robe, with her clothes cradled neatly in her arms. She was just about to pass us when I stuck out my arm and stopped her. "May I ask where you come from?" With a wan, polite smile, she replied "Düsseldorf," and continued on her way.

None of the writers allowed himself to laugh, though I thought one or two blushed at the irony of the situation. A bit tense, struggling awkwardly to reconstruct the earlier atmosphere of comradely warmth, we strolled through the dark Balkan night, the president and four distinguished delegates of the writers' organization established after World War I by H. G. Wells, George Bernard Shaw, Henri Barbusse and other war-weary writers as an attempt to apply the universalist tradition of literature to the melting down of those geographical and psychological barriers of nationalism for whose perpetuation humanity has always spent its noblest courage, and its most ferocious savagery.

1994

Let's Privatize Congress

It is great news, this idea of selling a House office building now that the Republicans are dissolving so many committees and firing their staffs. But I wouldn't be surprised if this is only the opening wedge for a campaign to privatize Congress. Yes, let the free market openly raise its magnificent head in the most sacred precincts of the Welfare State.

The compelling reasons for privatizing Congress are perfectly evident. Everybody hates it, only slightly less than they hate the president. Everybody, that is, who talks on the radio, plus millions of the silent who only listen and hate in private.

Congress has brought on this hatred, mainly by hypocrisy. For example, members are covered by complete government-run health insurance—while the same kind of coverage for the voters was defeated, with the voters' consent and support, no less.

The voters, relieved that they are no longer menaced by inexpensive health insurance administered by the hated government, must nevertheless be confused about not getting what polls show they wanted.

The important point is that even though they are happy at being denied what they say they want, they also know that the campaign to defeat health insurance was financed by the big private health insurance companies to the tune of millions of dollars paid to congressional campaigns. The net result is that with all their happiness, the voters are also aware of a lingering sense of congressional hypocrisy.

Health care is only one of many similar issues—auto safety, the environment, education, the use of public lands, etc. The way each issue is decided affects the finances of one or another business, industry or profession, and these groups naturally tend to butter the bread of members of Congress.

We can do away with this hypocrisy by making Congress a private enterprise. Let each representative and senator openly represent, and have his salary paid by, whatever business group wishes to buy his vote. Then, with no excuses, we will really have the best representative system money can buy. No longer will absurdly expensive election campaigns be necessary. Anyone wanting the job of congressional representative of, say, the drug industry could make an appointment with the council of that industry and make his pitch.

The question arises whether we would need bother to go through the whole election procedure. But I think we must continue to ask the public to participate lest people become even more alienated than they are now, with only thirty-nine percent of the eligible voters going to the polls in November.

A privatized Congress might well attract a much higher percentage of voters than the present outmoded one does because the pall of hypocrisy would have been stripped away and a novel bracing honesty would attract voters to choose whichever representative of the auto or real estate industries or the date growers they feel most sympathy for.

Once Congress is privatized, the time would have come to do the same to the Supreme Court and the Justice Department. If each justice were openly hired by a sector of the economy to protect its interests, a simple bargaining process could settle everything. The Auto Industry justice, wishing to throw out a suit against General Motors or Ford, could agree to vote his support for the Agribusiness justice, who wanted to quash a suit by workers claiming to have been poisoned while picking cabbages.

Some will object that such a system of what might be called legalized corruption would leave out the public and its interests. But this is no longer a problem when you realize that there is no public and therefore no public interest in the old sense. As Margaret Thatcher once said, "There is no society," meaning that the public consists of individuals, all of whom have private interests that to some degree are hostile to the interests of other individuals.

Possible objections: the abstract idea of justice would disappear under a system that takes only private economic interests into account. Secondly, the corporate state, which this resembles, was Mussolini's concept and resulted in the looting of the public by private interests empowered by the state.

Objections to the objections: we already have a corporate state. All privatization would do would be to recognize it as a fact.

Conclusion: we are in bad trouble.

1995

On Mark Twain's Chapters
from My Autobiography

O ne of the books that as a teenager tore me from the football field to the library was *A Connecticut Yankee in King Arthur's Court*. It may be a flawed book, but it made a friend of Mark Twain for life, and if in later years I came to question the innate superiority of a scientific civilization over one based on supernatural faith, I must in the end bow before the undeniable—it is better to be vaccinated against cholera than to land in India with one's blood in its virginal purity.

I am not at all sure that every one of his sentences is golden, not to speak of his paragraphs, but he somehow managed—despite a steady underlying seriousness few writers have matched—to step around the pit of self-importance and to keep his membership in the ordinary human race in the front of his mind and his writing. His wit notwithstanding, he found the ways to let his feelings show, even his sentiments. In this he is not modern, incidentally, when so much of the late century's writing is one or another version of camp, our preferred tonality above all others. One cannot, for example, read his anguished record of his daughter Susy's death and its effects upon him without admiring not only his stoicism in being able to write at all on so painful a subject, but his maintaining so fine a balance between a flow of genuine feeling and the restraint of a man trying to stay lucid after a mortal blow to his sanity. But one must beware of ascribing too definite a purpose in Mark Twain's writing; he wrote, or affected to, for a living, but in reality because he had to, in the way water has to boil when it is heated.

He seems always to have been an observer of himself, albeit an often mystified one, as well as of the world. "I was born reserved as to endearments of speech and caresses, and hers [his young wife's] broke upon me as the summer waves break upon Gibraltar. I was reared in that atmosphere of reserve. . . . I never knew a member of my father's family to kiss another member of it except once, and that at a death-bed." And indeed, it was only to ask to be allowed to die that the kiss was given by the dying man.

He is cool but without the duplicity of camp, which after all is a strategy of indicating feeling in place of feeling very much, thus escaping any commitment which might make embarrassingly visible the heart on the sleeve, or worse yet the absence of any heart at all. Twain's style is different. He admits to his feelings, and in full-throatedly saying so he often moves us just before he makes sure to mock himself. But what supports this acerbic distancing is his announced role as a lifelong witness to his experience rather than a participant. I suppose what also keeps his sentiment from overflowing is his incredible truthfulness. One never feels one is being worked over, pumped for sympathy or anything else. He seems to be saying, quite simply, Here are the facts of myself on this occasion. And of course he manages to express this distancing through what might be called his confessional laughter. Speaking of the large prices paid at auction for some of his old letters, and comparing them to the lower prices brought by General Grant's: "I can't rise to General Grant's lofty place in the estimation of this nation, but it is a deep happiness to me to know that when it comes to epistolary literature he can't sit in the front seat along with me." He has not only beaten Grant out but is enjoying it, and that's funny because its truth threatens our defenses against admitting the pleasure of besting someone we respect.

Clemens, as this autobiography reminds us again and again, was an alienated man, but with the difference that he admits to sharing the absurdities himself which he has observed and often ruthlessly criticizes in others. He seems to have seen his role, and probably the role of literature in general, differently than most cultural observers presently see theirs. He is not using his alienation from the public illusions of his hour in order to reject the country implicitly as though he could live without it, but manifestly in order to correct it. The notion of a lost generation, for instance, something which recrudesces with almost every generation from the expatriates of the Twenties to the Beats and onward, would be beyond his imagining; he is very much part of what needs changing. But by the onset of the twentieth century the human race had not yet crossed over the line at which its insanities could no longer be easily forgiven. I can think of two possible reasons that he stops short of giving up on the whole race, including its corrupted politics; first, because doomsday thinking was not yet the style which would come on after the two world wars, plus the fascist and communist depredations and the dawning awareness among the civilized of the physical and psychic damage of racism; and second, because Clemens wrote much more like a father than a son. He doesn't seem to be sitting in class taunting the teacher but standing at the head of it challenging his students to acknowledge their own humanity, that is, their immemorial attraction to the untrue. Nor does he spare himself, except indirectly by virtue of bringing up, time and again and in a host of disguises, the whole matter of lying. If you peel off some of its hilarity, his book is a litany of treachery, deceit, mendacity unmasked—odd if you think of him as the American Homer, the writer *sui generis,* more than any other the surveyor who marked the boundaries of American literature.

He can't stop his boasting, especially now in his old age, quickly following up by puncturing whatever balloon he has just inflated. Tracing his lineage, whose distinction in Britain he has just been bragging about, he quickly comes down to earth with "But I am forgetting the first Clemens— the one that stands furthest back toward the original *first* Clemens, which was Adam."

Clemens, a second son, writes as though he were the eldest. His older brother, Orion, was a touchingly inept man who flew from perch to perch all his life and never found one where he felt comfortable, and Henry, two years younger, was apparently a rather dull fellow whose role in the family was to bore their mother with his tedious goodness until she turned for relief to Sam and his pranks, wisecracks and unexpectedness. Looking back over his seventy years, Clemens seems to see himself as the preferred child, and maybe this helps account for the air of confident, abundant love which lies just below the surface of these recollections. If a more skeptical author would be hard to find—"Carlyle said 'a lie cannot live.' It shows that he did not know how to tell them"—he can speak in almost the same breath of his daughter's death in some of the most nakedly painful prose imaginable: "It is one of the mysteries of our nature that a man, all unprepared, can receive a thunder-stroke like that and live." His hard-edged, hard-eyed contempt seems not to have interfered with admissions of grief, empathy, limitless affection and weakness. Perhaps this accounts for the devotion he seems never to have lost among his countrymen. In the end readers love love.

Apart from his never completing it, I am not sure—not that it matters—that this is an autobiography in any proper sense. It is rather a string of riffs on themes that rise and fall out of consciousness. That it was not written but dictated, talked out, no doubt helps explain the lack of formal structure. But this looseness tends to lend the text more credence as a spontaneous record of the author's own contradictions as well as those of his time. It is interesting to note what he apparently felt were the limits that a prudish churchgoing America would expect him to observe. The Clemens childrens' fifteen-year-old German nanny was "a clear-souled little maiden and without offense, notwithstanding her profanities, and she was loaded to the eyebrows with them. . . . She was always scattering her profanities around, and they were such a satisfaction to me that I never dreamed of such a thing as modifying her." Yet revealing his admiration for a cussing young woman was one thing, quoting her in plain English was another. One day, finishing with the tedious job of braiding the girls' hair, the nanny exploded to heaven, "Gott sei Dank ich bin fertig mit'm Gott verdammtes Haar!" To which Clemens added, "I believe I am not brave enough to translate it." If the nanny's expostulation—"Thank God I am finished with this goddamned hair"—really breached the propriety of the time, I wonder whether some of Clemens's popularity reflected a near-scandalous titillation with the shock of his candor. Through most or all of his writing life, after all, nothing of a respectable woman's body could be seen outside her bedroom except her hands and face, and there was hardly a household furnishing, from a lamp to a window shade to a drape to a chair seat, whose modesty was not suggested by a discreet fringe.

Mark Twain could not have existed anywhere but in America not only because the very web of his work is woven out of our geography, our spaces, rivers, mountains; it is also because there are no sexually alive women in his writings. His women are ideals, vapors, mothers and aunts who are almost always wise protectors of hearth and home, or virginal girls who are never pursued or are not old enough to be married. It is not a question of hostility toward women on his part; they seem never to threaten him at all. It is more likely the simple blindness of the culture toward the feminine, which, as with practically every other American trait, he exemplified.

American prudery, needless to say, is still alive just beneath the surface, awaiting the hypocrite's rousing touch. But nowadays it takes other forms, some of them of political importance. Early in Bill Clinton's presidency he was nearly brought down by charges of having had sex some years ago with a lady of doubtful morals. Had the real and pretended feelings of moral outrage evoked by this charge been permitted to skew the images of our former chief executives, we should have been without the services of—let's see now—Washington, Jefferson, probably Jackson, Cleveland, Harding, Roosevelt, Eisenhower, and Kennedy, among others, which would have left us to the characterological flavorings of Chester Arthur, Calvin Coolidge, Herbert Hoover and Richard Nixon. Admittedly, we might pepper the pot with Harry Truman, but what improvement a president's marital fidelity or lack of it bestows upon his official service it is not possible to speculate. All we can be sure of is that since some time around the Kennedy administration, the American press, obedient as ever to the zeitgeist, has done what it could not have done in Clemens's time—stationed itself at the keyholes of politicians' bedroom doors and reported the findings. That the public weal is benefited is doubtful; what is clear is that stoking suspicion of hanky-panky makes it easier to kid the public that a villain who never cheats on his wife (Nixon, for instance) is thereby to be granted high moral grades as public servant—an invitation to calamity.

Who was Mark Twain writing for? The question becomes important when one realizes that he is still selling in the millions and certainly sold in the hundreds of thousands during his lifetime. To be sure, he is plain-spoken, but there is an elegance here and an irony whose appreciation requires an uncustomary patience in a contemporary reader. As universally popular as he was, he vigorously disdained the major political parties of his time and their leaders. Was there more tolerance in America then, or simply greater self-certainty? Clemens's eagerness for popularity notwithstanding, he declared himself a mugwump, in effect a political independent of a kind some would have condemned for an aristocratic contempt of rank-and-file party adherents, i.e., the very people themselves. Manifestly he refused to pander to the loyalists of any party, to the point where almost every reference to a party is touched with ridicule. Yet he was clearly passionate about the need for honest men in government in an age when corruption was rife, and there was no surrender, at least none that is obvious, to cynicism and despair, for he was always quick to note the honest citizen who deserved his compliment.

It has been noted before that the final years of a century are often touched with foreboding of the millennial judgment approaching, the last days. This was the case as the century turned in America. The democratic promise was being overwhelmed by the greed of unprincipled, socially irresponsible forces, the moneygrubbers, the little foxes who spoil the vineyards, uncontrolled capitalism. "The Gilded Age" was an enduring title invented by Mark Twain much earlier, and his last books are indeed darkened by forebodings of the ruin of the country's early promise. In this autobiography is probably his most unmitigated prophecy of approaching doom.

> Human nature being what it is, I suppose we must expect to drift into monarchy by and by. It is a saddening thought, but we cannot change our nature; we are all alike, we human beings; and in our blood and bone we carry the seeds out of which monarchies and aristocracies are grown: worship of gauds, titles, distinctions, power. We have to worship these things and their possessors, we are all born so, and we cannot help it. We have to be despised by somebody whom we regard as above us, or we are not happy; we have to have somebody to worship and envy, or we cannot be content. . . . Like all other nations, we worship money and the possessors of it—they being our aristocracy, and we have to have one. We like to read about rich people in the papers. . . . "Rich Woman Fell Down Cellar—Not Hurt." The falling down the cellar is of no interest to us when the woman is not rich.

The republic, he continues, is inexorably heading for monarchy, "but I believe that if we obstruct these encroachments and steadily resist them the monarchy can be postponed for a good while yet." His political awareness was of course acute, and for all his scoffing at any direct influence of his own on public events, it seems implicit that he hoped his work would be useful in the struggle to maintain a democracy. But what did his audience make of this commitment? Or did they simply skip over it to enjoy his humor and tales? After all, some of his heartiest admirers were the great millionaire capitalists of the time as well as the leading politicians, men whose like manned the legislatures which, as the common saying went, were the best that money could buy.

Clemens was always the artist first and foremost, and the artist is a liar who, in Harold Clurman's phrase, tells lies that are like truth. Here as elsewhere in Clemens's canon there are a number of charming, innocuous-seeming stories which, intentionally or not, are metaphors of the artist's moral situation. There is his story of the mesmerist who performed in Hannibal when he was a boy of fourteen and wanted to stand before the town dripping with glamour. The mesmerist would select members of the audience, put them in trances, and control their actions by his commands. The young Clemens eagerly submitted himself, but unlike others, he could never manage to escape his stubborn consciousness. Finally, in order to astound the credulous audience, he faked a hypnotic state, pretending to carry out the mesmerist's orders. So convincing was his spirited acting that he quickly became a favorite subject for the mesmerist, who obviously knew a good thing when he saw it. But not everyone in the audience was convinced. A clutch of elderly men thought he was faking until in one of his trances he began recalling the details of a long-forgotten theater fire which he had once overheard them talking about, unbeknownst to them. Amazed by his "vision" of an event which only they were old enough to have witnessed, they rallied to his side and helped lift him triumphantly over any doubters in the audience.

But having hit once, he had to repeat. One evening, spotting a local bully who had been making his life miserable, he fell into his usual trance and then suddenly grabbed a rusty revolver off a prop table, leaped from the stage and took out after his persecutor, who fled in terror. Uproar! But the mesmerist assured the frightened audience that the Clemens boy could not possibly have done any damage because he had been under mesmeric control the whole time and would have been stopped by the great mind-pilot before he could shoot anybody. Clemens had now become a veritable star in the mesmerized-performer business, walking proof of the power of hypnosis. "It is curious," he writes. "When the magician's engagement closed there was but one person in the village who did not believe in mesmerism, and I was the one." And here speaks the artist surrounded by his trunks filled with stringed puppets, his technique, and his bag of tricks which sweep the public imagination as mere fact never can. Again, the human mind loves the lie which ironically can be made beautiful in the shape of art.

It needs no special psychiatric sensibility to note that his first subject after this public triumph of his boyhood is his mother, and how he entertained her with his lies. Visiting the lady thirty-five years after these "evil exploits of mine"—and after an unexplained hiatus of more than ten years during which he failed to visit her—he is filled with remorse, not only for having ignored her but for having convinced her, his own mother, with the lie that he was so famously mesmerized so long ago. He resolves to confess himself. The consequence is typical Clemens, and a bit strange.

By this time he had long felt revulsion at his ill-earned fame in Hannibal, based on fraud as it indeed had been. It is very odd, the depth of this self-revulsion at what would seem a boyish prank, and stranger still that he sustained the sensation for nearly four decades. "How easy it is to make people believe a lie, and how hard it is to undo that work again!" Only after much anguish can he bring himself to tell her the truth, in dread "of the sorrow that would rise in her face and the shame that would look out of her eyes," but "after long and troubled reflection" he makes his confession.

Naturally, being Clemens's mother, she rejects the confession, calmly insisting that after so many years he can't possibly remember accurately what happened, and that as a witness to his victory she is sure he earned it honestly and was certainly under the mesmerist's control. Her turning his guilt away alarms him. He protests that he had no "vision" at all of the theater fire as he pretended, but merely overheard the men talking about it some time earlier. And more, the mesmerist's trick of pushing needles into his arm while he showed no pain was also a fraud, for he was in fact in agony, just as he would be now if she stuck pins into his flesh.

But she is tranquilly adamant in her belief in him. "I was nettled, to have my costly truthfulness flung out of the market in this placid and confident way when I was expecting to get a profit out of it." In short, she denies him absolution in favor of his artistic triumph, his power and fame which she loves, and far more than she loves his picky purity. In effect, she rejects the real him and the bared soul he has offered her. And here is the artist's complicated disgust with his art, the disgust mixed with equal amounts of pride plus the feeling of control over the imaginations of other people and his guilt at having planted images in their minds which he alone knows are hot air molded to beautiful and sometimes meaningful forms. It is all a lie, a lie like truth. Again, there is a certain indefinable sadness an inch beneath Mark Twain's happy art, like a painful longing for some elusive reconciliation which lends it an indefinable depth. There is hardly a story in this autobiography which does not pose the lie against the truth; and the victory of the lie leaves everyone basking contentedly in life's normative stasis. The victory of untruth and illusion simply doesn't matter one way or the other in the long scheme of things, and yet it is important to Clemens that there be honest people in the world.

Reading along, one becomes aware of being spoken to by this book, that it is really a chat, something that in our day could easily be turned into half a dozen tapes to be played in the car. It is wonderfully visual, full of recollected pictures, the best kind of listening. You can just about hear him laughing, or his voice growing husky in the sad parts. Clearly there are long rambles with no particular thematic relevance beyond the simple pleasure of the telling, like rummaging through cabinets and closets and trying on discarded shoes, old gloves and a half-remembered jacket or two.

He thinks he once remembered his brother Henry walking into a fire when he was six months old; it took years for him to realize that walking is impossible at that age. But memory, he believes, has no morals and no rules. "When I was younger I could remember anything, whether it had happened or not; but my faculties are decaying now, and soon I shall be so I cannot remember any but the things that happened." But of course there are more rules to memory than his pre-Freudian time suspects. At another point in his ramble he has the remarkable experience of dreaming yet again of Henry's death and of his lying in a metal coffin and being covered with white flowers, with a red rose in the center. This is followed by Clemens's great relief at realizing, within the dream, that it is only a dream. But a short time later the dream turns out to have been prophetic. His brother has indeed died, possibly as a result of the ineptitude of a young physician, and is laid out, with no help from Clemens but precisely as in his dream, in a metal coffin, with white flowers covering him and a red rose in their center.

In view of recent objections to Clemens's attitudes toward slavery and black people, it comes as a surprise to read his apparently spontaneous words about them, written, as far as I am aware, not in any defensive spirit but simply as memorable fact no different from other recollections in his mind at the moment, the turn of the century. Of the slave after whom he modeled Jim as well as other of his black characters, a man whom life has badly used, and who "has endured . . . with the patience and friendliness and loyalty which were his birthright," Clemens says, "It was [from him] that I got my strong liking for his race and my appreciation of certain of its fine qualities. This feeling and this estimate have stood the test of sixty years and more and have suffered no impairment. The black face is as welcome to me now as it was then." One can't help sensing a subconscious agenda behind such remarks (there are others like it), a personal affirmation before the majority of Americans, who by the turn of the century—a time when American black life was as hopelessly oppressive as South Africa's would later be—were light-years away from so warm and positive an opinion.

In essence, the book is a valediction. There is overall a tone of farewell, of a life's work done. Naturally, Clemens can't sustain this idea too long and is soon back to his old habit of making things up out of half-remembered fragments of his life and writing. And the book is at the same time a confession, unique in his works, of the superstitious streak that accompanied his lifelong skepticism.

> I think that in *Tom Sawyer* I starved Injun Joe to death in a cave. But that may have been to meet the exigencies of romantic literature. I can't remember now whether the real Injun Joe died in the cave or out of it, but I do remember that the news of his death reached me at a most unhappy time—that is to say, just at bedtime on a summer night when a prodigious storm of thunder and lightning accompanied by a deluging rain that turned the streets and lanes into rivers, caused me to repent and resolve to lead a better life. . . . By my teachings I perfectly well knew what all that wild riot was for—Satan had come to get Injun Joe. . . . With every glare of lightning I shrivelled and shrunk together in mortal terror, and in the interval of black darkness that followed I poured out my lamentings over my lost condition, and my supplications for just one more chance, with an energy and feeling and sincerity quite foreign to my nature.
>
> But in the morning I saw that it was a false alarm and concluded to resume business at the old stand and wait for another reminder.

The prophetic dreams in this book—I believe he mentions three that come to mind in this connection—all concern death, and each precedes the actual death of the person dreamed of, and in precisely the dream situation. Mark Twain at seventy was gathering his powers unto himself; the same man who went through deep depressions that may well have tempted him with suicide was demonstrating for his own benefit and for the world's his mastery over his life, including a touch of the prophetic gift—a tour through all that he had created, all that he had dreamed. There were sins he dared not speak of even now, but I doubt any other major writer has ever allowed the world so close a look at his own insides and the experiences which he acknowledges having used and transformed into his fiction.

The effect of this opening up of the secret files, so to speak, is in no way a weakening of the force of his art. Or so it seems to me. "Tom Sawyer" is still "Tom Sawyer" even after we know the real character's name without quotation marks.

Mark Twain was a performer, obviously, a man drawn happily toward center stage. Almost from the start of his career he moved about the country from one lecture platform to another, telling his stories, cracking his jokes. It was years before he was taken seriously—or took himself seriously—as an artist, let alone a major one who would be looked to for insights into America's always uncertain moral life and its shifting but everlasting hypocrisies. One has to wonder what would have become of him in our television age, when he may well have found fame as essentially a comedian, like Will Rogers, or a character with his own program, perhaps like Jack Benny or Bob Hope. Sam Clemens did not disdain money, not at all, and TV could have made him very rich, could have addicted him to the compromises that come and must come with that territory, could have fed his appetite for soft celebrity rather than the hard bed of art. He would have been pressured to round the edges of his satire so as to emphasize uplift for the folks, perhaps to spare some fraudulent politician his lash whose subcommittee might make trouble for the broadcasting industry. Or even simpler, he would have been told in very clear tones, as I and doubtless other writers have been told by a network producer, that American television does not want "art." (They pronounce the quotation marks.) And that he must eliminate diversions from the main drive of his stories and simplify his syntax lest the audience lose track of a too-lengthy sentence. One way or another he would surely have ended in a head-on crash on the information superhighway, there can be no doubt of that.

It isn't easy to say how strong his resistance would have been to the suborning of his talent by his own declared wish to capture the big audience rather than settling for a far easier triumph with a narrower and more elegant supportive clique that already agreed with him. That big audience today is facing the TV screen, not the book or the lecture platform. My own inclination is in his favor; I think he would certainly have fallen for the power and emoluments of national TV celebrity, but would have found his way home again. Because he was an artist, and one who fed upon his own soul as much as on what he observed, and the call of the soul was the most powerful emotion he knew.

Of course this estimate may be wrong. Orson Welles, another man of brilliance and also a performer, was basically neutered by the American entertainment business, and spent most of his creative powers at poolside thrilling other artists with his culture, his knowledge and the spectacle of a greatness that was always on the verge of retaking the stage but could not be reborn, at least in my opinion, because it had no spiritual support in a country where few people knew enough to want what he could give. All that is certain is that the country by and by would have tired of listening to the *Mark Twain Weekly Hour;* and if he wanted to remain a national prime-time asset, the bubbling up of his genuine material would have slowed in due time and he would have had to begin clawing at himself, scouring his memories to feed into the television maw, and would have ended in a wealthy, self-contemptuous defeat.

We had Mark Twain when it was still possible to have him as an artist intent on addressing the whole country without having to pay the price of celebrity and the inevitable desiccation of his talent. We had Mark Twain when it was still possible to have him as the celebrity he was and the respected artist at the same time; the culture would support such a phenomenon still. That he might have survived intact the crush of the bottom line of mass communications—which in theory would have attracted him—is not easy to imagine. So the treasure is intact, and our American luck, at least in this case, has held.

1996

Clinton in Salem

A number of commentators have seen a resemblance between the extravaganza around President Clinton and the witchcraft hysteria in Salem three hundred years ago. There are some similarities and some important differences.

The tone of iron vituperation and the gut-shuddering hatred are reminiscent of the fury of the Salem ministers roaring down on the Devil as though they would grind their heels into his face. Though there were never any witches while there certainly is a Bill Clinton, the underlying emotions are not all that different—the evident wish is to end the Evil One's very existence.

In both cases there is a kind of sublime relief in the unearthing of the culprit's hidden crimes. The Salem church, which effectively controlled the village, had been so fractious that minister after minister had fled the pulpit or been dismissed. But with the discovery of Satan in town, the people understood in a flash what the source of their troubles had been, and a new era of social peace opened before them—provided they could root out the diabolically corrupt. Suddenly paranoia ruled and all were suspect and no one was safe.

What is very different now is the public reaction. Rarely does just about every newspaper and television commentator agree so thoroughly. Be it *The New York Times, The Washington Post,* or the television and print tabloids whose normal business is reporting news of the gutter, media outlets all became highly moral in a single stroke, as though an electric charge had passed through iron filings, instantly pointing them all in the same direction. Not often does one sinner raise so many so quickly out of their moral slumber.

But what is strange and interesting is how the public, that great stallion that is so often led to water, this time dipped its head but refused to drink, perhaps scenting the stale smell of political manipulation.

It may also be that with so many American marriages ending in divorce, and most of those surely involving a mate in the wrong bed, an unspoken self-identification with this kind of marital misery has restrained people from losing all sympathy for their leader, disappointed as they might be in his behavior.

Despite the lashings of almost all the press and the mullahs of the religious right, the people seem largely to have withheld their righteous anger. This did not happen in Salem, where the members of the clergy, who were also the leaders of the community, were strangers to mercy and indeed to common sense, and helped drive the public into a lethal panic.

There is, I think, a parallel in the sexual element underlying each phenomenon. Witch-hunts are always spooked by women's horrifying sexuality awakened by the superstud Devil. In Europe, where tens of thousands perished in the hunts, broadsides showed the Devil with two phalluses, one above the other. And of course mankind's original downfall came about when the Filthy One corrupted the mother of mankind.

In Salem, witch-hunting ministers had the solemn duty to examine women's bodies for signs of the "Devil's Marks"—a suggestion of webbing, perhaps, between the toes, a mole behind an ear or between the legs, or a bite mark somewhere. I thought of this wonderfully holy exercise when Congress went pawing through Kenneth Starr's fiercely exact report on the president's intimate meetings with Monica Lewinsky. I guess nothing changes all that much.

In any case, those who think it trivial that Mr. Clinton lied about a mere affair are missing the point: it is precisely his imperious need of the female that has unnerved a lot of men, the mullahs especially, just as it has through the ages. This may also help to account for the support he still gets from women. He may be a bit kinky, but at least he's not the usual suit for whom the woman is a vase, decorative and unused.

Then there is the color element. Mr. Clinton, according to Toni Morrison, the Nobel Prize–winning novelist, is our first black president, the first to come from the broken home, the alcoholic mother, the under-the-bridge shadows of our ranking systems. He is also the most relaxed and unaffected with black people, whose company and culture he clearly enjoys.

His closeness to blacks may, in fact, have contributed to the relative racial harmony we have been enjoying these past few years. But it may also be part of the reason for his estrangement from his peers, and it may have helped uncork the sewer of contempt upon his head, the Starr report.

The Devil in Salem was white, but two of the few black people in the village were his first suspected consorts, John Indian and Tituba. Both were slaves. Tituba was tortured into naming women she had seen with the Devil, thus starting the hunt on its way. The conflation of female sexuality and blackness in a white world is an old story, and here it had lethal results.

In Mr. Clinton's case, there comes an overflowing of rage reminiscent of that earlier explosion. If he lied under oath he of course broke the law, but it seems impossible that the Founding Fathers would have required Congress, as a part of his punishment, to study what parts of a woman's body the president had touched. Except for this hatred of Mr. Clinton, which sometimes seems to mount to a hellish fear of him as unclean, a supernatural contaminator, it would surely have sufficed for Mr. Starr to report that he had had an affair and falsely denied it under oath.

The Salem paroxysm left the town ravaged, accursed and almost deserted, a place where no one would buy land or farm or build for one hundred years. Salem's citizens had acted out the mythology of their dark subconscious and had eaten their own—all in the name of God and good morals. It was a volcanic explosion of repressed steam that gave people license to speak openly in court of what formerly would have been shamefully caged in their hearts—for example, the woman who testified that her neighbor flew in through her window one balmy night and lay upon her and had his way. Suddenly this was godly testimony, and the work of heaven was to kill the neighbor.

Salem purified itself nearly to death, but in the end some good may have come of it. I am not historian enough to assert this as fact, but I have often wondered if the witch-hunt may have helped spawn, one hundred years later, the Bill of Rights, particularly the Fifth Amendment, which prohibits forcing a person to testify against himself—something that would have stopped the witch-hunt in its tracks. It may also have contributed to the wall of separation between church and state in America, for in Salem theocratic government had its last hurrah. Or so one may hope.

1998

Salesman *at Fifty*

As far as I know, nobody has figured out time. Not chronological time, of course—that's merely what the calendar tells—but real time, the kind that baffles the human mind when it confronts, as mine does now, the apparent number of months, weeks, and years that have elapsed since 1948, when I sat down to write a play about a salesman. I say "apparent" because I cannot find a means of absorbing the idea of half a century rolling away beneath my feet. Half a century is a very long time, yet I must already have been grown up way back then, indeed I must have been a few years past thirty, if my calculations are correct, and this fact I find indigestible.

A few words about the theatrical era that *Death of a Salesman* emerged from. The only theater available to a playwright in the late Forties was Broadway, the most ruthlessly commercialized theater in the world, with the Off-Broadway evolution still a decade away. That theater had one single audience, not two or three, as is the case today, catering to very different levels of age, culture, education, and intellectual sophistication. Its critics were more than likely to be ex–sports reporters or general journalists rather than scholars or specialists university-trained in criticism. So a play worked or it didn't, made them laugh or cry or left them bored. (It really isn't all that different today except that the reasoning is perhaps more elevated.) That unified audience was the same for musicals, farces, O'Neill's tragedies, or some imported British, French, or Middle European lament. Whatever its limitations, it was an audience that loved theater, and many of its members thought theatergoing not quite a luxury but an absolute necessity for a civilized life.

For playwriting, what I believe was important about that unified audience was that a writer with ambitions reaching beyond realistic, made-for-entertainment plays could not expect the support of a coterie of like-minded folk who would overlook his artistic lapses so long as his philosophical agenda tended to justify their own. That unified audience had come in from the rain to be entertained, and even instructed, if need be, provided the instruction was entertaining. But the writer had to keep in mind that his proofs, so to speak, had to be accessible both to the lawyers in the audience and to the plumbers, to the doctors and the housewives, to the college students and the kids at the Saturday matinee. One result of this mix was the ideal, if not the frequent fulfillment, of a kind of play that would be complete rather than fragmentary, an emotional rather than an intellectual experience, a play basically of heart with its ulterior moral gesture integrated with action rather than rhetoric. In fact, it was a Shakespearean ideal, a theater for anyone with an understanding of English and perhaps some common sense.

Some of the initial readers of the *Death of a Salesman* script were not at all sure that the audience of 1949 was going to follow its manipulations of time, for one thing. Josh Logan, a leading stage and film director of numerous hits, *Mister Roberts* and *South Pacific* among them, had greeted *All My Sons* two years earlier with great warmth, and invested a thousand dollars in *Salesman,* but when he read the script he apologetically withdrew five hundred. No audience, he felt, would follow the story, and no one would ever be sure whether Willy was imagining or really living through one or another scene in the play. Some thirty years later I would hear the same kind of reaction from the theater people in the Beijing People's Art Theater, where I had been invited to stage the play, which, in the view of many there, was not a play at all but a poem. It was only when they saw it played that its real dramatic nature came through.

In the 1949 Broadway audience there was more to worry about than their following the story. In one of his letters O'Neill had referred to that theater as a "showshop," a crude place where a very uncultivated, materialistic public cut off from its own spirituality gathered for a laugh or a tear. Clifford Odets, with his first successes surely the most hotly acclaimed playwright in Broadway history, would also end in bitter alienation from the whole system of Broadway production. The problem, in a word, was seriousness. There wasn't very much of it in the audience, and it was resented when it threatened to appear on the stage.

So it seemed. But *All My Sons* had all but convinced me that if one totally integrated a play's conceptual life with its emotional one so that there
was no perceptible dividing line between the two, such a play could reach
such an audience. In short, the play had to move forward not by following
a narrow, discrete line, but as a phalanx, all of its elements moving together simultaneously. There was no model I could adapt for this play, no
past history for the kind of work I felt it could become. What I had before
me was the way the mind—at least my mind—actually worked. One asks
a policeman for directions; as one listens, the hairs sticking out of his
nose become important, reminding one of a father, brother, son with the
same feature, and one's conflicts with him or one's friendship come to
mind, and all this over a period of seconds while objectively taking note of
how to get to where one wants to go. Initially based, as I explained in
Timebends, my autobiography, on an uncle of mine, Willy rapidly took over
my imagination and became something that has never existed before, a
salesman with his feet on the subway stairs and his head in the stars.

His language and that of the Loman family were liberative from any
enslavement to "the way people speak." There are some people who simply don't speak the way people speak. The Lomans, like their models in
life, are not content with who and what they are, but want to be other,
wealthier, more cultivated perhaps, closer to power. "I've been remiss,"
Biff says to Linda about his neglect of his father, and there would be many
who seized on this usage as proof of the playwright's tin ear or of some in-
authenticity in the play. But it is in Biff's mouth precisely because it is indeed an echo, a slightly misunderstood signal from above, from the more
serious and cultivated part of society, a signal indicating that he is now to
be taken with utmost seriousness, even remorseful of his past neglect. "Be
liked and you will never want" is also not quite from Brooklyn, but Willy
needs aphoristic authority at this point, and again, there is an echo of a—
for want of a better word—Victorian authority to back him up. These folk
are the innocent receivers of what they imagine as a more elegant past, a
time "finer" than theirs. As Jews light-years away from religion or a community that might have fostered Jewish identity, they exist in a spot that
probably most Americans feel they inhabit—on the sidewalk side of the
glass looking in at a well-lighted place.

As it has turned out, this play seems to have shown that most of the
world shares something similar to that condition. Having seen it in five or
six countries, and directed it in China and Sweden, neither of whose lan-

guages I know, it was both mystifying and gratifying to note that people everywhere react pretty much the same in the same places of the play. When I arrived in China to begin rehearsals the people in the American embassy, with two exceptions, were sure the Chinese were too culturally remote from the play to ever understand it. The American ambassador and the political officer thought otherwise, the first because he had been born and raised in China, and the second, I supposed, because it was his job to understand how Chinese thought about life. And what they were thinking turned out to be more or less what they were thinking in New York or London or Paris, namely that being human—a father, mother, son—is something most of us fail at most of the time, and a little mercy is eminently in order given the societies we live in, which purport to be stable and sound as mountains when in fact they are all trembling in a fast wind blowing mindlessly around the earth.

1999

The Crucible *in History*

It would probably never have occurred to me to write a play about the Salem witch trials of 1692 had I not seen some astonishing correspondences with that calamity in the America of the late Forties and early Fifties. There were other enticements for me in the Salem period, however; most especially the chance it offered to write in what was for me a practically new language, one that would require new muscles.

I was never a scholar or an historian, of course; my basic need was somehow to respond to a phenomenon which, with only small exaggeration, one could say was paralyzing a whole generation and in an amazingly short time was drying up the habits of trust and toleration in public discourse. I refer, of course, to the anticommunist rage that threatened to reach hysterical proportions and sometimes did. I can't remember anyone calling it an ideological war, but I think now that that is what it amounted to. Looking back at the period, I suppose we very rapidly passed over anything like a discussion or debate and into something quite different, a hunt not alone for subversive people but ideas and even a suspect language. The object, a shock at the time, was to destroy the least credibility of any and all ideas associated with socialism and communism, whose proponents had to be either knowing or unwitting agents of Soviet subversion. An ideological war is like guerrilla war, since the enemy is first of all an idea whose proponents are not in uniform but are disguised as ordinary citizens, a situation that can scare a lot of people to death.

I am not really equipped to deliver a history of Cold War America, which like any other period is packed with passionately held illusions and ideas distorted on all sides by fear. Suffice to say it was a time of great, no doubt unprecedented fear, but fear, like love, is mostly incommunicable once it has passed. So I shall try to limit myself, as far as possible, to speak of events as they struck me personally, for those are what finally created *The Crucible*.

One knew that congressional investigations of subversion had been going on since the Thirties. The Dies committee, beginning with Nazi subversion in America, ended up with a neverending and often silly investigation of communists. But the country in the Thirties was not under external threat, and nobody seemed to take seriously any menace from an American Communist Party that could hardly elect a dogcatcher. From my perspective, what changed everything was the victory of the Chinese communists in 1949. Inevitably, the Chinese Reds were seen as all but an arm of the expansionist post–World War II Soviet machine, and a look at the map would indeed show that an enormous new part of the planet had turned red.

"Who Lost China!" almost instantly became the Republican mantra. Who were the traitors inside the Democratic administrations, going back to Roosevelt, that had sold out our favorite Chinese, Chiang Kai-shek? This, I think, was the first notable injection of the idea of treason and foreign agents into domestic political discourse. To me the simplicity of it all was breathtaking. There had to be left-wing traitors in government, otherwise how could the Chinese—who, as everyone knew, loved Americans more than anybody—have turned against the pro-American Chiang Kai-shek in favor of a Soviet agent like Mao Tse-tung?

All I knew about China in 1949 was what I had read by Edgar Snow and Jack Belden and Teddy White and other American reporters. What it amounted to was that the Nationalist regime was feudal and thoroughly corrupt and that the Reds were basically a miserably exploited peasantry that at long last had risen up and thrown their exploiters into the sea. I thought it was a great idea. In any event, the idea of our "losing" China seemed the equivalent of a flea losing an elephant. Nevertheless, there was a growing uproar in and out of Congress. One read that the China Lobby, a wealthy support group backing Chiang Kai-shek's hopes to return to Beijing from Taiwan, was reportedly paying a lot of the bills and that Senator McCarthy was one of their most effective champions. The partisan political manipulation of a real issue was so patent that President Truman could dismiss the Republican scare as a "red herring." But it is an indication of its impact on the public mind that he soon had to retreat and institute a loyalty board of his own to investigate the allegiance of government employees.

To call the ensuing atmosphere paranoid is not to say that there was nothing real in the American–Soviet standoff. To be sure, I am far more willing than I was then, due to some experiences of my own with both sides, to credit both the American and Soviet leadership with enough ignorance of each other to have ignited a third world war. But there was something of the inauthentic, the spurious, and the invented in the conflict, if only because of the swiftness with which all values were being forced in a matter of months to literally reverse themselves. I recall some examples.

Death of a Salesman opened in February of 1949 and was hailed by nearly every newspaper and magazine; parenthetically, I should add that two exceptions come to mind, one Marxist, the other ex-Marxist. The Marxist was the *Daily Worker*, which found the play defeatist and lacking militant protest; the ex-Marxist, Mary McCarthy, who seemed outraged by the idea of elevating it to the status of tragedy and just hated it in general, particularly, I thought, because it was so popular. Real tragedy would have to close in two weeks. Anyway, several movie studios wanted it, and it was finally Columbia Pictures that bought it and engaged a great star, Fredric March, to play Willy.

In something like two years or less, as I recall, with the picture finished, I was asked by a terrified Columbia to sign an anticommunist declaration in order to ward off picket lines which apparently the American Legion was threatening to throw across the entrances of theaters showing the film. In the numerous phone calls that followed, the air of terror was heavy. It was the first intimation of what would soon follow. I declined to make any such statement, which, frankly, I found demeaning; what right had any organization to demand anyone's pledge of loyalty? I was sure the whole thing would soon go away, it was just too outrageous.

But instead of disappearing, the studio, it now developed, had actually made another film, a short which was to be shown with *Salesman*. This was called *The Life of a Salesman* and consisted of several lectures by City College School of Business professors. What they boiled down to was that selling was basically a joy, one of the most gratifying and useful of professions, and that Willy was simply a nut. Never in show business history has a studio spent so much good money to prove that its feature film was pointless. I threatened to sue (on what basis I had no idea), but of course the short could not be shown lest it bore the audience blind. But in less than two years *Death of a Salesman* had gone from a masterpiece to a pariah that was basically fraudulent.

In 1948, '49, '50, '51, I had the sensation of being trapped inside a perverse work of art, one of those Escher constructs in which it is impossible to know whether a stairway is going up or down. Practically everyone I knew, all survivors of the Great Depression of course as well as World War II, was somewhere within the conventions of the political left of center; one or two were Communist Party members, some were sort of fellow travelers, as I suppose I was, and most had had one or another brush with Marxist ideas or organizations. I have never been able to believe in the reality of these people being actual or putative traitors any more than *I* could be, yet others like them were being fired from teaching or other jobs in government or large corporations. The unreality of it all never left me. We were living in an art form, a metaphor that had no long history but, incredibly enough, suddenly gripped the country. So I suppose that in one sense *The Crucible* was an attempt to make life real again, palpable and structured—a work of art created in order to interpret an anterior work of art that was called reality but was not.

Again—it was the very swiftness of the change that lent it this unreality. Only three or four years earlier an American movie audience, on seeing a newsreel of—let's say—a Russian soldier or even Stalin saluting the Red Army, would have applauded, for that army had taken the brunt of the Nazi onslaught, as most people were aware. Now they would have looked on with fear or at least bewilderment, for the Russians had become the enemy of mankind, a menace to all that was good. It was the Germans who, with amazing rapidity, were turning good. Could this be real? And how to mentally deal with, for example, American authorities removing from German schoolbooks all mention of the Hitler decade?

In the unions, communists and their allies, who had been known as intrepid organizers, were now to be shorn of union membership and turned out as seditious, in effect. Harry Bridges, for example, the idol of West Coast longshoremen, whom he had all but single-handedly organized, would be subjected to court trial after court trial to drive him out of the country and back to his native Australia as an unadmitted communist. Academics, some of them prominent in their fields, were especially targeted, many forced to retire or simply fired for disloyalty; some of them communists, some fellow travelers, and inevitably, a certain number who were simply unaffiliated liberals who refused to sign one of the dozens of anticommunist pledges being required by college administrations.

The sweep went not only very wide but deep. By 1950 or thereabouts there were subjects one would do better to avoid and even words that were best left unspoken. The Spanish Civil War, for example, had quickly become a hot button. That war, as some of you may not recall, resulted from an attack in 1936 by the Spanish army upon the democratically elected Spanish government. After almost three years of terrible fighting, in which Nazi air force planes and Mussolini's troops helped him, the fascist Generalissimo Franco took power. Spain would become the very symbol of the struggle against fascism; but more and more one heard, after about 1950, that Franco's victory was actually a not unworthy triumph of anticommunists. This despite the common belief through the Thirties and Forties that had Franco been thrown back, opening Hitler's Atlantic flank to hostile democrats rather than allied fascists, his war against Europe might well have had to be postponed if not aborted.

Again, it was the swiftness of this change that made it so fictional to me. Occasionally these quick changes were rather comical, which didn't help one's sense of reality.

One day in 1950 or thereabouts a stranger called, asking to come and see me about some matter he would prefer not to talk about on the phone and dropping as one of his bona fides that he had fought in Spain. I figured he was in trouble politically and must be really desperate if he imagined that I could help him. (A few ill-informed people still imagined I had some clout of this kind.) He arrived at my Brooklyn Heights house, a bright, youngish fellow carrying a briefcase. We chatted for a few minutes and then got down to business. Opening his briefcase, he took out a large map of a Texas oil field, rolled it out on my desk, and pointing at various black dots explained that these were oil wells in which he was selling stock. When I confessed surprise that an idealistic antifascist fighter should be ending up as an oil stock salesman, he asked, "Why not?" and with a touch of noble sincerity added, "Once the workers take over they're going to need oil!" This was a harbinger of the wondrous rationalizations that I would have cause to recall as our future arrived.

I should add that my uneasy fictional view of things turned out not to be entirely unwarranted; some six or seven years later, I would be cited for contempt of Congress for refusing to identify writers I had met at one of the two communist writers' meetings I had attended many years before. Normally, these citations resulted in a trial in federal court that took half an hour to lead to inevitable convictions. But my lawyer, Joseph Rauh Jr., brought in a former senator, Harry M. Cain, who had been head of the loyalty board under Eisenhower, to testify as an expert witness that my plays showed no signs of having been written under communist discipline. Cain had a curious history; a decorated Korean War veteran and fierce anticommunist, he had been a sidekick of McCarthy's and a weekly poker partner of his. But disillusionment had worn him down when, as head of the loyalty board, he had had to deal with the hundreds of letters a week from people suspecting neighbors, friends, and relatives of communist sympathies. The idea of the whole country spying on itself began to depress him, and he came to feel that from his Washington window he was looking out at a terrified nation and worse—some substantial fraction of it was quite literally crazed. The climax for him came with a series of relentlessly persistent letters from a Baltimore postman complaining of having been fired for disloyalty. What bothered him was the handwriting, which was barely literate. Communists were bad people, but they were rarely illiterate. Finally Cain invited the man to his office and realized that the accusations were not credible; this led him to wonder about the hundreds of other accusations he had with little or no examination been regularly forwarding to the FBI. At last he went directly to Eisenhower and told him he was convinced that the loyalty board itself was incompatible with political liberty. The next morning he found that he himself had been fired.

But that was still six or seven years on. My brushes with the fictional world in which I lived went back to 1947, when *All My Sons*, as the result of protests by the Catholic War Veterans, was removed from the Army's theatrical repertoire in Europe as a threat to soldiers' morale—since it told the story of a manufacturer selling defective parts to the Air Force. In a few years a former officer in that theatrical troop wrote to inform me that not only had *All My Sons* been banned but an order was given that no other play written by me was to be produced by the Army. As far as the Army was concerned, I had simply disappeared as an American writer. But this would be a useful experience when, in the late Sixties, as president of International PEN, I would find myself commiserating with Soviet writers and those in other communist countries who had seen their names obliterated from the rosters of living authors.

But it is impossible, certainly not in this short time, to properly convey the fears that mark the period. Nobody was being shot, to be sure, although some were going to jail, where at least one, a man named William Remington, was murdered, by an inmate hoping to shorten his sentence for having killed a communist. Rather than physical fear it was the sense of impotence, which seemed to deepen with each passing week, of being unable to speak simply and accurately of the very recent past when being Left in America, and for that matter in Europe, was simply to be alive to the dilemmas of the day. To be sure, I had counted myself a radical since my years in college and had tried and failed to read *Das Kapital*; but the Marxist formulations had certainly given shape to my views of politics— which in fact meant that to understand a political phenomenon you had to look for the money. It also meant that you believed capitalism was quite possibly doomed, but between 1929 and around 1936 there were moments when *not* to believe that would put you in a political minority. I may have dreamed of a socialism where people no longer lived off another's labor, but I had never met a spy. As for the very idea of willingly subjecting my work not only to some party's discipline but to anyone's control, my repugnance was such that as a very young and indigent writer I had turned down fairly lucrative offers to work for Hollywood studios because of a helpless revulsion at the thought of someone other than myself literally owning the paper I was typing on. It would not be long, perhaps four or five years, before the fraudulence of Soviet cultural claims was as clear to me as they should have been earlier, but I would never find it believable, either in the Fifties or later, that with their thuggish self-righteousness and callous contempt for artists' freedoms, the unabashed Soviet way of controlling culture could be successfully exported to America, except, perhaps, in Madison Avenue advertising agencies. In any case, to believe in that danger I would have to share a bed with the Republican Right.

Which is not to say that there was not much sincerity in the fears people felt in the Fifties, and, as in most things human, much cynicism as well, if not corruption. The moral high ground, as in most things human, was wreathed in fog. But the fact remained that some greatly talented people were being driven out of the country to live and work in England, screenwriters like Carl Foreman and Donald Ogden Stewart, actors like Charlie Chaplin and Sam Wanamaker (who, incidentally, in his last years, led the campaign to build a copy of Shakespeare's theater on the Thames). I no longer recall the number of our political exiles, but there were more than too many.

My subpoena before the House committee came some four years after

The Crucible was produced, but I had been shot at more than once as a result of that play. Shortly after its production, the renewal of my outdated passport had been denied when I applied in order to go to Belgium, at the invitation of the Belgo-American Association, to attend the first European performance of the play. The stated grounds for confiscating my passport were that my presence abroad was not in the best interests of the United States. A rather farcical situation soon developed—and I should say that farce was always a step away from all the tragedies of the period. Since the play was the first and practically the only artistic evidence Europe had of resistance to what was considered a fascistic McCarthyism, the applause at the final curtain was intense and insistent, and since the newspapers had announced that I had accepted the invitation to be present, there were calls for the author. These went on and on until the American ambassador felt compelled to stand and take a bow. A species of insanity was spreading everywhere. Here was the ambassador, an officer of the State Department, acknowledging the applause for someone deemed by that department too dangerous to be present. It must surely have struck some of the audience as strange, however, that an author would be wearing a wide diplomatic sash diagonally across his chest; and the next morning's papers had loads of fun with the scene, which, of course, could hardly have advanced the best interests of the United States.

I should explain what I meant by the cynicism and corruption of the Red hunt. By 1956, when HUAC subpoenaed me, the tide was going out, and the committee was finding it difficult to make the front pages anymore. However, the news of my forthcoming marriage to Marilyn Monroe was too tempting to be passed up. That it had some connections with my being subpoenaed was confirmed when Chairman Walter of HUAC sent word to Joseph Rauh, my lawyer, that he would be inclined to cancel my hearing altogether if Miss Monroe would consent to have a picture taken with him. The offer having been declined, the good chairman, as my hearing came to an end, proceeded to entreat me to write less tragically about our country. This lecture cost me some $40,000 in lawyer's fees, a year's suspended sentence for contempt of Congress, and a five-hundred-dollar fine. Not to mention about a year of inanition in my creative life.

But back to the late Forties and early Fifties; my fictional view of the period, my sense of its unreality was, like any impotence, a psychologically painful experience. A very similar paralysis at a certain point descended on Salem.

A new cautionary diction was swiftly ensconced in our way of talking to one another. In a country that a bit more than a quarter of a century earlier had given three million votes to Eugene Debs, the Socialist presidential candidate, the very word "socialism" was all but taboo. Words had gotten fearsome. As I would learn directly from students and faculty in Ann Arbor on a 1953 reporting visit for *Holiday* magazine, students were actually avoiding renting rooms in the houses run by the housing cooperative for fear of being labeled communist, so darkly suggestive was the word "cooperative." On hearing this, even I was amazed. But there was more—the head of orientation at the university told me that the FBI had enlisted professors to report on students voicing left-wing opinions and— some more comedy—they had also engaged students to report on professors with the same views. When I published these facts in *Holiday*, the Pontiac division of General Motors threatened to withdraw all advertising from the magazine if I ever appeared in it again; Ted Patrick, its editor, promptly badgered me for another piece, but I didn't know the reason why for some years.

It was a time—as I would learn only decades later from my FBI record, obtained under the Freedom of Information Act—when the FBI shadowed a guest of mine from a dinner party in my Brooklyn Heights house. The guest's name was blacked out, and I have been puzzling ever since about his identity. The point is that reading my FBI record in the Seventies I was not really surprised to learn this. In the Fifties everybody over forty believed that his phone was being tapped by the FBI, and they were probably right.

What is important here is that none of this was secret; everybody had a good idea of what was happening but, like me, felt helpless to reverse it. And to this moment I don't think I can adequately communicate the sheer density of the atmosphere of the time, for the outrageous had so suddenly become the accepted norm.

In the early Fifties, for example, with Elia Kazan, who had directed *All My Sons* and *Death of a Salesman*, I submitted a film script to Harry Cohn, the head of Columbia Pictures. It described the murderous corruption in the gangster-ridden Brooklyn longshoremen's union, whose leadership a group of rebel workers was trying to overthrow. Cohn read the script and called us to Hollywood, where he simply and casually informed us that, incredibly enough, he had first had the script vetted by the FBI and that they had seen nothing subversive in it; on the other hand, however, the head of the AFL motion picture unions in Hollywood, Roy Brewer, had condemned it outright as totally untrue communist propaganda, since, quite simply, there were no gangsters on the Brooklyn waterfront. Cohn, no stranger to the ways of gangsterism, having survived an upbringing in the tough, famously crime-ridden Five Points area of Manhattan, opined that Brewer was quite naturally only trying to protect Joe Ryan, his brother AFL union leader, the head of the AFL Brooklyn longshoremen. Brewer also threatened to call a strike of projectionists in any theater daring to show the film, no idle threat since he controlled *their* union. (Ryan, incidentally, would shortly go to Sing Sing prison for gangsterism. But that was not yet.) Meanwhile Cohn offered his solution to our problem with Brewer; he would produce the film if I would agree to make one simple change— the gangsters in the union were to be changed to communists. This would not be easy; for one thing, I knew all the communists on the waterfront; there was a total of two of them (both of whom, incidentally, in the following decade became millionaire businessmen).

And so I had to withdraw the script, which prompted an indignant telegram from Cohn: "As soon as we try to make the script pro-American you pull out." One understood not only the threat in those words but the cynicism; he certainly knew that it was the Mafia that controlled waterfront labor. Nevertheless, had I been a screenwriter in Hollywood, my career would have ended with this refusal to perform this patriotic idiocy. I have to say that there were days when I wondered if we would end in an unacknowledged, perhaps even comfortable American fascism.

But the theater had no such complications, no blacklist, not yet anyway; and I longed to respond to this climate of fear if only to protect my sanity. But where to find a transcendent concept? As I saw it, the difficulty was that we had grown so detached from any hard reality I knew about. It had become a world of signals, gestures, loaded symbolic words, and of rites and rituals. After all, the accusations of Party membership of film writers, actors, and directors never mentioned treasonous acts of any sort; what was in their brains was the question, and this created a kind of gestural phantom land. I did not yet think of it this way at the time, but looking back I think we had entered an ideological war, as I have said, and in such wars it was ideas and not necessarily actions that arouse anger and fear. And this was the heart of the darkness—that it had come rather quickly to be believed that a massive, profoundly organized conspiracy was in place and being carried forward mainly by a concealed phalanx of intellectuals, including labor people, teachers, professionals of all sorts, sworn to undermine the American government. And it was precisely the invisibility of ideas that was helping to frighten so many people. How could a play deal with this mirage world?

There was a fundamental absurdity in the Salem witch-hunt, of course, since witches don't exist, but this only helped relate it more to what we were going through. I can't recall the date anymore, but to one of the Un-American Activities Committee hearings, several Hollywood writers brought piles of their film scripts for the committee to parse for any sign of Marxist propaganda. Of course there would hardly be anything that provocative in a Hollywood movie of the time, but in any case the committee refused to read the scripts, which I imagined was a further humiliation for the writers. But what a cruel irony, that these terribly serious Party members or sympathizers, in the attempt to prove themselves patriotic Americans, should feel compelled to demonstrate that their work was totally innocuous!

Paranoia breeds paranoia, of course, but below paranoia there lies a bristling, unwelcome truth, a truth so repugnant as to produce fantasies of persecution in order to conceal its existence. For example, the unwelcome truth denied by the Right was that the Hollywood writers accused of subversion were not a menace to the country or even the bearers of meaningful change. They wrote not propaganda but entertainment, some of it of a mildly liberal cast, to be sure, but most of it mindless; or when it was political, as with Preston Sturges or Frank Capra, entirely un-Marxist. In any real assessment, the worst they could do was contribute some money to Party coffers. But most Hollywood writers were only occasionally employed, and one doubted that their contributions could have made any difference to a party so completely disregarded by the American public and, in the bargain, so thoroughly impregnated by the FBI. Yet they had to be portrayed as an imminent danger to the republic.

As for the Left, its unacknowledged truth was more important for me. If nobody was being shot in our ideological war but merely vivisected by a headline or two, it struck me as odd, if understandable, that the accused were largely unable to passionately cry out their faith in the ideals of socialism. Attacks on the committees' right to demand that a citizen reveal his political beliefs, yes; but as for the idealistic canon of their own convictions, the accused were largely mute. It was a silence, incidentally, that in the public mind probably tended to confirm the committees' characterization of them as conspirators wrapping themselves in darkness. In their defense, the committees instantly shut down as irrelevant any attempts to explicate their ideas, any idealistic displays; but even outside, in public statements beyond the hearings, they relied almost wholly on legalistic defenses rather than the articles of the faith in which they unquestionably believed. The rare exception, like Paul Robeson's forthright declaration of faith in socialism as a cure for racism, was a rocket that momentarily lit up the sky, but even this, it must be said, was dimmed by his adamant refusal to recognize, at least publicly, what he knew to be the murder of two Soviet Jewish artists, his good friends, under Stalin's anti-Semitic decrees. It was one of the cruel twists of the time that while he would not in Washington display his outrage at the murders of his friends, he could in Moscow choose to sing a song in Yiddish that the whole public knew was his protest against Soviet anti-Semitism.

In a word, the disciplined avoidances of the Left bespoke a guilt that the Right found a way to exploit. A similar guilt seems to reside in all sorts of American dissidents, from Jehovah's Witnesses to homosexuals, no doubt because there is indeed an unacknowledged hostility in them toward the majority for whose cherished norms they feel contempt. It may be that guilt, perhaps, helped to account to some degree for the absence in our theater of plays that in any meaningful way confronted the deepening hysteria, which after all was the main event in our culture. Here was a significant part of a whole generation being forced to the wall, with hardly a word about it written for the stage. But it may simply have been the difficulty of finding a dramatic locution, a working symbolization that might illuminate the complex fog of the unspoken in which we were living.

To put it differently, stuffed in the pockets of both sides was a hidden agenda. On the Right it was, quite simply, their zeal to finally disgrace and wipe out what remained of New Deal attitudes, particularly that dreadful tendency in Americans to use government to help the helpless and to set limits around the more flagrant excesses of unbridled capitalism. Instead, their advertised goal was the defense of liberty against communism.

What the Left was not saying was that they were in truth dedicated to replacing capitalism with a society based on Marxist principles, and this could well mean the suppression of non-Marxists for the good of mankind. Instead, they were simply espousing constitutional protections against self-incrimination. Thus the fresh wind of a debate of any real content was not blowing through these hearings or these terrible years. The result was miasma, and on the Left, the guilt of the wholly or partially insincere. The Right, of course, convinced as it always is of its persecution, is certain that it represents the incoherent and stifled but genuine wishes of the majority and is thus a stranger to guilt.

How to express all this, and much more, on a stage? I began to despair of my own paralysis. I was a fisherman without a hook, a seaman without a sail.

On a lucky afternoon I happened upon a book, *The Devil in Massachusetts*, by Marion Starkey, a narrative of the Salem witch-hunt of 1692. I knew this story from my college reading more than a decade earlier, but now in this changed and darkened America it turned a wholly new aspect toward me, namely, the poetry of the hunt. Poetry may seem an odd word for a witch-hunt, but I saw now that there was something of the marvelous in the spectacle of a whole village, if not an entire province, whose imagination was literally captured by a vision of something that wasn't there.

In time to come the very notion of equating the Red hunt with the witch-hunt would be condemned by some as a deception. There certainly were communists, and there never were witches. But the deeper I moved into the 1690s, the further away drifted the America of the 1950s, and rather than the appeal of analogy I found something somewhat different to draw my curiosity and excitement.

First of all, anyone standing up in the Salem of 1692 who denied that witches existed would have faced immediate arrest, the hardest interrogation, and quite possibly the rope. Every authority—the church in New England, the kings of England and Europe, legal scholars like Lord Coke—not only confirmed their existence but never questioned the necessity of executing them when discovered. And of course, there was the authority of the Bible itself [Exodus 22:18]: "Thou shalt not suffer a witch to live." To deny witches was to deny the existence of the Devil's age-old war against God, and this, in effect, left God without an opposite and stripped him of his first purpose—which was to protect the Christian religion and good order in the world. Without evil, what need was there for the good? Without the Devil's ceaseless plotting, who needed God? The existence of witches actually went to prove the existence of God's war with evil. Indeed, it became obvious that to dismiss witchcraft was to forgo any understanding of how it came to pass that tens of thousands had been murdered as witches in Europe, from Scandinavia across to England, down through France and Spain. And to dismiss any relation to the hunt for subversives was to shut down an insight into not only the remarkably similar emotions but literally the numerous identical practices, both by officials and victims, in both outbreaks.

Of course there were witches, if not to most of us then certainly to everyone in Salem; and of course there were communists, but what was the content of their menace? That to me became the issue. Having been deeply influenced as a student by a Marxist approach to society (if less so as I grew older) and having known any number of Marxists and numerous sympathizers, I could simply not accept that these people were spies or even prepared to do the will of the Soviets in some future crisis. That such people had thought to find some hope of a higher ethic in the Soviets was not simply an American but a worldwide irony of catastrophic moral proportions, for their like could be found all over Europe and Asia. But as the Fifties dawned, they were stuck with the past they had chosen or been led into. Part of the unreality of the great anti-Left sweep of the Fifties was that it picked up a lot of people to expose and disgrace who had already in their hearts turned away from a pro-Soviet past but had no stomach for naming others who had merely shared their illusions. In short, then, the whole business for me remained what Truman had initially called it, not a moral crusade but a political red herring.

Nevertheless, the hunt captured some significant part of the American imagination, and its power demanded respect. And turning to Salem was like looking into a petri dish, a sort of embalmed stasis with its principal moving forces caught in stillness. One had to wonder what the human imagination fed on that could inspire neighbors and old friends to suddenly emerge overnight as hell's own furies secretly bent on the torture and destruction of Christians. More than a political metaphor, more than a moral tale, *The Crucible,* as it developed for me over the period of more than a year, became the awesome evidence of the power of the inflamed human imagination, the poetry of suggestion, and finally the tragedy of heroic resistance to a society possessed to the point of ruin.

As I stood in the stillness of the Salem courthouse, surrounded by the miasmic swirl of the images of the 1950s but with my head in 1692, what the two eras had in common was gradually gaining definition. In both was the menace of concealed plots, but most startling were the similarities in the rituals of defense and the investigative routines. Three hundred years apart, both prosecutions were alleging membership in a secret, disloyal group; should the accused confess, his honesty could be proved only in precisely the same way—by naming former confederates, nothing less. Thus the informer became the very proof of the plot and the investigation's necessity.

Finally, in both eras, since the enemy was first and foremost an idea, normal evidentiary proof of disloyal actions was either deemphasized, left in limbo, or not required at all; and indeed, actions finally became completely irrelevant; in the end, the charge itself, suspicion itself, all but became the evidence of disloyalty.

And, most interestingly, in the absence of provable disloyal actions both societies reached for very similar remedies. Something called the Attorney General's List was promulgated, a list of communist-front organizations, membership in which was declared not so much illegal as reason to suspect subversive conduct or intentions. If membership in an organization could not be called illegal, it could at least be made disgusting enough to lose you your job and reputation.

One might wonder whether many spies would be likely to be joining communist fronts, but liberals very possibly might and indeed had done so at various turns in the road, frequently making common cause with the Left and with communists during the New Deal period a decade earlier. The witch-hunt in 1692 had a not dissimilar evidentiary problem but a far more poetic solution. Most suspected people named by others as members of the Devil's conspiracy had not been shown to have actually *done* anything—not poisoning wells, setting barns on fire, sickening cattle, aborting babies or calves, nor somehow undermining the virtue of wives (the Devil having a double, phenomenally active penis, as everybody knew). Rather than acts, these suspect folk needed only to have had the bad luck to have been "seen" by witnesses consorting with the Devil. The witnesses might be dismally addled hysterics, but they might also be sober citizens who'd somehow gotten themselves suspected of practicing witchcraft and could clear themselves only by confessing and naming coconspirators. But, as in the Fifties, there was a supply of nonhysterical lawyers in and around the witch-hunt, as well as Harvard-educated ministers, and as accusations piled up one obvious fact was more and more irritating to them; as they well knew, the normal fulcrum of any criminal prosecution, namely, acts, deeds, crimes, and witnesses thereto, was simply missing. As for ordinary people, as devout as they might be and strictly literal about Biblical injunctions, they still clung to the old habit of expecting some sort of proof that an accused was guilty, in this case, of being an accomplice of the Devil.

To the rescue came not an Attorney General's List but a piece of poetry smacking of both legalistic and religious validity; it was called "spectral evidence." Spectral evidence, in normal jurisprudence, had been carefully winnowed out of the prosecutorial armory by judges and lawyers as being too manifestly open to fabrication. But now, with society under this hellish attack, the fateful decision was made to bring it back in, and the effect was like the bursting of a dam. Suddenly all the prosecution needed do was produce a witness who claimed to have seen not an accused person but what was called his familiar spirit, his living ghost, as it were, in the act of poisoning a pig or throwing a burning brand into a barn full of hay. You could be at home asleep in your bed, but your spirit could be crawling through your neighbor's bedroom window to feel up his wife. The owner of that wandering spirit was thereupon obliged to account to the court for its crime. With the entrance of spectral evidence, the air was quickly filled with the malign spirits of those identified by good Christians as confederates of the Beast, and with this, of course, the Devil himself really did dance happily into Salem village and proceeded to take the place apart.

And in no time at all, people in Salem began *looking* at each other with new eyes and *hearing* sounds from neighbors' throats that they had never heard before and *thinking* about each other with new insights far deeper than their former blind innocence toward one another could have given them. And now, naturally, a lot of things that had been bewildering before suddenly made sense. Why, for instance, had London annulled all property deeds, causing everybody to be fighting with everybody else over boundary lines? Why was the congregation forever turning in on itself in fierce doctrinal fights and bitter arguments with ministers who one after another had had to flee the contentiousness of Salemites? Clearly, it was the Devil who had been muddling people's brains to set them against each other. But now, now at last, with the Lord's help, they had the gift of sight; the afflicted children had opened up their eyes to the plot in which, unknowingly, like innocent birds in a net, they were all caught. Now, with the admission of spectral evidence, they could turn to the traitors among them and run them to their deaths.

I spent some ten days in the Salem courthouse reading the crudely recorded trials of the 1692 outbreak, and it was striking how totally absent was the least sense of irony, let alone humor. I can't recall whether it was the provincial governor's nephew or son who with a college friend had come from Boston to watch the strange proceedings; at one point both boys burst out laughing at some absurd testimony. They were promptly jailed and were saved only by friends galloping down from Boston with a bribe for a guard, who let them escape from a very possible hanging.

Irony and humor were not exactly at a premium in the Fifties either. I was in my lawyer's office one afternoon to sign some contract, and a lawyer in the next office was asked to come in and notarize my signature. While this man was stamping the pages, I continued a discussion with my lawyer about the Broadway theater, which at one point I said was corrupt, that the art of theater had been totally displaced by the bottom line, that being all that really mattered anymore. Looking up at me, the notarizing lawyer said, "That's a communist position, you know." I started to laugh until I saw the constraint in my lawyer's face, and despite myself I quickly sobered up.

I am glad, of course, that I managed to write *The Crucible,* but looking back I have often wished I'd had the temperament to have done an absurd comedy, since that is what the situation often deserved. There is something funny in the two sophisticated young Bostonians deciding to trot down to Salem to look in on the uproar among the provincials, failing to realize that they had entered a new age, a new kind of consciousness. I made a not dissimilar mistake as the Fifties dawned, and I continued to make it. A young film producer I didn't know asked me to write a script for a film about what was then called juvenile delinquency. A mystifying, unprecedented outbreak of gang violence had exploded all over New York. The city, in return for a good percentage of the profits, had contracted with this producer to open police stations, schools, and so on to his camera. I spent the summer of 1955 on Brooklyn streets, wrote an outline, which, incidentally, was much praised by the Catholic Youth Organization's leadership, and was ready to proceed with the script when an attack on me as a disloyal leftist was opened in the *New York World-Telegram and Sun.* The cry went up that so long as I was the screenwriter the city must cancel its contract with the producer. A hearing was arranged, attended by some twenty-two city commissioners, including those of the police, fire, welfare, and not least the sanitation departments, as well as two judges. At the long conference table there also sat a lady in sneakers and a sweater who produced a thick folder of petitions and statements I had signed, going back to my college years, provided to her, she said, by the House Un-American Activities Committee. I defended myself; I thought I was making some sense when the lady began literally screaming that I was killing the boys in Korea. She meant that I *personally* was doing it, as I could tell from the froth at the corners of her mouth, the fury in her eyes, and her finger pointing straight into my face. The vote was taken and came up one short of continuing the city's collaboration, and the film was killed that afternoon. As we were filing out, the two judges came up and offered their sympathy. I always wondered whether the crucial vote against me came from the sanitation department. But it was not a total loss; it would soon help with the writing of *The Crucible,* the suffocating sensation of helplessness before the spectacle of the impossible coming to pass.

Since you, or some of you, are historians, I have emphasized history in these remarks, but I doubt if I'd have written the play had the question of language not so powerfully drawn me on. The trial record in the Salem courthouse, of which I was allowed to borrow a photocopy, was written by ministers in a primitive shorthand. This condensation gave emphasis to a gnarled, densely packed language that suggested the country accents of a hard people. (A few years on, when Laurence Olivier staged his London production, he used the gruff Northumberland accent.) In any event, to lose oneself day after day in that record of human delusion was to know a fear, not perhaps for one's safety precisely but of the spectacle of perfectly intelligent people giving themselves over to a rapture of such murderous credulity. It was as though the absence of real evidence was itself a release from the burdens of this world; in love with the invisible, they moved behind their priests closer to that mystical communion that is anarchy and is called God. Evidence, in contrast, is effort; leaping to conclusions is a wonderful pleasure; and for a while there was a highly charged joy in Salem, for now that they could see through everything to the frightful plot being daily laid bare in court sessions, their days, formerly so eventless and long, were swallowed up in hourly revelations, news, surprises. *The Crucible,* I think, is less a polemic than it might have been had it not been filled with wonder at the protean imagination of man.

As a commercial entertainment, the play failed, of course. To start with, the title: Nobody knew what a crucible was. Most of the critics, as sometimes does happen, never caught on to the play's ironical substructure, and the ones who did were nervous about validating a work that was so unkind to the same basic principles as underlay the current hunt for Reds, sanctified as it was. On opening night, old acquaintances shunned me in the theater lobby, and even without air-conditioning the house was noticeably cool. But the problem was also with the temperature of the production. The director, a great name in the theater of the Twenties, Thirties, and into the Forties, had decided that the play, which he believed a classic, should be staged like what he called a Dutch painting. In Dutch paintings of groups, everyone is always looking front. We knew this from the picture on the wooden boxes of Dutch Masters cigars. Unfortunately, on a stage such rigidity only propels an audience to the exits. It would be several years before a gang of young actors, setting up chairs in the ballroom of the McAlpin Hotel, set fire to the audience and convinced the critics; and the play at last took off and soon found its place in the world. There were cheering critics this time, but now of course McCarthy was dead, and the fever on whose waves of heat he had spread his wings had cooled, and more and more people found it possible to face the dying embers and read the terrible message in them.

It is said that no one would buy land in Salem for a hundred years. The very ground was accursed. Salem's people, in the language of the time, had broke charity with one another.

But the Devil, as he usually does after such paroxysms, had the last laugh. Salem refuses to fade into history. A few years ago the foundation of an old colonial-era church in a town near Salem began to sag. The contractor engaged to make repairs dug out some of the loose stones and crawled underneath to inspect matters. There he discovered what looked like barely buried human skeletons. Harvard scientists were called in and confirmed that the remains of some twenty-two people were under the church. Now no one has ever known exactly where in Salem the gibbet was located, but the bodies of the twenty-two people hanged there for practicing witchcraft had never been found. Moreover, according to one legend, as their ultimate punishment they were denied Christian burial.

The scientists wanted to remove the skeletons and try to identify them. But some quite aged parishioners, descendants not only of the witchcraft victims but no doubt of their persecutors as well, were adamantly opposed. The younger church members were all for it but decided to wait until the elders had passed away rather than start a ruckus about the matter. In short, even after three centuries, the thing, it seems, cannot find its serene, uncomplicated end.

And, indeed, something very similar occurred in Salem three hundred years ago. After the hunt had blown itself out, after Cotton Mather, having whipped up the hysteria to and beyond the point of murder, finally conceded that demanding the admission of spectral evidence had been his dreadful mistake, the legislature awarded to some, though not all, of the victims' families a few pounds' damages along with a mild apology: "Sorry we hanged your mother," and so forth. But in the true Salem style of solemn bewilderment, this gesture apparently lacked a certain requisite disorder, so they also included reparations to some informers whose false accusations had hanged people. Victims and victimizers, it was all the same in the end. I suppose it was just the good old American habit of trying to keep everybody happy.

The Crucible is my most-produced play, here and abroad. It seems to be one of the few shards of the so-called McCarthy period that survives. And it is part of the play's history, I think, that to people in so many parts of the world its story seems so like their own. I think it was in the mid-Seventies—dates at my age take on the viscosity of poached eggs—but in any case, I happened to be at my publishers when another Grove Press author came in. Her eyes filled with tears at our introduction, and she hastened to explain: She was Yuen Cheng, author of *Life and Death in Shanghai*, the story of her six-year solitary confinement during the Cultural Revolution. It seems that on her release, an old friend, a theater director, took her to see a new production of his in Shanghai, *The Crucible*, a play and author she had never heard of. As she listened to it, the interrogations sounded so precisely the same as the ones she and others had been subject to by the Cultural Revolutionaries that she couldn't believe a non-Chinese had written it. And picking up the English text, she was amazed, she said, not least by the publication date, which of course was more than a decade before the Cultural Revolution. A highly educated woman, she had been living with the conviction that such a perversion of just procedure could happen only in the China of a debauched revolution! I have had similar reactions from Russians, South Africans, Latin Americans and others who have endured dictatorships, so universal is the methodology of terror portrayed in *The Crucible*. In fact, I used to think, half seriously—although it was not far from the truth—that you could tell when a dictator was about to take power in a Latin American country or when one had just been overthrown, by whether *The Crucible* was suddenly being produced there.

The net of it all, I suppose, is that I have come, rather reluctantly, to respect delusion, not least of all my own. There are no passions quite as hot and pleasurable as those of the deluded. Compared with the bliss of delusion—its vivid colors, blazing lights, explosions, whistles, and sheer liberating joys—the dull search for evidence is a deadly bore. In *Time-bends,* my autobiography, I have written at some length about my dealings with Soviet cultural controllers and writers when as president of International PEN I would attempt to impress its democratic values upon them in their treatment of writers. Moving about there and in East Germany, Hungary, and Czechoslovakia in communist times, it was only by main force that I could dredge up memories of my old idealism, which I had attached to what in reality had turned out to be little more than a half-feudal society led by an unelected elite. How could this possibly be? I can only think that a man in a rushing river will grasp at any floating thing passing by. History, or whatever piece of its debris one happens to connect with, is a great part of the answer. For me it was my particular relation to the collapse of key institutions in the Great Depression, the sometimes scary anti-Semitism I kept running into and the Left's thankful condemnation of it, the Spanish Civil War and the all-but-declared pro-fascist sympathies of the British, and Roosevelt's unacknowledged collaboration with their arms blockade of the republic (the so-called Non-Intervention Policy). Indeed, on Franco's victory, Roosevelt told Secretary of the Interior Harold Ickes, according to Ickes's autobiography, that his Spanish policy was "the worst mistake I ever made." In a word, out of the Great Crash of 1929, America and the world seemed to awaken to a new sense of social responsibility, something which to the young seemed very much like love. My heart was with the Left if only because the Right hated me enough to want to kill me, as the Germans amply proved. And now, of course, the most blatant and foulest anti-Semitism is in Russia, leaving people like me filled not so much with surprise as a kind of wonder at the incredible amount of hope there once was and how it disappeared and whether in time it will ever come again, attached to some new illusion.

And so there is hardly a week that passes when I don't ask the unanswerable—what am I now convinced of that will turn out to be ridiculous? And yet one can't forever stand on the shore; at some point, even if filled with indecision, skepticism, reservation and doubt, you either jump in or concede that life is forever elsewhere.

Which I daresay was one of the major impulses behind the decision to attempt *The Crucible*. Salem village, that pious, devout settlement at the very edge of white civilization, had taught me—three centuries before the Russo–American rivalry and the issues it raised—that a kind of built-in pestilence was nestled in the human mind, a fatality forever awaiting the right conditions for its always unique, forever unprecedented outbreak of alarm, suspicion, and murder. And to people wherever the play is performed, on any of the six continents, there is always a certain amazement that the same terror that had happened to them had happened before to others. It is all very strange. On the other hand, the Devil is known to lure people into forgetting precisely what it is vital for them to remember—how else could his endless reappearances always come with such marvelous surprise?

1999

The Price—*The Power of the Past*

The sources of a play are both obvious and mysterious. *The Price* is first of all about a group of people recollected, as it were, in tranquillity. The central figures, the New York cop Victor Franz and his elder brother, Walter, are not precise portraits of people I knew long, long ago but close enough, and Gregory Solomon, the old furniture dealer, is as close as I could get to reproducing a dealer's Russian-Yiddish accent that still tickles me whenever I hear it in memory.

First, the bare bones of the play's story: the Great Crash of 1929 left Victor and Walter to care for their widowed father, who had been ruined in the stock market collapse and was helpless to cope with life. While Victor, loyal to the father, dropped out of college to earn a living for them both and ended up on the police force, Walter went on to become a wealthy surgeon.

The play begins decades later on the attic floor of the decrepit brownstone where the cop and his father had lived, surrounded by piles of furniture from their old apartment that the father had clung to. Now the building, owned by the father's brother, is to be torn down, so the furniture must be sold.

The conflict of how to divide the proceeds cuts open the long-buried lives of both men, as well as that of Victor's wife, Esther, and reveals the choices each has made and the price each has paid. Through it all weaves the antic ninety-year-old furniture dealer Gregory Solomon, who is yards ahead of them as he tries to shepherd them away from the abyss toward which he knows they are heading.

Behind the play—almost any play—are more or less secret responses to other works of the time, and these may emerge as disguised imitation or as outright rejection of the dominating forms of the hour. *The Price* was written in 1967, and since nobody is going to care anymore, it may as well be admitted that in some part it was a reaction to two big events that had come to overshadow all others in that decade. One was the seemingly permanent and morally agonizing Vietnam War, the other a surge of avant-garde plays that to one or another degree fit the absurd styles. I was moved to write a play that might confront and confound both.

I enjoyed watching some of the absurd plays—my first theater experiences were with vaudeville in the Twenties, after all, and absurdist comics like Bert Williams and Willie Howard, with their delicious proto–shaggy-dog stories and skits, were favorites. More, for a while in the Thirties our own William Saroyan, who with all his failings was an authentic American inventor of a domestic absurdist attitude, had held the stage. One would not soon forget his *Time* magazine subscription salesman reading—not without passion—the entire page-long list of names of *Time*'s reporters, editors, subeditors, fact checkers, department heads and dozens of lesser employees, to a pair of Ozark hillbillies dressed in their rags, seated on their rotting porch and listening with rapt incomprehension.

But the Sixties was a time when a play with recognizable characters, a beginning, middle and end was routinely condemned as "well made" or ludicrously old-fashioned. (That plays with no characters, beginning or end were not called "badly made" was inevitable when the detonation of despised rules in all things was a requisite for recognition as modern. That beginnings, middles, and ends might not be mere rules but a replication of the rise and fall of human life did not frequently come up.)

Often against my will, however, I found myself enjoying the new abstract theater; for one thing, it was moving us closer to a state of dream, and for dreams I had nothing but respect. But as the dying continued in Vietnam with no adequate resistance to it in the country, the theater, so it seemed to me, risked trivialization by failing to confront the bleeding, at least in a way that could reach most people. In its way, *Hair* had done so by offering a laid-back lifestyle opposed to the aggressive military-corporate one. But one had to feel the absence—not only in theater but everywhere—of any interest in what had surely given birth to Vietnam, namely, its roots in the past.

Indeed, the very idea of an operating continuity between past and present in any human behavior was démodé and close to a laughably old-fashioned irrelevancy. My impression, in fact, was that playwrights were

either uninterested in or incapable of presenting antecedent material altogether. Like the movies, plays seemed to exist entirely in the now; characters had either no past or none that could somehow be directing present
actions. It was as though the culture had decreed amnesia as the ultimate
mark of reality.

As the corpses piled up, it became cruelly impolite if not unpatriotic
to suggest the obvious, that we were fighting the past; our rigid anticommunist theology, born of another time two decades earlier, made it a sin to
consider Vietnamese Reds as nationalists rather than Moscow's and Beijing's yapping dogs. We were fighting in a state of forgetfulness, quite as
though we had not aborted a national election in Vietnam and divided the
country into separate halves when it became clear that Ho Chi Minh would
be the overwhelming favorite for the presidency. This was the reality on
the ground, but unfortunately it had to be recalled in order to matter. And
so fifty thousand Americans, not to mention millions of Vietnamese, paid
with their lives to support a myth and a bellicose denial.

As always, it was the young who paid. I was fifty-three in 1968, and if
the war would cost me nothing materially, it wore away at the confidence
that in the end Reason had to return lest all be lost. I was not sure of that
anymore. Reason itself had become unaesthetic, something art must at
any cost avoid.

The Price grew out of a need to reconfirm the power of the past, the
seedbed of current reality, and the way to possibly reaffirm cause and effect in an insane world. It seemed to me that if, through the mists of denial,
the bow of the ancient ship of reality could emerge, the spectacle might
once again hold some beauty for an audience. If the play does not utter the
word Vietnam, it speaks to a spirit of unearthing the real that seemed to
have very nearly gone from our lives.

Which is not to deny that the primary force driving *The Price* was a
tangle of memories of people. Still, these things move together, idea feeding characters and characters deepening idea.

Nineteen sixty-eight, when the play is set, was already nearly forty
years since the Great Crash, the onset of the transformed America of the
Depression decade. It was then that the people in this play had made the
choices whose consequences they had now to confront. The Thirties had
been a time when we learned the fear of doom and had stopped being kids
for a while; the time, in short, when, as I once noted about the era, the
birds came home to roost and the past became present. And that Depres-

sion cataclysm, incidentally, seemed to teach that life indeed had beginnings, middles and a consequential end.

Plays leave a wake behind them as they pass into history, with odd objects bobbing about in it. Many of these, in the case of *The Price*, are oddly funny for such a serious work. I had just finished writing it and with my wife, Inge Morath, went to the Caribbean for a week's vacation. Hurrying onto the beach in our first hour there, we noticed a man standing ankle-deep in the water, dressed in shorts and a wide-brimmed plantation hat, who looked a lot like Mel Brooks. In fact, he *was* Mel Brooks. After a few minutes' chat I asked if there was any fishing here. "Oh, God, yes," he said, "yesterday there was one came in right there," and he pointed a yard away in the shallow water. "Must have been three feet long. He was dead. But he may be over there today," he added, pointing down the beach.

He wanted to know if I was writing, and I said we were casting a new play called *The Price*, and he asked what it was about. "Well," I said, "there are these two brothers . . ."

"Stop, I'm crying!" he yelled, frightening all the Protestants lying on the beach.

Then there was the letter from the Turkish translator, who assured me that he had made only one change in the text. At the very end, he wrote, after the two brothers nearly come to blows and part forever, unreconciled and angry, there follows a quiet, rather elegiac moment with the old furniture dealer, the cop, and his wife.

Just as they are leaving the stage, the translator explained, he had to bring back the elder brother, Walter, to fall tearfully into the cop's arms. This, because the audience would fear that *the actors themselves* would have had to have a vendetta that could only end in a killing if they parted as unreconciled as the script required. And so, out of the depths, rose the Turkish past . . .

1999

Notes on Realism

Twenty-five years ago I used to defend Broadway against its detractors, because it was where American theatrical innovation almost always began, the rest of the country timorously following behind. Now the Broadway producer is scared stiff, and in those rare cases when he does produce a serious play—Harold Pinter's *Betrayal*, or Tony Kushner's *Angels in America*—it needs to have proven itself somewhere else, such as Texas or London. A play likely to alienate some part of the audience, as so many great plays have done, or whose style is strange or requires some effort to penetrate, simply will not get produced on today's Broadway. George Bernard Shaw once remarked that businessmen always want to talk about art, but playwrights want to talk about business. This is inevitable, especially now, when one knows, for example, that a play like my *Crucible* would be inconceivable, with its cast of twenty-one and its four large sets. Put another way, the aesthetic of that kind of play is beyond the reach now of the commercial theater, though it would be a mistake to think that serious, expensive-to-mount plays like this were exactly welcome in the theater of the Forties or earlier. On the contrary, producers then as now prayed for the next *Life with Father*, a genial comedy with a smaller cast and one set. The difference is that there existed then a handful of producers, most notably Kermit Bloomgarden and Robert Whitehead, who longed for artistically ambitious and socially interesting plays and could put their money where their mouth was. The nub of the problem is that a "straight" play could be mounted in those times for well under $50,000, as opposed to the $1 million or more frequently required today.

Directly and more subtly, theatrical economics translates into theatrical style, unless one is thinking of closet drama put on for a few recondite friends. Fantastic production costs have combined almost lethally with the rise to near total domination of a single paper, the *New York Times*, and its critic over a play's fate, so that stylistic innovation has been left to small and Off-Broadway venues, where the risk of financial loss is lessened. It seems to me that a resulting confusion has crept into the reviewing and discussion of the various styles of playwriting in fashion today. "Realism" is now a put-down; "poetic" is praise. "Experimental" is attractive; "traditional" is not. "Metaphorical" is intriguing, though perhaps not so much as "lyrical," "nonlinear," "dreamlike," and "surreal." It is almost as if "realism" can hardly be poetic, or as if the "poetic" is not, at its best, more real than the merely "realistic" and, at its worst, more conventional beneath its elusive or unfathomable skin. It would be impossible in a small essay to comb out all this fur, but perhaps at least some of the fundamental fault lines, as well as the overlaps among various approaches to the art, can be illuminated by examining a tiny bit of the history of age-old stylistic strategies employed by playwrights to trap reality on the stage.

Perhaps the obvious needs stating first: There is no such thing as "reality" in any theatrical exhibition that can properly be called a play. The reason for this is that stage time is not, and cannot be, street time. In street time, Willy Loman's story would take sixty-two years to play out instead of two and a half hours. Thus, whether a play strives for straight realism or for some more abstracted style, with the very act of condensation the artificial enters even as the first of its lines is being written. The only important question is the nature of that artificiality and how it is acknowledged by the play, and what ought to be judged is not the extent to which the artifice is "nonlinear" or "metaphorical" or "dreamlike" but rather its efficiency in getting across the playwright's vision of life. This in turn raises questions about a style's suitability to its subject and about the kind of language—what variation on "real" speech—the playwright chooses.

When I began writing plays in the late Thirties, "realism" was the reigning style in the English-language commercial theater, which was just about all the theater there was at the time in America and Britain. Theater could still be thought of then as a popular art, though one knew (and this was long before television) that something of its mass appeal had gone out of it, and a lot of its Twenties glamour, too. In general, one blamed the movies, which had stolen theater's audience and thus its civic power, such as it was, as well as its cultural influence. Despite the obvious fact that our audience was predominantly middle class, we continued to believe that we were making theater for an audience comprising a representative variety of New York City people and even beyond; in other words, theatergoers of many different cultural and educational levels. In New York, where plays had a ticket price of 55 cents to $4.40 (as opposed to $40 to $100 today), one somehow took for granted that a professor might be sitting next to a housewife, a priest beside a skilled worker, or a grammar school teacher, or a business executive, or a student. This perception of a democratic audience, accurate or not, influenced the writing of plays directed at the commonsensical experience of everyday people. (Black or Asian or Hispanic faces were not represented, of course, but these were beyond the consciousness of the prevailing culture.) Even into the Forties, production costs were relatively within reason; plays such as *All My Sons* or *Death of a Salesman,* for example, cost between $20,000 and $40,000 to produce, a budget small enough to be raised among half a dozen modest contributors who could afford to lose their investment with some embarrassment but reasonably little pain, given the killing they occasionally would make.

We were torn, those of us who tried to convince ourselves that we were carrying on the time-honored tradition of theater as a civic art rather than as a purely commercial exercise, because to attract even the fitful interest of a Broadway producer, and thus to engage the audience, we had to bow to realism, even if we admired and wished to explore the more "poetic" forms. An Expressionist like the German Ernst Toller, for example, would not have been read past his sixth page by a Broadway producer or, for that matter, by a producer in London. There is not one "important" playwright of Toller's era who was then, or is now, welcome in the commercial theater, not Chekhov, not Ibsen, not Hauptmann, not Pirandello, Strindberg, Turgenev, or even Shaw.

To perform a Beckett play like *Waiting for Godot* in the proximity of today's Broadway, one has to have a cast of movie stars for a very short run, as was done a little while back at Lincoln Center with Robin Williams, Steve Martin, F. Murray Abraham, Bill Irwin, and Lukas Haas. Things were probably worse half a century ago or more. One need only read Eugene O'Neill's letters castigating the "showshop" mentality of Broadway and the narrow compass of the American theater audience's imagination, or Shaw's ridiculing of British provincialism, to understand that for some mysterious reason the Anglo-Saxon culture has regarded theater as an entertainment first and last, an art of escape with none of the Continental or

Russian involvement in moral or philosophical obligations. The English-language theater was, in fact, almost pridefully commercial; it was a profit-making enterprise wedded to a form whose "realistic" veneer would be universally recognized. Musicals were the exception—they alone had the happy license to part from reality, at least to some extent—but for straight plays even satire was uncommercial enough to merit George Kaufman's definition of it as what closes on Saturday night.

The point is that what we think of as "straight realism" was tiresome half a century ago but nonetheless went unquestioned as a reflection of life by audience and reviewer alike. At a time when "experimental" is all that need be said of a play for it to gain serious consideration, it is not a bad idea to confess that an extraordinarily few such researches have achieved any kind of enduring life. It is not quite enough to know how to escape restrictions; sooner or later one also has to think of arriving somewhere.

American theater's one formal innovation in the Thirties, and probably the single exception to realism's domination, was the WPA's Living Newspaper. An epic in presentational form, written like movies by groups of writers under an editor-producer rather than individually, the Living Newspaper dealt exuberantly with social issues such as public ownership of electrical power, labor unions, agriculture, and medicine, and was extremely popular. The WPA was government-subsidized, using unemployed actors, designers, and technicians, and had no need to make a profit, so a show could call upon large casts and elaborate production elements. And the ticket price was low. It could send Orson Welles, for example, into Harlem storefronts with a big cast playing *Macbeth,* charging a quarter a seat. Theater-for-profit was hardly affected by what might be called this epic-populist approach, because, then as now, it was simply too expensive to produce commercially.

My own first playwriting attempt was purely mimetic, a realistic play about my own family. It won me some prizes and productions, but, interestingly, I could not wait to turn at once to a stylized treatment of life in a gigantic prison—modeled on Jackson state penitentiary in Michigan, near Ann Arbor, where I was in school. Jackson, with something like six thousand inmates, was the largest prison in the United States. I had visited the place over weekends with a friend, who, having taken one psychology course in college, was appointed its lone psychologist. The theme of my play, *The Great Disobedience,* was that prisons existed to make desperate workingmen insane. There was a chorus of sane prisoners chanting from a high overpass above the stage and a counterchorus of the insane trying to draw the other into their ranks. Inevitably, I discovered a strange problem of dramatic language, which could not engage so vast a human disaster with speech born in a warm kitchen. And this led to the question of whether the essential pressure toward poetic dramatic language, if not toward stylization itself, came from the inclusion of society as a major element in a play's story or vision. Manifestly, prose realism was the language of the individual and of private life; poetry, the language of the man in the crowd, in society. Put another way, prose was the language of family relations; it was the inclusion of the larger world beyond that naturally opened a play to the poetic. Was it possible to create a style that would at once deeply engage an American audience that insisted on a recognizable reality of characters, locales, and themes while at the same time opening the stage to considerations of public morality and the mythic social fates—in short, to the invisible?

Of course, this was hardly my preoccupation alone. I doubt there was ever a time when so much discussion went on about form and style. T. S. Eliot was writing his verse plays; Auden and Isherwood, their own. The poetic mimesis of Sean O'Casey was most popular, and W. B. Yeats's dialogue was studied and praised, if not very often produced. The realism of Broadway—and the Strand and the Boulevard theater of France—was detested by the would-be poetic dramatists of my generation, just as it had always been since it came into vogue in the nineteenth century. What did this realism really come down to? A play devoid of symbolic or metaphysical persons and situations, its main virtue verisimilitude, with no revolutionary implications for society. Quite simply, conventional realism was conventional because it avowedly or implicitly supported convention. But it could just as easily do something quite different, or so it seemed. We thought of it as the perfect style for an unchallenging, simple-minded, linear, middle-class, conformist view of life. What I found confusing at the time, however, was that it was not so very long before the term "realism" came to be applied to the revolutionary style of playwrights like Ibsen, Chekhov, and, quite frequently, Strindberg, writers whose whole thrust was in opposition to the bourgeois status quo and the hypocrisies on which it stood.

Clifford Odets, for a few years in the mid-Thirties, was more wildly and lavishly celebrated than any playwright before or since. For younger writers such as myself, Odets was the trailblazer not just because of his

declared radicalism but because of the fact that his plays were so manifestly *written*. But there was a misapprehension behind his popularity, too;
since his characters were the very exemplars of realistic theater, lacking
strangeness or stylish elegance, Odets was called a realist—indeed, a
kind of reporter, no less, of Jewish life in the Bronx. I had never lived in
the Bronx, but the speech of Brooklyn Jews could not have been much different, and it had no resemblance whatever to the way Odets's people
spoke:

> I'm super-disgusted with you!
> A man hits his wife and it is the first step to fascism!
> Look in the papers! On every side the clouds of war—
> Ask yourself a pertinent remark: could a boy make a living play-
> ing this instrument [a violin] in our competitive civilization
> today?
> I think I'll run across the street and pick up an eight-cylinder
> lunch.

Odets was turning dialogue into his personal jazz, and the surprised
audience roared with delight. But had any Bronxite—or anyone else—
ever really exclaimed, "God's teeth, no!" or, "What exhaust pipe did he
crawl out of?" or, "I feel like I'm shot from a cannon"?

Inevitably, in a theater defined by realism, this had to be mistakenly
labeled as simply a kind of reported news from the netherworld. But of
course it was a poet's invented diction, with slashes of imagery of a sort
never heard before, onstage or off. Odets's fervent ambition was to burst
the bounds of Broadway while remaining inside its embrace, there being
no other theatrical place in America for him to go. When the time came,
as it probably had to, when some of the surprise was no longer there and
when critics took the same pleasure in putting him down as they had in
building him up, he found himself homeless on Broadway, and he left for
the movies.

I suppose his fate may have had some effect on my own explorations
into "alternative" forms as I came out of the Thirties. All I knew for sure
was that the word "poetry" wasn't enough if a play's underlying structure
was a fractured one, a concept not fully realized. A real play was the discovery of the unity of its contradictions, and the essential poetry, the first
poetry, was the synthesis of even the least of its parts to form a symbolic

meaning. A certain consistency was implicit. The oak does not sprout maple leaves, and a certain kind of self-conscious lyricism does not belong in a realistic work. In short, I had come to believe that if one could create a very strong unity in a work, any audience could be led anywhere. Ideally, a good play must offer as sound an emotional proof of its thesis as a law cases does factually, and you couldn't really do that with words alone, lovely as they might be.

Odets's contribution, ironically, was not his realistic portrayal of social reality—his alleged aim—but his willingness to be artificial; he brought back artificiality, if you will, just as ten years later Tennessee Williams did so with his birdsong from the magnolias. But Williams had an advantage: his language could be far more faithful to its real-world sources. Southern people really did love to talk, and often elaborately, and in accents much like Amanda's in *The Glass Menagerie:*

> But Laura is, thank heavens, not only pretty but also very domestic. I'm not at all. I never was a bit. I never could make a thing but angel-food cake. Well, in the South we had so many servants. Gone, gone, gone. All vestige of gracious living! Gone completely! I wasn't prepared for what the future brought me. All my gentlemen callers were sons of planters and so of course I assumed that I would be married to one and raise my family on a large piece of land with plenty of servants. But man proposes—and woman accepts the proposal! To vary that old, old saying a little bit—I married no planter! I married a man who worked for the telephone company! That gallantly smiling gentleman over there! [*Points to husband's picture*] A telephone man who—fell in love with long distance! Now he travels and I don't even know where!

This, too, was called realism, but then how did it differ from the conventional realistic play? Clearly the very action of Williams's plays, certainly the best of them, was working toward the building of a symbolic meaning that would express both the psychological development of his characters and his personal specter of a menacing America struggling with its own repressed sexuality. His earliest work is shot through with the left-wing attitudes of the time, which he managed gradually to fuse with his own vulnerability, his pain and anxiety at being overwhelmed and defeated by a crazy violence that underlay the American, one might say the whole Western, ethos. Without that confession of his pain and anxiety—his tragic vision—his words alone would have seemed, I think, flowery and excessively romantic.

To consider such writers as purely private, self-involved persons is to disserve the truth. Odets when he began thought his egalitarian Marxism would heal America and create its new community, and Williams unfurled the banner of a forlorn but gallant resistance to the mendacity and the violence aimed at the oddball, the poet, the sexual dissident. But it may as well be admitted that in their different ways both men in the bitter end unwittingly collaborated with the monster they believed was trying to destroy them.

O'Neill, of course, was an aesthetic rebel, but his socialism was private and did not inform his plays (though *The Hairy Ape* is surely an anticapitalist work). It was his formal experiments and tragic ambience that set him apart. But O'Neill was a totally isolated phenomenon in the Broadway theater as a maker and user of new and old theatrical forms. Odets, on the other hand, while describing himself as a man of the Left, was, with the possible exception of his first produced play, *Waiting for Lefty,* no innovator where form was concerned. His was a poetic realism, but it was still bound to recognizably real types in actual social relationships. And this was perhaps inevitable; as both actor and revolutionary he had his eye on the great public and the reconstitution of power once a failed capitalism had been brought down. In the Depression, it was all but impossible for a Left writer not to think of the act of writing as a fulcrum for social change. Odets saw himself not only as a political realist but as an anarchic poet, a word-nurse (he kept a file of startling locutions) whose novel twists of language would lift his work into the skies. O'Neill, on the other hand, was not the revolutionary but the rebel, a despairing anarchist who, if he glimpsed any salvation, knew that it could come only with the tragic cleansing of the life-lie that is permanently ensconced in the human condition. Since, unlike Odets, he did not obligate himself to even foreshadow some new and better polity in place of the present corrupt one, he was free to explore all sorts of theatrical means by which to set forth the extant situation of the damned—that is, the Americans. Moreover, if O'Neill wanted his plays to register in the here and now, as he surely did, they need not necessarily be popular to justify his having written them, for he was hunting the sounding whale of ultimate meaning, and he expected to suffer for it (and to be misunderstood) as his models, like Strindberg, had. As much as any playwright could be, O'Neill seemed hardened to the possibility of failure, pledged as he was to drag the theater into the unfamiliar world of spirit and metaphysic.

A critical or box-office failure for Odets meant rejection of a far more personal kind, a spit in the eye by an ungrateful and self-satisfied bourgeois society. A failed play was a denial of what Odets was owed, for he was chasing the public no differently than did his bourgeois and nonrevolutionary contemporaries, a public as fickle as it always was and is. O'Neill could say, as he did, that he was interested in relations not among men but between Man and God. For America, in his view, was damned, from virtue estranged by fixations on gain, racism, social climbing, and the rest of the materialist agenda.

A good style for O'Neill was basically a question of the apt use of metaphor, imagery, and argot. "I wish to God I could write like that!" he wrote to O'Casey, who, incidentally, would no doubt have called himself a "realistic" writer in the sense that he was trying to turn Irish attention to Irish reality. But like Williams, O'Casey came from a culture that loved talk and sucked on language like a sweet candy:

MRS. GOGAN: Oh, you've got a cold on you, Fluther.

FLUTHER: Ah, it's only a little one.

MRS. GOGAN: You'd want to be careful, all th' same. I knew a woman, a big lump of a woman, red-faced and round-bodied, a little awkward on her feet; you'd think, to look at her, she could put out her two arms an' lift a two-storied house on th' top of her head; got a ticklin' in her throat, an' a little cough, an' th' next mornin' she had a little catchin' in her chest, an' they had just time to wet her lips with a little rum, an' off she went.

Even in the most mundane of conversational exchanges, O'Casey sought, and as often as not found, the lift of poetry. Indeed, that was the whole point—that the significantly poetic sprang from the raw and real experience of ordinary people. J. M. Synge, O'Casey's forerunner at the turn of the century, had struck a similar chord. Synge was in a supremely conscious revolt against the banality of most theater language. As he wrote, the popular imagination was still fiery and magnificent, and tender; so that those of us who wish to write start with a chance that is not given to writers in places where the springtime of the local life has been forgotten, and the harvest is a memory only, and the straw has been turned into bricks.

Synge rejected the then-dominant Ibsen and Zola for their realism with "joyless and pallid words" and instead, as in *Riders to the Sea,* when the women are lamenting the deaths of so many of their men working the angry sea, wrote

> MAURYA: In the big world the old people do be leaving things after them for their sons and children, but in this place it is the young men do be leaving things behind for them that do be old.

Here it might be useful to remember that James Joyce, another Irish poet, revered Ibsen notwithstanding the pallor of his words in English, for Joyce had, by learning Ibsen's Norwegian, penetrated the poetic structure of the plays and their outcry against the spiritual failure of the modern world.

The advent of the Absurd and of Beckett and his followers both obscured and illuminated the traditional discussion of theater style. The Beckett difference, as it might be called, was to introduce humble people, or social sufferers—bums, in fact—with the plainest of language arranged so as to announce and develop pure theme. His could be called a presentational thematic play, announcing what it was about and never straying very far from what it sought to prove or what his instinct had led him to confirm. Beckett had parted with the time-honored tradition of inferential playwriting, in which the author's thematic intentions were inferred from a seemingly autonomous story whose climax consisted of the joining together of story and the finally revealed underlying theme. With Beckett, the story *was* the theme, inseparably so, from page one. Moreover, he blatantly interpreted the story himself in his dialogue.

By the Fifties, the notion that an elevated tone or diction was required for an escape from common realism was discarded in favor of the most common, undecorated speech. But it was not the traditional speech of realistic plays. Rather, it was a speech bent almost out of recognition by a surreal deracination. The Absurdist approach at first seemed to me to be celebrating the impotence of human hopes, even the futility of action it-self. All but the flimsiest connectiveness between utterances was eventu-ally eliminated, creating an atmosphere of sinister danger (in Pinter) or (in Beckett) the threatening sense of immanence familiar from bad dreams. Man was unique because he tripped over himself, and it was quite as though the emphatic absence of purpose in the characters had created a loss of syntax. I take it that in later years Beckett took pains to clarify this impression of human futility, emphasizing the struggle against inertia as his theme. In any case, however ridiculous so much of his dialogue is, the tenderness of feeling in his work is emphatically not that of the cynic or the hard ironist.

Beckett fused style and meaning organically, the dominating theme of *Godot* being stasis and the struggle to overcome humanity's endlessly repe-titious paralysis before the need to act and change. We hear this theme as blatantly as a train announcement and as stripped clean as a bleached bone.

ESTRAGON: Then adieu.
POZZO: Adieu.
VLADIMIR: Adieu.
POZZO: Adieu.
VLADIMIR: Adieu.
POZZO: Adieu.
ESTRAGON: Adieu.
Silence.
POZZO: And thank you.
VLADIMIR: Thank *YOU*.
POZZO: Not at all.
ESTRAGON: Yes yes.
POZZO: No no.
VLADIMIR: Yes yes.
ESTRAGON: No no.
Silence.
POZZO: I don't seem to be able . . . (*long hesitation*) . . . to depart.
ESTRAGON: Such is life.

This is a vaudeville at the edge of the cliff, but vaudeville anyway, so I may be forgiven for being reminded of Jimmy Durante's ditty—"Didja ever get the feelin' that you wanted to go? But you wanted to stay? But you wanted to go?" Here is a language shorn of metaphor, simile, everything but its instructions, so the listener may hear the theme like a nail drawn across a pane of glass. *Godot* does not make the mistake of so many of its imitators; in its flight from realism it does not leave structure behind.

My own tendency has been to shift styles according to the nature of my subject. *All My Sons, The Crucible, A View from the Bridge, Death of a Salesman, The Price, The American Clock,* my earliest work like *The Golden Years,* about the destruction of Mexico by the Spaniards, and the more recent plays like *The Creation of the World, Some Kind of Love Story, The Last Yankee,* and *Broken Glass* all differ greatly in their language. I have done this in order to find speech that springs naturally out of the characters and their backgrounds rather than imposing a general style. If my approach to playwriting is partly literary, I hope it is well hidden.

It is necessary to employ the artificial in order to arrive at the real. More than one actor in my plays has told me that it is surprisingly difficult to memorize their dialogue. The speeches sound like real, almost reported talk when in fact they are intensely composed, compressed into a sequential inevitability that seems natural but isn't. But all this, important though it may be, is slightly to one side of the point. Experimental or traditional, the real question to ask of a work is whether it brings news, something truly felt by its author, an invention on his part or an echo.

The struggle with what might be called reportorial realism, written "the way people talk," is at least as old as the century. And although realism can land us further from common reality than can the most fantastic caprice, in the end stylization in the theater will be justified not by its novelty—at least not for long—but by the degree to which it illuminates how life works in our time. How a thing is said is only as new as what it is saying. The proof of this is the deep pile of experimental plays of two, three, five, ten years ago, which can only be appreciated anymore by the scholar-specialist. It is a pile, incidentally, no smaller than the one for so many conventionally realistic plays of the same era. Finding truth is no easier now when we are totally free to use any stylistic means at hand than it was a century or half a century ago, when a play had to be "real" to be read at all and had to make sense to sensible people.

Call it a question of personal taste rather than principle, but I think that in theater work there is an optimum balance between two kinds of approaches: One is the traditional attempt to fill characters with acknowledged emotion, "as in life." The other is in effect to evacuate emotion from characters, merely referring to their subjective life rather than acting it out, the so-called camp style. In his speculative prose, Brecht, for one, called for such a drying-out of script and acting, but except in his most agitprop and forgettable plays he failed or declined to practice this method. The strict containment not of emotion but of emotionalism is the hallmark of the Greek tragic plays, of Molière and Racine and the Japanese Noh plays, whereas Shakespeare, it seems to me, is the balance, the fusion of idea and feeling. In short, it is by no means the abstracting of emotion I dislike; it is the lack of feeling and the substitution of fashionably alienated ironies in its place.

There has been a plethora of plays in recent years whose claim to modernity is based on indicated rather than felt emotion. The assumption, I suppose, is that this *sec* quality lends a play an intellectuality it may or may not have earned and in any case rescues it from the banality of work aimed at the audience's belly rather than its head. The big devil to be avoided is sentimentality, emotion unearned.

Theater, like politics, is always the art of the possible. And when economics makes it impossible to employ more than four or five actors in a single unchanging set, when competition for actors by TV and films prevents them from maturing in theater work, when the cost of advertising makes it effectively impossible for a play to survive without nearly unanimous critical praise, it seems to me a shame to dismiss a play that is not camp simply because it moves an audience. Can't it be art if it moves people? If the pun can be pardoned, man lives not by head alone, and the balance between the two modes, one aimed at the mind and one the flesh, as it were, is what will interpret life more fully. After all, at least part of what we ask of a modern play is to show us what life now *feels* like.

Ultimately, every assault on the human mystery falls back to the ground, changing little, but the flight of the arrow continues claiming our attention over a longer time when its direction is toward the castle of reality rather than the wayward air.

1999

Subsidized Theatre

The commercial system of theatrical production in New York is some two centuries old. In contrast, theatre has been carried on in various parts of the West for a couple of thousand years but under very different production circumstances. The New York system is thus a sport, something created to reflect a vibrant capitalism with its joy in risk-taking and the excitement of the win-all-or-lose-all rodeo. We have arrived—in New York—at the expiration time of that theatrical way of life as far as straight plays are concerned. The system no longer works for non-musical theatre and hasn't in years. The time has come to consider alternatives.

I have sometimes wondered if there ever was what one could call a "healthy" theatrical circumstance. The classical Greek situation, turning out one masterpiece after another, usually appears to us as serene, like some great ship cruising stormy seas unperturbed by the tons of water crashing down on its decks. But then one recalls stories of the *choreaqi*, the men of wealth chosen for the honor of paying the bills for the chorus, who tried as best they could to duck the distinction. And to read almost any twenty pages of Aristophanes is to sense the backbiting and posturing and nastiness surrounding Greek theatre. Much the same mess seems to have prevailed in Elizabethan times, and Molière's, Strindberg's, Chekhov's, Shaw's, O'Casey's, just as in our own.

Theatre production these days is a problem with not even an acceptable definition let alone a solution. The theatre owner will tell you that it is simply that costs are too high even as he takes fifty-two percent of the gross. Nor is the stagehand or author or actor likely to look to himself for the source of the difficulty. All one can say is that the play that cost less than forty thousand to produce a generation ago now comes in at a million and a half or even two million and rising, the price of a ticket soaring from four or six dollars to seventy-five and up. It is a system which has almost literally eaten its own body alive.

In the belly of the beast, as always, is the money and the conflicts it breeds. Where the state finances production, as it partially does in England and other parts of the world, its built-in urge to censor has to be curbed; where private investment does so, it is greed that must be bridled lest it lead down into the swamp of theatrical triviality where the great mass of the public is alleged to live and hence the promise of the biggest returns. Theatre is born to trouble as the sparks fly upward, but we are in more than trouble now and an altogether new spirit will have to infuse those interested in changing—perhaps saving is the word—the production of plays on a professional level.

Amid the gratitude, which I share, for the annual arrival of fine British plays on and off Broadway, it is useful to remember that every one of them, practically with no exceptions, came out of subsidized theatres. It is not possible to imagine that a Pinter, a Stoppard, a Hare, a Frayn, would have been nurtured in London's commercial West End. They are all too chancey and their audiences admittedly too limited to warrant investment-for-profit. The British public, in short, has been financing a significant part of New York's theatre for a long time now.

The minds of probably most American politicians—and even some critics and editorialists—seem to curdle at the idea of subsidizing any art, least of all theatre. To them, subsidized theatre seems to imply a crutch to help hold erect failed artists who can't make it in the tough, Darwinian for-profit arena. After all, a good number of people have gotten rich on doing theatre work, why can't these mendicants? And besides, isn't theatre attendance on Broadway higher than ever? And if almost all the increase has gone to musicals, then so be it—the public has decided it doesn't want straight plays. The system operates like any other market and if one can't manage on its terms maybe he ought to give up and go into another line of work.

With the richest theatre in America unable to produce a single new straight play season after season, leaving only a very occasional revival on the boards in that category, one is given the reason as being the failure of playwrights who somehow have forgotten how to do the job. That hundreds, thousands of plays are written in this country every year, without a single one good enough for professional production in our greatest entertainment city, is nothing short of a statistical marvel. So extreme is the situation that one is driven to drastic explanations; is it possible, one wonders, that this generation of New York producers, who will travel to England or even Australia to sign up a new hit play, are not competent to read and judge a script but only its reviews, or by having sat in the midst of a laughing or weeping audience to decide to reach for their contracts? I find this illiteracy far more likely than the idea that the playwriting art has simply gone to earth forever in a United States of two hundred and fifty million souls.

For reasons I can't pretend to understand, there are never more than a handful of playwrights in any age. Poets, novelists, essayists show up in numbers, but playwrights come in two's and three's. We presently have many more than this handful but the most commercialized theatre in the world has no place for them. Can it be that the commercial organization of professional theatre is, in fact, preventing the flowering of theatre, most especially in New York, where theatre is so important to the economy as well as the spirit of the place?

But why bother even to complain about the Broadway theatre when it is clearly so artistically bankrupt where production of original straight plays is concerned? There are good reasons for caring, most of them forgotten. In the two- or three-hundred seat off-Broadway theatre, whatever its charm, it is next to impossible to produce plays with casts larger than half a dozen, not to mention those requiring multiple sets. Thus, the esthetic of playwriting itself is affected by this total commercialization, and playwriting becomes of necessity a constricted technique. I do not believe that, for example, most of my own plays would have found production on today's Broadway, and what would one do with *The Crucible* on a shoebox stage with its twenty-one characters and several sets? I don't think *Salesman* would have been produced by the present breed of Broadway producers because it is too sad—and in fact even in 1949 there was pressure to find a more upbeat title, the producer actually paying to poll theatre audiences asking if they'd like to see a play called *Death of a Salesman*. Practically none, quite naturally, said they would. Off-Broadway has its uses but creating plays of breadth and physical size is not one of them. Broadway theatres, on the other hand, once welcomed plays of size, which of course is not to deny that in any age the producer's dream is a very funny play with a cast of two in one set.

As things stand now, it is almost impossible to imagine an actor making a lifelong career acting in the theatre. The off-Broadway theatre is basically subsidized by people without families to support, its young underpaid actors whose eye is really on television or films, not theatre. Much is made of the great British actors, but almost without exception the Oliviers, Richardsons, Gielguds, Gambons, Guinnesses came out of subsidized theatres where they developed their craft in great roles in classic plays. There is no play in New York where anything like this kind of muscle building is possible. We have wonderfully talented actors who do incredible things in the three- or four-week rehearsal period normally allowed them, but if a bottom-line theatre, which is what we have, cannot afford longer rehearsals it doesn't justify making a virtue of our deprivation.

If we have theatres, we don't have Theatre, which is not real estate but a collection of people of talent whose main interest and devotion is the creation of something beautiful. This is difficult to discuss because it is basically about an atmosphere. Playwrights as different as Clifford Odets and Eugene O'Neill have hated the absolute commercialization of New York theatre, and it is hard to think of any artist who has loved it, including some who have made fortunes out of it. My own impression is that the atmosphere has in some ways degenerated even further than when the earlier generation complained of it. Perhaps it is the immensity of the investment required now, but where there was once a certain comity between producer and artist, a certain collaborative equality between people with different but complimentary functions, it seems now like merely one more employer-employee relationship. A real power shift seems to be taking place. Producers speak now of having "given" a production to an author, quite as though profit-making were not at all involved in driving the deal but the generosity and largesse of one who is not only the holder of a lease on a theatre building but the proprietor of the art itself. There is some dangerous, if superficial, logic in this; the businessman is always around but the author, director, and actors vanish sometimes for years before they show up again with a new play and new roles. So that the illusion can easily grow that the business of theatre is business, and the art rather incidental. Indeed, the pressure is actually on now by certain producers to junk the traditional royalty arrangements with authors, who of course have for several generations retained ownership and control of their scripts, and to replace it with the producer's taking over if not actual ownership then the right to make any script changes he desires. Some think we are moving into the Hollywood system, where the producer buys or commissions scripts and the author moves down to the bottom of the totem pole, without control or contractual rights once he is paid. Indeed, the Hollywood system sprang from the old Broadway practice of producers buying plays and even attaching their names to them as authors, as the famed John Golden did for many a year before the Dramatists Guild was organized to protect writers.

Broadway has been pronounced dead too many times for me to do so again, but one thing is new—its impotence before the challenge to produce new plays. It is now a secondhand merchandiser of plays from abroad or, on occasion, one of the off-Broadway theatres. That there is an audience there can be no question—the success of revivals of famous, proven works over the past decade has shown that a sizable number of people want to see straight plays on Broadway. It is the production system that has broken. It needs replacement by a new, broader vision, a rededication to essentials—the writer, the director, the actor, the audience. Whoever can bring these elements together deserves praise and gratitude, but excepting for occasional flukes, the risks have clearly grown too great now for private capital alone to manage anymore. Something not particularly novel, of course, but rather as old as theatre itself awaits us—at least partial subsidization of production by either private or public funds or a mixture of both.

Having worked in two great state-subsidized theatres—in China and Sweden, where I directed *Death of a Salesman*—I can testify to some of their failings as well as their virtues. Inevitably, their worst problem, I think, is bureaucracy. People nestle into state jobs and can't be blasted out of them regardless of competency or even sobriety. (In Stockholm I had two drunks operating a hidden platform on my *Salesman* set, and on their cue to lower a bed they were found in the basement playing a bleary, oblivious card game. As union men they could not be fired, but one of them felt he had so humiliated himself that he resigned his position.) It is hard to see any ready solution to this dilemma. But friction arises with anything that moves, and these theatres are nevertheless often capable of work far beyond what any New York theatre can presently contemplate. Ingmar Bergman's *Peer Gynt* and the *Teahouse* of the Beijing People's Art Theatre, which I happened to see, were of a conceptual grandeur, a lyricism and exactitude of acting that simply cannot be achieved in our hit-and-run, semihysterical production process. They were reminders once again that every play of the European masters of the nineteenth and twentieth centuries has come out of subsidized theatres. From Brecht to Strindberg and Ibsen and reaching back to Shakespeare and the Greeks, there was a partial or complete state subsidy or, as in Elizabethan times, a noble patronage supporting the art.

But there may not necessarily be one single solution to the problem. It has to be said that in our hazardous, high-stakes gambling house called Broadway the thrill of the dice throw can be exhilarating, and in times past when productions did not yet bear killing costs the flow of new American plays was greatly admired by theatre folk in other countries. But that was then and this is now.

My own experience indicates that the best system is most probably a mixed one, with the private commercial theatre coexisting with the subsidized one. Their functions may often overlap but in general the private theatre would most likely offer entertainment while the other would be free to pursue its more difficult theatrical dreams.

The subsidized theatre can indeed settle into an institutionalized stupor if allowed to drift that way, but the British, for one, have shown that it need not, or at least not for long. In any case, if there are other alternatives than I have named to the present system, let them be heard and debated.

Theatre is not going to die. To paraphrase Carl Sandburg, there will always be the young strangers, people desperate to act, to interpret what they have seen, and now and again a writer gathering stray beams of light into a flaming focal point. Most of these now dream of the filmic media, but some of that attraction is due to the present theatre system which ignores or repels the young rather than working to open itself to them. Whole generations have passed now which have gone through the taste-forming years of youth without having seen a play, but only film. Would people want music who have never heard music? A responsible subsidized theatre would, as it does elsewhere, open the world of plays to students. If it was always at bottom an entertainment machine devised to make money and fame for a few, commercial production nevertheless did keep open a certain space for writers, directors, and actors with serious intentions and visions of a world they passionately wished to make real. No more. That whole developmental function has simply been passed along to off-Broadway and academia while commercial Broadway waits to skim off some floating drops of cream.

2000

Index